THE COMMERCIAL LOBBYISTS

THE COMMERCIAL LOBBYISTS

Politics for Profit in Britain

edited by
Grant Jordan

ABERDEEN UNIVERSITY PRESS
Member of Maxwell Macmillan Pergamon Publishing Corporation

First published 1991
Aberdeen University Press

British Library Cataloguing in Publication Data

Jordan, Grant
  The Commercial Lobbyists: politics for profit in Britain
  1. Great Britain. Parliament. House of Commons.
  Members. Lobbying
  I. Title
  328.41078

ISBN   0 08 037984 2

Typeset by University of Aberdeen Central Printing Service

Printed by Billings & Sons Ltd

Contents

Preface

This collection is primarily about the commercial 'for hire' lobbyists who work for a variety of clients representing views to Government or Parliament. The book is based on the same sense of 'something stirring' that has prompted the House of Commons Select Committee on Members' Interests to look twice at the issue in the past few years. (See the First Report from the Select Committee on Members' Interests, 1984-5, HC 408 and Select Committee on Members' Interests, *Parliamentary Lobbying,* 1988 HC 518, 1989 HC 44). In 1987 it was noted,

> ... there is increasing lobbying activity in Westminster, that it will continue to increase, and that conflicts of interest will more frequently confront Members. (HC 110, 1986-7, para 10).

One member of the 1989/90 Committee, Robert Adley, told *The Observer* (9th April, 1989) that the evidence had lead the Committee to the conclusion, 'We have an uneasy feeling that the place is being perverted by commercial pressures.'

The chapters here are written by a mixture of practitioners and academics. It was thought that it was important to obtain the views of those 'in the game' as there has yet to be a substantial academic inquiry into the impact of these firms. The book length studies of the phenomenon so far have been from the 'practical' side of the fence – Ian Greer, *Right to be Heard* (1985) and Charles Miller, *Lobbying Government* (1987).

As editor I am very grateful to all contributors but especially to Austin Mitchell, Ian Greer, Charles Miller, Martin Smith and Barney Holbeche who have had to squeeze this contribution to wider public awareness into already busy professional lives in which publication is a luxury. As the chapters show there is no firm division of views between those active professionally and those not. There are concerns that are noted by both types of participant and a dis-consensus over remedies divides both sets of contributors.

If the collection does not resolve the vital question of *impact* (has the mushrooming of activity actually changed *outcomes*?), and if it reports a debate on styles of lobbying and the need for regulation rather than agreed conclusions, it is hoped the discussion of such themes is itself useful. The collection seeks to put commercial lobbying in a context of policy making by consultation and wide ranging policy discussion. If one approaches the work of professional lobbyists with a notion that Government evolves policy only through intra-party politics or by civil servants attempting to define or distil the public interest, then the proliferation of lobbyists may be disturbing. If one accepts that policy making is normally a complex series of negotiations among civil servants and interested bodies, then one might still be concerned at specific activities of lobbyists, but lobbying in general would appear less controversial. In this light the activities are perhaps at worst only a spot of grey on an already murky canvass. It is not the argument in this book that commercial lobbying *is* British politics. But the claim is that the study of such lobbying is necessary for a full understanding of the British decision-making process.

Much of the press attention of lobbyists concerns their activities in the Houses of Parliament, but the conclusion of the various contributions herein is that the prime target for effective lobbying has to be the Government and Civil Service rather than back benchers (though Conservative back benchers can force their Government to re-consider). The argument is caught by Austin Mitchell, MP, in a review of Alf Dub's (1989) book on lobbying. Of Parliamentary lobbying he notes:

> ... is it all worth while? The processes are fascinating, the lobbying self-inflating and feeding on itself. Yet under our elective dictatorship, the legislature is still basically a rubber stamp in the hands of the executive ... So lobby as we might, set procedural traps as we might, work as we might, at the end of the day we are largely impotent. As long as the Prime Minister carries her party with her – not very difficult when they're as docile as this and eager for promotion – we have all the intellectual satisfaction of heckling a steam roller.
>
> *(The House Magazine*, 6th March, 1989)

The controversy over lobbying in the House is thus not a measure of the importance of the House in policy making but reflects unease that the relationships of those interested in policy changes and target MPs are too often accompanied by financial links. *The Observer* (9th April, 1989) noted 'two out of three MPs now have some sort of paid employment, and one in every three MPs acts as a parliamentary consultant to some commercial or professional organisation.'

It may be thought that the description in the contributions of techniques is, in total, repetitive. But there was no clear unanimity when the chapters were initially discussed. That a common pattern does emerge should be taken to be confirmation of the thrust of the argument. But there is by no means absolute unanimity. Not far below the gentlemanly exposition of the contributions by Charles Miller and Ian Greer there is a fundamental difference in their evaluation of the Parliamentary strategy. Alan Doig has a rather more tart view of the profession than is palatable to most within.

This work is completed before the Select Committee on Members' Interests makes its second Report on this subject. Clearly there would have been great profit in waiting for the report – but the work of the committee has been delayed beyond the publishing schedule. And the delay perhaps tells us something about the eventual output. Had the committee been able to make easy and dramatic recommendations the report would have been already out. The delay reflects the committee's discovery that no easy options exist.

My thanks are again due to Lorna Cardno for her typing (and re-typing) and to Jeanne Caesar whose last minute intervention helped provide a more practical slant to my contributions. Other commitments prevented Jane Sargent from making a planned contribution to this collection, but she gave very useful advice. Very late in the preparation of the typescript I had the opportunity to discuss these matters with Professor Lewis Dexter at Dalhousie University. This was a considerable privilege and I only regret that I did not have the advice much earlier.

The project began with a small panel at the Political Studies Association Conference held at the University of Aberdeen in 1987, but most of the papers were invited after the success of the panel. Thanks are due to the other participants. Professor Jeremy Richardson of Strathclyde University was co-organiser of that panel and, yet again, merits my personal thanks. Derek Kemp and Marjorie Leith were of great assistance in the business of turning our papers into book form. Whatever deficiencies remain are the responsibility of the editor : that there are not considerably more is the responsibility of these two.

Finally, this book is dedicated to Ian and Eileen Taylor. There should be some reward for their welcome interest over such a prolonged period – and for the wine donated by Taylor's Auctions (Montrose) to the 1987 dinner of the Political Studies Association.

PART I : Introduction and Comparisons

INTRODUCTION:
The View From The Lobbied: A Consumer's Guide

AUSTIN MITCHELL MP

What we need in the study of commercial lobbying is light, more light and still more light. To know what goes on is invaluable in an area all too obscure and even more emotive. Purists and constitutionalists find lobbying itself distasteful, though how anyone could make the institutions work or let their own light so shine before men that they may see their good works without it, is never explained. Commercial lobbying for reward is assumed to be somehow reprehensible or disreputable. Yet lobbying is not just an inevitable part of politics, it is politics. Politics themselves are becoming increasingly professional. So is lobbying. So we are really saying that lobbying is a good thing when done for principled or party purposes but somehow sordid, money grubbing and unworthy, done for reward or commercial purposes. Des Wilson good; Ian Greer naughty. Alarm bells ring with cash registers. Particularly on my side of the House, where we assume that the lower the income the higher the moral principles and the less lobbied (as Labour is) the more virtuous. We prefer hair shirts to sloganised T shirts and see incompetence as a symptom of sincerity.

In reality, lobbying has increased, is increasing, and is not going to be diminished. Even our vaunted constitution is really a framework of lobbying; for the constitution is, essentially, whatever governments can get away with. Lobbying, persuasion and opinion manipulation are the tugs at the sleeve of power. Government itself is a lobby. It can't be director in a pluralistic society and whether its role is as manager, or another player, it has to persuade, influence, lobby for its objectives. Departments are lobbied, particularly by the network of pressure and interest groups which cluster round most. They are also lobbiers, now bullying their lobbies where they once tried to be nice to them. Ministers play the same game for interests, policies, careers; and even political parties take on an American role as lobbies, as umbrellas beneath which lobbies group, and as prey and battleground for lobbies: C.N.D., Low Pay, Low Tax, Business, Unions, anti-hunting, anti-nuclear power.

Parliament, behind its obscuring cloak of dignity and respectability, has changed from the great forum of the nation into the playground of its pressure groups. The House of Lords, a collection of lobbyists dignified by ermine and age and made portunate, in the case of life peers by low pay, in the case of the rest by office, background, experience. So whether as Directors, representatives of organisations or simple function bookers, the Lords is an ermine-lined lobby pool. MPs, who try to be tribunes of the people, are both prey of pressure groups and participants in the game, as cause pushers and influence peddlers. The latest *Register of Members' Interests* indicates that 52 Tory MPs are connected with trade associations, 50 are lobbyists of various forms, and 164 'consultants', all high proportions in a party where Ministers put interests into cold storage; indeed Richard Alexander (Newark) has advertised for a consultancy in the *House Magazine*. The corresponding figures for Labour (which does not advertise) are 28, 20 and 30, dwarfed by the 148 sponsored by unions at the low pay, unskilled, end of the lobbying industry. That phenomenon underlines another side of the problem. No-one's hands are clean: lobbying motes cannot easily be plucked out when sponsorship beams obscure the view and rotten boroughs still exist in constituencies dependent on union money. Who can be squeamish about lobbying perks when so many have wives on their own staff payrolls to keep the cash in the family? A few of those most vociferous on lobbying have been Euro MPs with two sets of expenses, and part of a system which is a noisy lobby on perpetual pilgrimage between Strasbourg, Luxembourg and Brussels.

The conclusion must, therefore, be that an advanced pluralistic society with a division of interests and roles breeds lobbying as it does interest and pressure group politics. It is the undergrowth and an increasingly large element of the substance, of politics. Both will become more professional as politics do. The difference between nations is not so much the scale of the phenomenon but the way it conforms to the contours of the institutions and grows out of the social base of politics. It seems more active in the USA because federalism and the separation of powers provide many points of leverage and leak, openness shows all that goes on, the looseness of coalition parties eases disciplines. On the Continent everything appears quieter. Corporate politics are more disciplined and structured, coalition government more a matter of consultation than assertion of will and endless arguments over ideology. The battle is less likely to break surface because the lobby is built into the system, so that everything works more smoothly. Deals drive out rows.

Here, secrecy obscures, but *a priori,* a dominant, centralised, executive must drive lobbying down the ladder, particularly in a period of government by will. It spills out as rearguard actions appealing, usually vainly, to a comparatively impotent wider democracy. Institutionally Britain is strongly centralised but socially we are awkward, individualistic and disorganised. Corporate structures are weaker. Neither the TUC nor the CBI have the strength or discipline to be effective corporate players. They view success as triumph over the other side, being fixated with each other. Neither can come to deals and deliver, as counterparts do in Europe, or Australasia. British corporatism reached its peak in the 1970s and never extended much beyond pay and inflation. Even that imposed such strain that it collapsed in a Luddite revolt on the left, an intellectual counter-revolution on the right.

They brought in a government which boosted lobbying by triggering a vigorous demolition of corporatism. It imposed free market policies by an exercise of power, will and advertising. It lashed out at vested interests with its handbag. All of which boosted the lobbyists. A strong-willed government doing more, put more cats among more pigeons, while as Charles Miller describes, the old boy network, which business particularly had relied on for friends at court, was disintegrating and discounted, forcing firms to hire help. Commercial lobbying is not distinct from cause lobbying. Causes too hire help as do professions where threatened, and most changes have commercial consequences. Getting lead out of petrol may be a good environmental cause but oil companies which have expanded capacity to produce lead free petrol to find sales below expectations are ever ready to push it. Environmental and health issues have consequences for industry, financial institutions and professions. So does the level of public spending. God writes me a lot of letters calling for the preservation of the English Sunday; all long, hand written and different. Mammon prefers printed forms handed out at DIY stores. Sincerity, and thought, have gone into God's epistles. Yet Mammon's more numerous efforts encapsulate a widespread popular desire which might not express itself if someone wasn't paid to help it.

Prime Ministers were traditionally lobbied by their friends. Mrs Thatcher's friends – Tim Bell, Gordon Reece – were available for hire and contacts at the top must be at least a subconscious part of their sales appeal. Saatchi's political repute enhances the value of the wide ranging portfolio of services and consultancies which endears them to organisations like the Bar or British Rail with difficult cases to sell. Lobbying blurs into public relations, crisis management, services and the advice given by Tim Bell or David Hart to Sir Ian MacGregor during the coal strike or by Gordon Reece to Westland. All involved media massage, strategy and image building.

Saatchi's have endeavoured to develop their consultancy services but have never packaged them into a super consultancy. The high powered lobbying which advises on strategies rather than doing donkey work has not taken institutional form in specialised firms advising clients on the whole development and projection of their case: what chords to strike, what keys to press. Such firms exist in America where corporate and political campaigning overlap, but not yet here. What we have done is to professionalise the skills of the Parliamentary researchers, the ejected politician and even the current practitioner, who all offer themselves as guides to the wonderful world of Parliament, to the complexities of development, regional and European, financing (much like jungle guides though without machete knives) or who specialise on their former parliamentary interests as consultants. What is on offer here is expertise, contacts, and information services: the last being probably the aspect most in demand. Here I must declare an interest. *The House Magazine*, of which I am an associate editor, has its own information service. Few MPs are expert enough to offer specialised consultancy of any value but many offer themselves as Sherpas to expeditions, big and small. All this is not dissimilar to the House's seventy barristers, plying for hire. Except that lobbyists work on longer contracts and usually posthumously, after losing seats.

Smaller firms, surprisingly ignorant of parliamentary and political realities, are prone to hire the help of the proliferation of consulting firms, agents and advisers. So too are local government units, and also firms coming in from outside the UK, particularly the Japanese who are anxious to understand the natives. Large British companies needing such services prefer to have it 'in house' as the Law Society has done when it took on Walter Merrick, critic turned gamekeeper, after its conveyancing defeat, to organise a more effective (and far lower profile) campaign against the conveyancing aspects of the Lord Chancellor's legal reforms. In business the bumper crop of ex-Cabinet Ministers, usually Tory but also a few disillusioned Labour (the still illusioned do public service things), are recruited as directors. This is more likely to be for contacts and influence even though their dismissal is often due to a failure of both than for business value. Indeed, Douglas Strachan, the director of ProNed (Promotion of Non-Executive Directors) has said that 'Politicians make rotten non-executive directors – they really have no idea of what the job is all about'.

Full time senior company officers are also brought in from PR politics, the professional version in Central Office and Transport House (R I P), or from Departmental PR. They chat up politicians, hang round the political fringe and pick up large tabs at party conferences. In a few areas of business, Dunlop is one instance, companies have poached civil servants or military brass, nominally for expertise, in fact for contacts and knowledge of the government machine. Here is the area most open to abuse. Controls are laxer than in America where the seepage is more common. They depend too much on the integrity of sound chaps and the wisdom of 'old boy' networks and trust. They do not cover effectively the new 'consultants' often operating freelance in the defence field and so not employed directly by anyone.

The wise lobbyist gravitates to power. In Britain that lies with the executive, Ministers, departments, public bodies. Here, as is established in other chapters (especially Chapter 11), successful lobbying aims at influence on Departments before policy is placed on the Parliamentary conveyor belt. There, changes have to be effected against a Government majority and entrenched civil service opinion. So the range of topics where Parliament is a sensible place to seek change (as opposed to being the last chance) is few. The best lobbyists should not need to seek concessions because they have influenced the Department. Civil servants did in the past see their function as delivering what is pleasing to their client groups, less so now when Government's restless interventionism puts cats into every available pigeon loft. Thus Barney Holbeche claims that the NFU does not get things all their own way from MAFF but they have for a long period, until Government determined to cut spending. Mrs Thatcher took up reform of the CAP reducing their automatic support for Brussels and food safety became an issue. It was because Mrs Currie attacked the agricultural producers and spoke up for the consumers that she both highlighted the extent of MAFF's conspiracy with the producers, and had, herself, to go, a sacrificial victim to their anger. A case so unusual that it completely wrongfooted the Labour Party which at first had gone into battle against her, then belatedly switched to her defence.

Parliament is a court of appeal for those who fail at the real centre of power. Its most powerful leverage is exercised within the governing party, the fringes of the court whose support is necessary to get proposals through. In recent years, several ministers with reform proposals – Lord Young with the brewers, Nicholas Ridley with water privatisation; Lord Mackay with legal reform – have had a hard time from their own party which has modified their decision. The House itself is less important, the forum for their rows and recriminations after the decisions are taken. Commercial lobbying usually spills over into caucus and out to consumers as part of wider public campaigns, often on questions of survival, takeover, monopoly enquiries (Rowntree, Plessey, the Brewers, Credit Cards) or on government contracts, particularly in the defence field, such as Westland, GEC's Nimrod radar aircraft, frigate building, the Challenger tank replacement, ICL and computer contracts, or prescribing of drugs in the NHS. The instinctive response is usually to drape the cause in the flag and fight in Parliament and through the media on jobs, contracts, constituency and national interests. This has mixed results: TSR2 lost, Concorde half saved and then lost, the British Challenger's successor reprieved though not yet authorised, Rowntree lost, Plessey reprieved and the Brewers' winning a mild reprieve which doesn't leave them too bitter since they retain most of their tied houses and an association with the rest despite Lord Young's initial 'inclination' to accept a Monopolies and Merger Report which wanted divestment of over 2,000 tied houses. Interestingly many of these battles are now shifting, at least in part, to the European front as growing EC competence makes the Commission more influential in commercial matters. Parliament will, therefore, become shriller and more assertive because its influence will be even less in a multi theatre struggle.

The Thatcher Government's restless reformism added a new market for lobbyists from threatened professions and institutions, most spectacularly the Bar threatened with solicitor competition, the Law Society threatened with Building Society competition and the BMA opposing the health service reform. All posed as true friends of the consumer but the BMA working through the patients waged the most politically effective campaign, to the great annoyance of government and its MPs. However, the Bar with some help from Saatchi and more from the judges, actually had more success in modifying initial Government intentions.

All this is negative. Positive successes in prodding government into doing something it might not otherwise have done seem to be rare. The Port Employer's campaign to end the National Dock Labour Scheme built up steady pressure over three years. Failing with ministers they turned to MPs. An Early Day Motion was signed by the majority of Conservatives, and this led to the sudden abolition decision in April 1989 and a bill passed by the end of June which became the opportunity for a purge of the docks with redundancy paid by the taxpayer. Privatisation, too, was a lobbying process as nationalised industries worked to push themselves up the agenda. Roy Watts, of Thames Water, lobbied for privatisation and then to change Government's mind on the formula while Contract Prison Plc lobbied to break down the Home Office resistance. How many of these operations, positive or negative, were handled by commercial lobbyists is not clear. Yet there is little indication that they could have added much. The voice of strong concern comes over clearly on its own and is best voiced directly and personally rather than filtered through middlemen. MPs do not have to be persuaded to participate on such issues. They clamour to do so.

As a consumer I am unimpressed by commercial lobbying in Parliament. Of course Labour is less likely to be lobbied than the Conservatives except in last resort situations, where we can be the kiss of death, so my view may be distorted. It is clear that commercial lobbying has increased almost exponentially, though it is still neither obsessive nor intrusive and some of it seems to me to perform as a talisman or lucky charm to ward off insecurity rather than through any cool assessment of its value. Rather than being a problem it helps to educate MPs, albeit one sidedly. It provides them with information, contacts, inside dope. It is helpful where government itself is grudging. Any Member worth his salt can easily evaluate what's true and necessary and what is special pleading and unlikely. Nevertheless it is hardly effective. The complaint then is not that there is lobbying. That is both defensible and inevitable. It is that lobbying is so often done so badly. As Charles Miller argues, it is the client that often needs protection and not the political system.

The *House Buyer's Bill* of 1983-4 provided a vivid example, for a Private Member's Bill requires an MP to be Government Department, whip, propagandist and lobbyist. That job is too big for anyone. Campaigning is impossible without professional help which in my case came from David Tench and Penny Duckham of the Consumers' Association. They provided briefs, circulated MPs (for we are restricted to six letters a day internally) and financed opinion polls to indicate how popular and necessary my bill was, countering the Law Society's own polls showing how much people enjoyed handing highly respected solicitors large sums of money for conveyancing. All this was invaluable. On the other side, the Law Society hired professional lobbyists and their advice combined with the Society's own self-righteous impetuosity to produce a mass lobbying effort – the details of which all leaked to me because the solicitors were divided. Solicitors attended MPs' surgeries to the great annoyance of many. They pressurised individual MPs, alienating them. They produced a foolish statement that MPs should be 'stopped' voting for my bill which provided me with a point of 'privilege' which was useless in parliamentary terms but invaluable as publicity. The bill would probably not have got 100 MPs for closure and survived its second reading had the Law Society not put so many backs up in its text book example of how not to do it.

No MP need ever eat alone, or pay the bill. In the constituency, local firms are becoming more anxious to keep in touch, particularly the bigger national ones. In London, trade associations, head offices, and professional lobbyists take over the tab. Parliamentary researchers and party staff disappear into the lobbying world, giving up the theory for the practicals, and earning more for it. Yet I am suspicious of lobbyists who promise introductions to men of power and then arrange functions at the House of Commons, where the catering is dreary, attended by me and people like me. My own efforts and unbalanced activity are at the disposal of anything which benefits my constituency. Indeed, it would be insulting to be paid, bribed or even fed, to do my job and I would, and do, resent intermediaries who come between me and local firms or causes.

Both the role and the nature of Members of Parliament have changed. Interest based on long experience is now relegated to the House of Lords, a geriatric cess pit of vested interests where badly paid life peers supplement their meagre incomes by plying for hire, and lobbyists, directors, and senior professionals have no need to register. Indeed it is almost as if interest is sanctified by ermine. Downstairs MPs are elected younger, before they have established themselves in any field or career, other than politics. This professional political class has lost its old role of relaying public opinion to government because opinion polls are far more accurate and sensitive than MPs, who are rather like cushions bearing the impress of whoever last sat on them. Constituency demands have grown, though they are mostly of a low order: social work, message bearing, occasionally mediating, plus intermittent unskilled promotion work for their area since development has become cut throat competition for footloose industry and jobs.

So they throw themselves into lobbying and Parliament becomes the apparent focal point for lobbying not because it is powerful but because it is the only open part of Government, the place where the arguments are put and tested, the location where the personnel of power, and its threads, come together, and the place where rearguard actions against executive decisions are fought. MPs are amateur lobbyists with nothing much to lobby, except each other. Yet lobbying skills are becoming a marketable proposition. Firms, businessmen, organisations, even local government, are depressingly ignorant of political processes, surprisingly in awe of Parliament, and even prone to believe that their case is best advanced by hiring help: be it PR, Ad agency, or the kind of television training for executives which has them all saying 'I'm glad you asked me that question'. In each sphere it is legitimate to question the value they got for their money. Nowhere more so than in political lobbying.

All this explains the concentration. Yet it does not indicate influence, Parliament has so little power. Members might have monkey wrenches to throw into the works, but not too many. They can't throw them all at once. Possession of such offensive weapons is largely confined to backbenchers of the governing party. Governments really defer only to those they fear. Today that is only the electorate. The executive controls the legislature and MPs are there to heckle from the Kop: commenting on the play but hardly influencing the game. Who would hire hecklers? Except the naive or those with a bad case. Which is why it is so little use to wine and dine MPs. There is such a thing as a free lunch. For MPs. Because they have so little to give in return – except their own whines for the dine plus the undoubtful charm and pleasure of their company. They do have powers but those of the minor, tinkering, bodging, mechanic not the man of destiny. They can ask questions. Some do obsessively to highlight issues or get information. They can draw attention to problems. Particularly once things have been spelled out to them. They can move amendments to legislation, and such major measures as the *Finance Bill* and the occasional Financial Services or Companies' Bill become the focus of major lobbyists with Tory backbenchers working hard at their keep. Usually they are allowed to make gestures which are regularly withdrawn for they can be successful only with Labour support which is withheld, except on issues of principle. MPs can urge points of view, with some deterioration in the style and the grammar and carry messages to the great, even if they do get garbled. The literate can sign Early Day Motions. They regularly do, on anything, for an increasing number of organisations are checking signatures and demanding new ones. They can fly kites in Ten Minute Rule Bills. They can even introduce real legislation, so anyone coming at the head of the ballot for Private Members Bills is suddenly very desirable. The ability to withdraw such a bill and make way for others is also a power and one which I have personally been offered - a bribe in the shape of a substantial donation to the Grimsby Labour Party's appeal if I would withdraw a Bill I was going to pull anyway, to expedite another in which the bookmakers had a strong interest. As for the bills themselves, of course, no one would sully the Procedure with the Austin Mitchell *Imports PLC (Compulsory Trebling of Profits and Conferment of Permanent Statutory Monopoly) Bill*. Yet the highest principles have commercial consequences, therefore many bills come gift wrapped with a professional campaign to back them.

Large public pressure groups, the Police Federation, the Insurance Industry, the Banks, the Oil companies, the Trade Associations, the Unions, the Co-op, the Bookies, have enough need of a voice in Parliament to pay someone. They buy 'prestige', access, and a voice, rather than influence. I assumed it was rather the ability MPs have to write impressive letters on headed notepaper or the contact in local government. Yet who now takes much notice of either? Such minor services can, and should, be available without charge to just causes and commercial interest which further the constituency. The best lobbyists, like Des Wilson, are those who do it for causes, not cash. They are effective because passion and conviction carry more weight than money or oil on the wheels of power ever could. So what is really needed commercially is what cannot be bought: an inside track. Newly available ex-Cabinet Ministers are only joggers on it. Yet they are usually snapped up for directorships, or as ornaments, rather than channels of real influence. What Jim Prior achieved for GEC is not immediately obvious but Norman Tebbit's role at Blue Arrow might not have been unconnected with the DTI enquiry.

In default of detailed case studies evidence must be anecdotal and impressionistic, even after the archives are opened. Much influence is ascribed but little found. Our vested interests still prefer the prehistoric battles of class and party to the subtle chess games of influence-peddling. On minor matters, and on rearguard actions when all else has failed, they will lobby clumsily. On major matters: running of the economy, interest rates, economic survival, they rally behind party lines, or concentrate on triumphing over the other side in the old class/interest struggle of an 'us and them' society. The 1979-81 deflation closed much of British manufacturing capacity andbankrupted many firms but all the machinery of influence, consultation and lobbying of the CBI and of the old boy network were unable to stop, or even check it. In America's open system Reagan reversed the same policies in eighteen months. It is difficult to compare the scale of the lobbying effort focusing on Parliament with that directed at Whitehall. Charles Miller argues for the importance of Whitehall but secrecy makes it difficult to assess its influence. So it may be that the Parliamentary side seems so important just because it is open and we know more about it. Perhaps, though, Parliament is an active field of lobbying because it is there, and the growing lobbying effort has nowhere else to focus. Perhaps, too, the lobbyists are incompetent, and the lobbyers unaware of their own interest, duped by the professionals and overawed by their own deference and ignorance. In this sense lobbying is a self-sustaining, self-generating process which could even be an inverse ratio to the power of its locus, witness the scale of the effort now focusing on the European Parliament.

'I am lobbied therefore I am important' could give Parliament a more useful role than it naturally possesses in Britain's strong executive system. Why not, therefore, enjoy it? The new breed of professional MPs want it, and its financial pickings, plus the feeling of importance and the information flows it brings. Televising the Commons has increased its importance, not because MPs will be wearing sponsored T shirts, but because they can put over a sympathetic argument and because an institution has only to appear on television to be assumed to be important: rather like the Eurovision Song Contest. Or the Lords.

Other developments are also possible. Information services are really late, rather than early, warning systems because by the time regulations and bills reach Parliament they are largely cut and dried. Yet if MPs could shape them in advance in committee, as they do in New Zealand, their job, and the lobbying, would both be more effective. Lobbying is already focusing on the departmental select committees, though these are really a means of educating MPs in a specialist area and examining the intellectual bases of government policy (a fairly short job with this one). All this will develop as the House becomes more specialised, its main restraint being the inability of MPs to carry a much heavier work load. Even here the lobbyists could help and provision of research assistance is not unknown already. Indeed, suspicion about the scale of this and the privileged access it conferred on some lobbyists (and to Pamella Bordes) was one of the reasons why MPs have now been restricted to three passes for assistants.

We can't stop it. Let's use it and ensure that it stays above board; interesting but impotent, like eunuchs in a harem. The old checks of honour, disinterest and declaration of vested interest are as dead as Poulson. The old defences of privilege and 'conduct unbecoming' are useless. Indeed they could kill everyone in sight if they were trundled into action. Taste is no control: it didn't cause Sir Marcus Fox to give up his consultancy work, though to be fair only taste required him to. So the only effective restraint which can be enforced is openness, rather than controls which are impossible to police. Register all interests of MPs, including their income, and for the MP consultants and lobbyists who they consult for and lobby. Register all lobbyists and organise them in a 'lobby' like the press lobby, restrained by the same sort of club rules and self-discipline. Most complaints about poor and unethical lobbying come from within the lobbying industry. As lobbyists in this collection of essays show, there is concern that the bad can drive out the good. So MPs can assist the more responsible firms by their own behaviour and responses to lobbying. Abuses can exist because members are not selective enough with whom they 'sup'. So, give MPs the ability to cope with it which means better paid and better backed MPs who are neither bribable nor grubbing for meals, theatre tickets, jobs or help on the side. Lobbying is no problem if MPs are less dependent and better equipped to do the job, rather than having to turn to lobbyists for help.

Those are all the safeguards we need. Provided the supreme one remains in place. MPs are neither saleable nor bribable because they are impotent. They have nothing to sell. I blame Bagehot for giving the wrong impression of lobbying (that it is a detraction from lofty independence) and for painting an inaccurate picture of MPs as having influence because Parliamentary debate means something. Bagehot is dead. So is his picture. MPs can be influenced, though usually by media panics on such issues as child abuse, Rotweillers, football hooliganism, rather than by more subtle lobbies. MPs have been bought in the past, and I don't see principles as being higher today, while there are many younger MPs eager to get on and make a bob or two. Yet MPs are worth buying only for minor DIY jobs because they have no power. I wouldn't trust Honourable Members an inch if they did.

1 The Professional Persuaders

GRANT JORDAN

Introduction

> In the United States, though lobbying is perfectly legitimate in theory, yet the secrecy and want of personal responsibility, the confusion and want of system in the committees, make it rapidly degenerate into a process of intrigue, and fall into the hands of the worst men. It is so disagreeable and humiliating that all men shrink from it, unless those who are stimulated by direct personal interest; and these soon throw away all scruples. The most dangerous men are ex-members, who know how things are managed.
> (Advice received by James Bryce in the writing of *The American Commonwealth*, 1888, Vol. 1, p.558).

While the Shorter Oxford has a bland definition of 'the lobby' which limits the meaning to the neutral exerting of influence, it does cite a more hostile Bryce-like source of 1884 which ran, 'The lobby and corruption are legitimate subjects for satire.' Common uses of the term – like the dictionary definitions – smuggle in a suspicion in the small print. One American lobbyist has complained in his memoirs:

> My mother has never introduced me to her friends as 'My son, the lobbyist'. My son, the Washington Representative, maybe. Or the Legislative Consultant. Or the Government Relations Counsel. But never as the Lobbyist. I can't say I blame her ...
> (cited in Schlozman and Tierney, 1986, p.261).

Though he sees the portrayal as unfair a leading commercial lobbyist and a contributor to this volume, Ian Greer, pointed out in an earlier book that there is a common picture of the '... lobbyist as a somewhat shady or sinister individual, working furtively behind the scenes on behalf of equally shady clients whose objectives are not always seen to be in the best public interest.' It might be worth noting that this slight undercurrent of sharp practice is not entirely harmful for the industry; after all in attracting clients it is useful if they think that it is only decorum that stops the lobbyist from claiming that he or she can provide an unfair advantage.

That lobbying is still a suspect activity in Britain was demonstrated by a powerful call by Anthony Howard in September 1989. He argued that far from being 'an accepted part of the democratic process', lobbying represented a gross affront to it. He claimed that in suggesting it is possible to buy a service that will improve the chances of favourable outcomes, there is the necessary implication that the lobbyist's trade must be regarded as 'not just distasteful but an insidious one, too'. Howard says that there has always been a belief held by some that democracy is no more than a sham – and that the lobbyists and their publicity were lending aid and comfort to that suspicion. He concluded that in that sense the lobbyist could not be anything but an enemy of democracy. (The *Independent*, 23rd September, 1989).

This book is aimed at stimulating more notice of the activity of commercial lobbyists in Britain. On the whole the thrust of this book is that lobbying is inevitable: the supply of expert comment on the likely practical impact of proposals is often useful for the development of public policies (as well as useful for the narrow interests of those in whose name the lobbying is conducted). However there is no unanimity among the authors collected here. There are worries that the lobbyists give an unfair advantage to those who can afford their services. There is also however the rather different worry that some lobbying entrepreneurs are a bigger threat to their clients than they are to the public interest: that their expensive activities are not only ill directed but even counter productive.

Concern is also found in Strasbourg as well as Westminster. David Martin, MEP, who is a member of the bureau responsible for regulations governing the European Parliament has called for an official register of the wheeler-dealers with the cheque books. (*Observer*, 1st October, 1989). Another MEP was reported as being stunned when he discovered the extent of the lobby influence. He said, 'It has reached the stage where lobbyists are queueing up to buy us dinner and bend our ears on all sorts of issues'. Mr Martin was quoted saying, 'I am not opposed to lobbyists, but a register is essential if big businesses and multi-national companies are to be prevented from seeming to purchase legislation that benefits them... There is so much legislation now about harmonisation of technical standards... A company has a lot to gain by having its standard accepted...'

This is all an echo of the worries expressed domestically.

In that it is often, and correctly, assumed that our growing lobbying industry means that we are following American practice, this introduction particularly selects cues and clues from the American literature. (But it is worth noting the distinctive role in the US of interest groups and lobbyists as sources of campaign finance: British groups have no comparable role – and hence diminished access). This US orientation is reinforced by a chapter from Professor Graham Wilson who has studied interest groups on both sides of the Atlantic – and also by explicit comparisons made by Wyn Grant in Chapter 5. In Britain we are (even) less aware of the lobbying conducted in Canada. A chapter by Professor Paul Pross demonstrates however, not only its importance there, but the attention given there to ethical issues. In Britain we seem slower to confront these.

Canada moved to register lobbying in 1988 after a period of controversy that seems to have started with the activities of Frank Moores of GCI (Government Consultants International). Moores was a former premier of Newfoundland who moved to operate in Ottawa when Prime Minister Mulroney took over. According to John Sawatsky (1987), he was one of the few men in Canada who could pick up the phone and reach the PM.

His behaviour caused media concern when it appeared that he could deliver a fishing licence transfer for £3,000 and when he kept on consultancies with Norair, Wardair and a Munich plane maker (MMB) when appointed to the board of Air Canada.

Sawatsky says, (1987, p.317):

> Whether the image was justified or not Frank Moores symbolized the quick fix school of lobbying. Nobody produced evidence of influence peddling but everybody suspected it.

The Canadian material thus reflects the same unease as has arisen in Britain – but with the difference that if Canadian MPs worked for fees as in Britain for specific companies, the political culture would define this as scandal.

The starting point of this book is accurately recorded by the title – *The Commercial Lobbyists*. The commercial lobbyist takes up – subject to personal reservations – any causes, corporate or promotional, that seek professional assistance. (In Chapter 3 Graham Wilson uses an alternative term – *contract* lobbyist). The companies we have in mind tend to operate by seeking to influence civil servants, Ministers, and, to a lesser degree, Members of Parliament. They are not routinely active in large campaigns oriented towards building up public pressure. Such public awareness campaigns tend to be the realm of the PR rather than the lobbying consultant.

Though the activities of these multi client lobbyists are more controversial than those of the 'in-house' lobbyist who works wholly for one employer, there is often considerable overlap in their operations. Therefore it seemed useful to extend our survey of the service and operations of the 'for hire' lobbyists with those of 'in-house' operations. Thus we have a chapter by Wyn Grant which describes the growth of the 'governmental relations function' within major companies. Inevitably the activities, tactics and strategies, of these professional lobbyists with one interest in dealing with the political system are not dissimilar from those of the 'bought- in' lobbyists. Likewise the activities of professional 'in-house' lobbyists for trade associations and public bodies such as NFU, the National Consumer Council or the Food and Drink Federation, or whatever, are similar to those of the major corporate lobbyists. (See chapters by Holbeche and Smith). A profile of the Director-General of the Building Societies Association, Mark Boleat, in *The Observer* (8th January, 1989) obscurely claimed that, 'He's not a lobbyist, more of a straightforward advocate.' He defined his own job as, 'working for the members .. (and) representing their interests to the media and – perhaps even more important – to government.' The line between the essence of the political work of the BSA and of a commercial consultancy is thus insubstantial. The profile went on to claim, *networking* is one of Boleat's particular strengths. The BSA wines and dines politicians of all hue ... 'We like to get to know politicians and civil servants who are rising.'

In late 1988 when the salmonella scare prompted the resignation of the Junior Minister at the Department of Health, Edwina Currie, press concern on the possibly overpowerful lobbying was aimed not only at the activities of the 'in-house' lobbyists of the NFU and the British Poultry Federation but also by commercial companies acting on their own account.

The salmonella saga in which the Government rejected its own 'stand on your own feet' instincts to give interim support of £20 million to the egg producers, shows the importance of Government to commercial concerns – and thereby gives the explanation of the attention paid by commerce to Government. Large companies can, in their own interests, be as active and effective as pressure groups or trade associations.

Examples of large politically aware companies in the egg-example included Dalgety and Unilever. Such organisations do not have to purchase lobbying skills from commercial consultancies: they also relate to the political system in other ways. The *Independent* (24th December, 1988) showed that the chairman of the owners of the largest selling egg brand, Dalgetys, was Sir Peter Carey, retired Permanent Secretary at the Department of Trade and Industry (1976-83). One of the top four poultry feed producers, J. Bibby and Sons, had a former Leader of the House Commons as a non-executive director. Unilever, owner of the biggest food producer BOCM Silcock, has former Cabinet Secretary, Lord Hunt, as an 'advisory director'. Pauls, part of Harrisons and Crosfield, another big feed supplier donated £9,700 to the Conservative Party funds in the last election year.

The *Sunday Times* (18th December, 1988) chose to focus on the activities of the National Farmers' Union. It recorded that even with a deterioration in the relationship between the NFU and the Conservative Party there were still 50 Tory MPs who kept close to their local NFU branches. The NFU passed their data on the 'Currie effect' to selected MPs including Robert Hicks, Robert Maxwell-Hyslop, Sir Peter Emery, Sir Hal Miller, Tim Boswell and David Curry. The NFU wrote to 200 MPs and many were given telephone briefings. The NFU's six poultry specialists were able to mobilise the 46 county branches to contact their local Members.

The contacts were to officials as well as politicians. The *Sunday Times* asserted that the Ministry of Agriculture had always been little more than a mouthpiece for the farming lobby, and,'... that the lobby's hired guns on the Tory back benches' had served Mrs Currie's head on a plate. Teddy Taylor MP claimed, 'Any minister speaking for consumers in a manner displeasing to the National Farmers' Union seems to be a political health hazard.'

It is worth adding that the Agriculture Minister, John MacGregor, explicitly countered the agricultural *MAFFia* suspicion in an article in the *Daily Telegraph* (22nd December, 1988) by pointing out that a series of changes such as the reform of the Common Agricultural Policy had been introduced against farming resistance. 'So MAFF is not in anybody's pocket.' But even this rejection by the Minister of a too cosy picture, did confirm a 'special relationship':

> Of course we consult the industry on many matters, just as all Ministers sensibly consult those in their fields of responsibility who are affected by their actions.

How clse could a complicated new scheme thought up in the corridors of power work on the ground in deepest Somerset? But consultation and co-operation are different from collusion. When I invite comments from the National Farmers' Union and similar organisations in the industry I listen and often see a side to an issue which I, my fellow Ministers, and my officials had not previously been aware of.

Though he did go on to make the assurance that he also consulted and represented a wider range of interests, the impression was none the less that the fall in the real incomes of farmers meant that the Ministry saw its current role as a support to the industry rather than a critic.

A major area of lobbying concerns corporate take-overs which may be referred to the Monopolies Commission. The account of the Guinness bid for Distillers (Saunders, 1990) noted that the Guinness chairman had an essentially political problem in defeating the rival bidder, the Argyll Group:

...Roger Seelig and Gordon Reece made it perfectly clear that as far as I was concerned there was only one priority: given Argyll's political clout, employing Sir Alex Fletcher, ex DTI minister, and with Cranley Onslow, chairman of the Tories backbench 1922 committee on their board, I would have to do everything to avoid our bid being referred ...

However Guinness had their own political advantages with Sir Peter Carey, the former DTI Permanent Secretary, sitting on the board of their advisers, Morgan Grenfell. Sir Jack Lyons appears to have been a useful contact to political circles

Not only industry lobbies: the Royal Society for the Protection of Birds has two lobbyists with an office near Westminster. Their parliamentary liaison officer has described his work as follows;

I usually spend two days a week in Parliament. This week, for instance, it will be three. Lobbying is a growth industry in Britain and is becoming very competitive. If the RSPB wishes to continue strong in the conservation movement, then we need to keep abreast of modern trends in lobbying Parliamentarians.
(*Observer Scotland*, 29th January, 1989)

If there are problems of acceptable practice in this broad area it seems unlikely that they arise only when the lobbying is done by hired consultants. A glance at *The House Magazine* which deals with Parliament will find that organisations as varied as BAA, the Chemical Industries Association, the Brewers' Association and the Anti-Slavery Society offer information services for Members.

An example of the hybrid system that can develop beween 'in-house' and 'bought-in' lobbying was described to the Select Committee on Members' Interests in 1988, by British Airways' Director of Public Affairs,

> ... we work in a very political environment. Everything relating to our industry
> ... (is) decided upon by negotiations between Governments internationally.
> Our fares structure in some areas ... is dependent upon government policy. So
> the company divides its activities between what is called in the airline industry
> 'Government affairs', and the more general corporate parliamentary lobbying
> activities which I am responsible for ... A retainer is paid as consultants to
> British Airways to Ian Greer Associates ... Rather than employing a large
> number of parliamentary affairs officers in-house, I have one parliamentary
> affairs officer within the public affairs department.

Any weakness of the collection is not that some contributions stray from
the strict remit of the title – but that there has not been room to include
studies of the full time and professional lobbying that is done by moral or
'cause' interests. (Martin Smith's study in Chapter 7 of the National Consumer Council is the nearest to dealing with that sort of body). They too usually work on the basis of timely advice in the pre legislative stages that marks
out the most successful lobbying operations. The naive idea that 'cause'
groups do not lobby can be corrected by referring to the examples above or
the point made in a letter by Jonathan Porritt of Friends of the Earth and Des
Wilson of Campaign for Lead Free Air to *The Sunday Telegraph* (19th September, 1988). There they said:

> ... our organisations win far more battles than they lose because of the high
> priority we put on detailed and authoritative research. And we gain support
> precisely because we are prepared to try to solve the problems together. Thus,
> CLEAR's involvement with the petroleum industry, let alone Friends of the
> Earth's co-sponsorship of a conference with the National Coal Board, its
> patient negotiations with the Timber Trade Federation, regular meetings with
> the National Farmers' Union *and endless sessions with the Department of the
> Environment.* (emphasis added).

Is there a British industry?
One no longer really needs to produce much evidence in support of the
claim that a commercial lobbying industry has grown up in Britain. It is all
too obvious. In an article in the *House Magazine* in November 1985 Norman
Tebbit complained of the 'present day hot-bed of lobbying in and around our
political life.' When the Thames Water Authority wanted to oppose the idea
of a National Rivers Authority as part of the privatised water industry, they
hired Ian Greer and Associates. When in November 1987 the P & O group
wanted to ensure that Tory MPs stayed up to vote in an all-night debate on
their Private Bill to extend the Felixstowe Docks, their lobbying advisers,
Charles Barker Watney and Powell, organised a champagne party – though
in the event this was cancelled after protests by the Opposition that this was
'buying votes'. The Director of Public Relations for British Airways told the
Select Committee on Members' Interests in July 1988 that more than 50 MPs
are entertained by BA on a regular basis. According to the *Daily Telegraph*
(16th July, 1988):

Almost every MP benefits from its hospitality at some point, ... This can include being wined and dined at the airline's expense, free trips or being upgraded to club or first class when travelling on Parliamentary business. Among the 'excursions' offered to MPs recently was a day-trip to Toulouse to mark the delivery of British Airways first A320 airbus. MPs were also flown to Rio when BA took over British Caledonian's South American routes, and to Atlanta, Georgia, to discuss American aviation. The MPs are normally drawn from specialist committees covering aviation, tourism and trade whose interests could be relevant to BA's operation. Other Members with local constituency interests are also targetted.

There is a tendency in traditional political science circles to discount the importance of technical changes to detailed legislation – which are the main business of the lobbyists – but the idea that there are political agenda items which are put forward by political parties – and which are more significant and different from those put forward by interests – is questionable in two ways. Firstly, it should not be assumed that the degree of partisan controversy is a measure of objective importance. Secondly, it is clear that the party shop window can be filled by sectional interests. For example Kate Ascher (1988, p.49) gives the following account of the 'selling' of 'contracting out' to the Conservative Party:

Private sector contractors and their trade associations played the foremost role in the lobbying campaign. At least three separate industries – catering, cleaning and textile maintenance – were involved in lobbying efforts in the early 1980s. Contracting firms fought their war on a number of separate battle fields. Party conferences and meetings with ministers were favoured, but they also used local authority and NHS exhibitions and seminars. Informal lobbying through Conservative Party channels helped secure some parliamentary support, but the most visible means by which contractors furthered their cause was through paid lobbyists. A few hired Michael Forsyth Associates to do their public relations work for them, while others went directly to the House of Commons to find suitable 'lobbyists' among the endless back-benches of the Conservative Party. Some looked to civil servants ... The Contract Cleaning and Maintenance Association (CCMA), for example, recruited John Hall from the Ministry of Defence; formerly in charge of monitoring the contracting out of cleaning in MOD buildings, Hall became the CCMA's Secretary-General. Another example involves Hospital Hygiene Services (HHS), a cleaning firm based in Yorkshire, which hired one of the DHSS administrators responsible for putting together the Department's competitive cleaning circular.

The idea of prison privatisation was advanced by former Conservative Central Office staff, Tony Hutt and Anne Strutt, who lobbied for Contract Prisons Plc – a company chaired by Sir Edward Gardner. (Wise, 1989) If the lobbying industry does not make the pages of every day's press, it at least seems to manage a weekly mention in the Sunday editions. (The next chapter suggests that this routinisation of lobbying is in large measure a post Second World War development.) There is a 'me-too' pressure for the increase in the frequency of lobbying. If one's opponents are employing a lobbying consultancy, then the assumption is that one is not giving 100% if one refrains from hiring a counter-consultant.

There is a widespread view that not only is there more lobbying than in the past but it has changed its character. In his evidence to the Select Committee on Members' Interests in 1988, Stanley Orme MP (Chairman of the Parliamentary Labour Party) argued:

> Organisations that used to lobby Members were themselves the organisations and they approached you; it might have been the engineering or building industry or whatever. Now we get approached, all Members do, with very glossy headed notepaper from consultants and those consultants are Parliamentary consultants. They pick up people who have themselves worked here ... they pick up people, like civil servants, and they have Members of Parliament who may also be consultants to them ... I feel that therefore the professional lobbying organisations have become much more Americanised ...

In summary therefore this book is mainly about the operations of the professional consultants who act as intermediaries and advisers to the interest groups and interests – often but certainly not exclusively business based who are attempting to influence governmental policy or decisions. However the boundaries cannot be firm. The *function* of lobbying is often undertaken by non lobbying organisations – eg merchant banks operating on take-over proposals. The lobbying firms have no monopoly.

The scale of the new industry

Besides those firms represented by chapters in this book – Ian Greer and Associates, The Public Policy Consultants – the industry includes (or included as the list of titles alters monthly) GJW, Market Access International, Sallingbury Casey, Countrywide Political Communications, CSM Parliamentary Consultants, Good Relations, Shandwick Public Affairs, Wedgwood Markham, Profile Corporate and Political Relations Ltd, Westminster Strategy, etc. In 1988 bodies like the Royal Institute for Public Administration and the Institute of Directors were offering seminars for those who required advice on the nature of Whitehall lobbying.

A survey report to the Select Committee on Members' Interests in 1988 showed that about a half of the 350 interest groups sampled, 'said they were worried about the lobbying world getting too crowded.'(HC, 518-iii, p.27) It has been estimated that the business was worth some £9.75-10 million by 1987. (*Select Committee on Members' Interests,* 518-vi, p.85). A survey published in the *Financial Times* in 1985 claimed that of 180 major British companies, 41% of them used political consultancies (paying them an average of

£28,000 p.a.) and 28% used public relations companies for work involving Government (paying them an average of £33,100 p.a.). David Rose in the *Guardian* in 1988 was quoted a fee of £40,000 as the scale of charges for an attempt to alter a major piece of legislation. A basic information service on parliamentary developments of relevance to a company might cost in the order of £4,000. A retainer of £2,500 a month – increasing to £5,000 if active lobbying is necessary – is apparently the sort of scale of charge to be expected. (*The Times*, 12th July, 1988). In 1984 the 'going rate' of payment for an MP to put down a written PQ was cited as about £200 with oral questions costing considerably more (*Observer*, 1st July, 1984). As an MP in 1986 Sir Alex Fletcher apparently met representatives of the Dutton-Forshaw Motor Group who were interested in purchasing Land Rover. He offered to help, '... negotiations with HMG, BL and other parties regarding the proposed aquisition ... of the Land Rover subsidiary of BL.' A report recorded a £5,000 'briefing fee', a £5,000-a-month retainer, and expenses. There was to be a minimum of £15,000 if the deal failed and a bonus of £25,000 – in addition to other fees – if it went ahead. (*Observer Scotland*, 23rd October, 1988). A consultancy to a group like National Licensed Victuallers Association is apparently worth £3,000 per year to an MP. (See reference to Stan Crowther in *Observer Magazine*, 14th October, 1990). The perk of the free travel seems as relevant as direct fees. The Bophuthatswana Government paid for around 12 trips there in 1989 by MPs. The *Observer Magazine* (14th October, 1990) estimated the cost per trip as £4,000. Another perk is research assistance with some 20 MPs having an assistant provided. This is admittedly pretty small change compared with the £156,000 reportedly given to (then) Senator John Tower for two years work in the US by British Aerospace. This fee was for helping them 'work the system' in selling civil aircraft and military equipment in America.

On the side of what a client can hope to get out of such a deal Charles Miller and Roger Hayes (1984) accepted as credible the claim by one consultancy that it had made £150 million for one of its clients in two years by simply negotiating with a willing Government. It was claimed that lobbying in 1988 on cable TV regulation produced concessions worth millions of pounds on franchise periods and advertising breaks. (*Observer*, 9th April, 1989). Lobbying is thus in part a logical response to the Government's discretion on purchasing, in creating product legislation, in setting regulatory frameworks, and establishing the relevant tax regimes for companies. For these reasons ostensibly private companies are very often effectively 'Government controlled'.

This activity of lobbying is certainly not new. In 1955 Lt Commander Powell of the then Messrs Watney and Powell described his work in the Institute of Public Relations Journal as a, 'consultant and adviser on Parliamentary affairs to a number of trade associations and societies'. (cited in Finer, 1958, p.53).There has however been a great increase in the numbers and visibility of lobbyists in the past decade. In the complicated financial dealings that has accompanied the realisation that here was a whole new profession waiting to be invented, GJW was bought out from its founders in 1987 for £6.5 million. The turnovers of Charles Barker and Sallingbury Casey are reportedly in excess of £750,000 and that of Ian Greer Associates in excess of £1.5 million.

However impressive though such multi zero numbers may look to the layman, Charles Miller has pointed out that the total sector turnover is probably only a quarter of that of the largest UK law firm. He suggests that this might account for the fact that lawyers have not made substantial inroads in this area where their drafting and advocacy skills would put them at an advantage. As noted above the existence of the lobby firm is a regular feature in press reports. Again this publicity reflects the sort of split personality of the profession. Just as it wants to be naughty and nice, it wants to move stealthily – and, for marketing reasons, to also boast of its successes. Much of the press reporting is however of a flavour that those lobbyists attempting to develop the prestige of the profession no doubt resent.

Who Lobbies?

Companies in the market are generally small in terms of staff numbers, with Public Policy Consultants 23 consultants (some part time), GJW with 20 staff and Ian Greer with 18, making them three of the larger. (Public Policy Consultants are now part of the consolidated group, The Public Policy Unit).The professional lobbyist very often seems to have spent his appenticeship on the fringes of one of the political parties though Miller and Hayes (1984) claim that too few of the profession come from an intimate background knowledge of the Government/ industry interface. An unpublished survey for *The Economist* has suggested that only PPC and GJW have recruited more than 50% of their executive staff from senior party, civil service, or House of Commons posts. Eight active MPs have been identified as owning or being partners in consultancies. Many others are themselves employed as consultants to such firms and, of course, far more are directly employed as consultants by interest groups or companies. There is not the bias to the law background that is so striking in the USA.

The number of relevant consultancies is probably no more than 25 – with something like a dozen companies being recognised as dominant. The precise number is difficult to establish because many general public relations companies would be prepared to act as lobbyists. There are also individuals – who might also work as research assistants to MPs – who would act in this area. In the 1987 report of the Public Relations Yearbook of the Public Relations Consultants Association 51 companies claimed expertise in public affairs, but not all PRCA members engaged in lobbying were on this list and not all on the list were very prominent in lobbying. Even more relevantly many of the most active lobbyists are not PRCA members.

The most prominent of the British individuals who have crossed from the world of party politics to that of non partisan professional persuasion are probably the co founders of Gifford Jeger Weeks (GJW). Andrew Gifford is a former aide to David Steel, Jenny Jeger worked in Jim Callaghan's private office and Wilf Weeks served in Tory Central Office and in Mr Heath's private office. Political Communication also seem to have attempted to develop a 'balanced ticket' with its two Joint Managing Directors, Douglas Smith and Fred Morgan, having Conservative and Labour Party backgrounds respectively. Ian Greer was a Conservative Party agent. Nicholas True at PPC was at the Conservative Research Department before acting as adviser to Lord Whitelaw and then the Department of Health. John Houston of Market Access International was a member of Christopher Tugendhat's *cabinet* in Brussels and an adviser to Geoffrey Howe. The Labour peer, Lord Parry, is active with PPC. Peter Luff formerly at Good Relations was a political adviser to Ted Heath and Peter Walker. Claude Simmond of Burson Marsteller was a former Board of Trade director of public relations and a member of the Conservative Party publicity committee. Former Labour Minister Lord Chalfont became a director of Shandwick Consultants. David Boddy of Market Access International is a former Director of Press and PR for the Conservative Party and political press secretary to Margaret Thatcher. Fred Silvester of Advocacy Partnership Ltd is a former Conservative Member. Paul Tyler of Good Relations was Liberal MP for Bodmin. In the House of Commons on 14th July, 1984 Dennis Canavan MP accused the Stirling Member Michael Forsyth of 'moonlighting' and using his Parliamentary role to further the interests of his consultancy. Forsyth, before becoming a Minister, had been prominent on the privatisation issue while his firm had as clients contract cleaning companies. Peter Fry, Conservative Member of Parliament for Wellingborough since 1969, is one of the most high profile of current MPs in the industry as Chairman of Countrywide Political Communication.

The following MPs have also declared interests in companies whose activities include parliamentary consultancy:

Jack Aspinall	John Gorst	David Nicholson
David Atkinson	Michael Grylls	Sir Julian Ridsdale
John Butcher	Dr Keith Hampson	Peter Rost
John Carlisle	Alan Haselhurst	Sir Giles Shaw
William Cash	Denis Howell	Sir Dudley Smith
Patrick Cormack	Robert Key	Keith Speed
Quentin Davies	Sir Michael McNair-Wilson	Malcom Thornton
Hugh Dykes	Michael Mates	Sir John Wheeler
Sir Marcus Fox	Sir Fergus Montgomery	Ann Widdecombe
George Gardiner	Michael Morris	Tim Yeo

(*Observer Magazine*, 14th October, 1990)

A questioner on the Select Committee on Members' Interests in 1988 queried the status of Sir Marcus Fox and Keith Speed as directors of Westminster Communications Ltd. (HC 518-vi, p.91). Sir Marcus dismissed such criticism as 'ludicrous'. He said, 'The only people who are making these attacks are a bunch of lefties.' (*Observer*, 9th April, 1989). In evidence to the Select Committee in 1988, Public Policy Consultants advised that the rules over the Register of Members' Interests be amended to force MPs to declare the full client list of any consultancy firm with which they are connected. They argued, 'It may be that some Members merely declare a directorship of XYZ Limited without declaring that XYZ is their consultancy vehicle and is employed by clients A, B, or C.'(HC 518-vi,p.85).

In March 1990 Michael Mates MP was criticized for the fact that while chairman of the Commons Select Committee on defence he had links (now severed) to a lobby company which attempts to help manufacturers secure MOD contracts. The company's promotional material apparently includes the claim that they, ...would construct a strategy to help secure future projects by parliamentary lobbying and influential communications with Ministers and the MOD. One member of the select committee argued, 'I had no idea the chairman was involved with a consultancy which gives, as an attribute, opening doors in terms of defence contracts. I shall be calling for his resignation, (The *Independent on Sunday*, 11th March).

There was criticism that even if the relationship between Mr Mates and the company was properly registered, the rules were too lax in permitting such a role for a committee chairman in the field of interest of the committee. More over though Mr Mates had registered his links to SGL Ltd he was criticized for failing to spell out the full name of SGL *Defence* Ltd.

This controversy made it very likely that the Select Committee on Members' Interests would recommend that chairmen of select committees should have no commercial links with relevant companies.

Other chairmen with links with their field of study includes Kenneth Warren, Chairman of the Select Committee on Trade and Industry who has business interests in Datapoint UK Ltd., Jerry Wiggin (Agriculture) who is a paid consultant to British Sugar.

It can be noted that for parliamentary consultants for any interest membership of a relevant Select Committee is at a premium. It has been argued that this gives a real power to the party whips – who can influence selection to the committees and can 'punish' a Member by keeping him off a particular committee and thereby damage his usefulness for outside interests.

The most controversial relationship between an MP and outside interests in recent years concerned John Browne, MP, who apologised to the House on 7th March 1990 for failing to declare British and Middle Eastern business dealings, but was nonetheless suspended from the House for 20 days. It is at least arguable that the press and public condemnation of Mr Browne was not for the technical failure to register – but because of suspicion of such activity by MPs – whether registered or not.

The Browne case was the start of the 'open season' of MP lobbyist hunting. Sir Peter Emery, chairman of Shenley Trust Services, was criticised for the company's activities for the Government of Bophuthatswana. Sir Marcus Fox, director of Westminster Communications Ltd, and a registered consultant to the cleaning contractors Brengreen (Holdings) Ltd was criticised for speaking in favour of 'contracting out'. (The *Independent on Sunday*, 25th February; *World in Action*, January 1990).

Keith Speed, MP, also a director of Westminster Communications, was criticized because while his constituents were affected by BR's proposed route for the Channel tunnel high-speed rail link, Westminster Communication clients included the Inter City division of BR. The Labour MP Gwyneth Dunwoody was criticized for claimed links to the anti rail link lobbying company Channel Communications and Planning. The *Independent on Sunday* (11th March) reported allegations that this relationship was not recorded on the parliamentary register.

In his evidence to the Select Committee on Members' Interests in May 1990, Ian Greer reported making six payments to three MPs who had introduced clients to his firm. He mentioned that other companies would do likewise. The Committee was told by Andrew Roth that Mr Greer paid a commission of between £5,000 and £10,000 to an MP for introducing British Airways to the firm in 1984.

Michael Colvin, a senior Conservative back bencher confirmed that he had introduced clients to Ian Greer Associates, but denied that there was payment for this role. (*Independent on Sunday*, 27th May, 1990). Mr Greer had told the Committee that he paid 5% of the first year fee for introductions. One Member had received 'thank you' payments in 1985, 1986 and 1990. Another had received payments in 1986 and a third had received payment in 1988.

One of those who received a one-off payment by Ian Greer Associates was Michael Grylls, MP. The *Third Report of the Select Committee on Members' Interests* (1989-90) felt that Mr Grylls' registration of this relationship was 'insufficiently detailed'.

Of course other MPs act as consultants for single issue trade associations, companies, or pressure groups. The Report on Members' Interests in 1984 established that there were 96 MPs employed as political consultants.(Jordan, 1985). A less strict definition of Parliamentary/political consultant would have added 20/25 more to the list. Even more might be added if board membership or trades union sponsorship was seen as a form of political role as it could be under some circumstances. Other job descriptions can also 'disguise' what is effectively a lobbying relationship using a more liberal interpretation of outside interest, the *Observer Magazine*, 14th October, 1990 found 220 MPs in that category.

One specific point of criticism about the activities of MPs as lobbyists is that they do not need to declare an interest when they ask a Parliamentary Question. In January 1990 *World in Action* claimed that in 1988 Tim Smith, MP asked 58 questions about computer contracts for Government Departments in furtherance of the interests of Price Waterhouse who were preparing a business plan in their companies division.

Even when MPs declare an interest in a debate (and there seems to be no effective sanctions when this convention is breached) they can still participate and vote in that debate. A declaration of interest recorded on the Register of Members' Interests need not be restated in debates.

Former Treasury Minister, Jock Bruce-Gardyne, (1986, p.86) has noted that lobbying is one of the few money making jobs suitable for back benchers – but in a role which can easily involve them in conflicts of interest and responsibility. *The Observer*, on 14th October, 1985, claimed that Cecil Parkinson's main job at Babcock and Wilcox had been to lobby for British Airways – which shared a chairman with Babcock and Wilcox. The role of MPs acting on behalf of clients proved controversial in various policy areas in recent years – e.g. 'Chunnel', reform of pub licensing hours, amendments to the *Finance Bill*.

In July 1988 the Labour Opposition complained to the Commons Committee of Privileges following claims in the debate on the *Finance Bill* that some of the 14 Conservative MPs tabling amendments and new clauses were acting for clients. The Labour spokesman, John Marek, asserted that Tory MPs:

> ... always seem to be pleading special cases, probably on behalf of clients in the gallery.

Of the MP for Beaconsfield he queried:

> I just wonder whether the sort of people to whom he is a consultant have an interest in the new clause being passed and in the gains that they would make if it were.

Another Labour front bencher, Nick Brown, said,

> It was our concern that it was companies, and not constituencies, that were being represented at this stage of the *Finance Bill*, and that it was property, not people, that were motivating the Members that moved the clauses.
>
> (*Independent*, 15th July 1988)

Civil servants who have moved across the desk to the visitors' armchair include Michael Casey who served in the DTI as an Under Secretary before moving to the newly created British Shipbuilders (and later to a private sector engineering company). He created his own lobbying company in 1983 and he is now chairman of the merged Sallingbury Casey. Also at Sallingbury Casey was Isaac Douek, who was a middle range civil servant at Trade and Industry. Sir Ronald Mason who was until 1983 Chief Scientist at the Ministry of Defence was also with Sallingbury for some time. Indeed he was still active in Whitehall committees including a Home Office committee on forensic science (See *Guardian*, 8th January, 1988). Sir Peter Woodfield is a consulting member of Public Policy Consultants from a Civil Service background (Prime Minister's Secretary 1961-5, Permanent Under Secretary of State N I Office, 1981-3 – and he re-entered Whitehall in 1988 to oversee the complaints arrangements for security services officers within the security services (HC 518-vi, p.90). Dorothy Drake at Profile is a former civil servant with experience as Chief Press Officer at the DHSS and the Office of Fair Trading. Ms Clare Wenner at GJW is a former MAFF civil servant. In earlier years Sir Frederick Kearns who was responsible for important British/EEC negotiations while in MAFF joined Lloyd-Hughes which was started by Sir Trevor Lloyd-Hughes who served as press secretary to Harold Wilson while the latter was PM. Ex House of Commons staff include Patrick Nealon who was formerly with the House of Commons Library, but is now Head of Research at Public Policy Consultants.

The 'in-house' lobby world of those who have a single employer is drawn from similar backgrounds. For example in 1981 the CBI recruited Keith McDowall who was then director of public affairs at British Shipbuilders. Earlier he had been director of information at the N Ireland Office, the Employment Department and elsewhere. His CBI responsibilities included 'public affairs' and 'parliamentary liaison'. He left a post as Deputy Director General of the CBI to create his own public affairs consultancy in 1988. Cyril Coffin was an Under Secretary at the Department of Prices and Consumer Protection and in other Departments before taking early retirement in 1977 to be Director-General of the Food Manufacturers' Federation and active in the CBI.

The Independent on Sunday (17th June, 1990) noted that the Food and Drink Policy Group of Sallingbury Casey had at least three former MAFF officials – William Mason, former Deputy Secretary, Shirley Stagg, former Principal Private Secretary to John MacGregor and (later) John Gummer and an Under Secretary, Gordon Myers.

The migration of civil servants into the activity of persuasion of the Government raises particular potential conflicts of interest and controversy over the recruitment by the defence industry of defence administrators. This, again, is not an ethical dilemma peculiar to the UK and it has been under scrutiny in the USA for some time.

Writing on the USA Berry (1984, p.127) observed,

> When you leave government and parlay that background into a lobbying job, it is usually at a much higher salary, and for a position designed to exploit your contacts with those you know in government ... The oil industry draws heavily on government employees to fill its top lobbying jobs ...

This pattern is by no means restricted to the oil and defence industries. Between 1945 and 1970, 21 of the 33 commissioners leaving the Federal Communications Commission became affiliated with the communications industry. Schlozman and Tierney (1986, p.269) show that 86% of their sample of American interest groups employed staff with experience in federal government, 46% had staff with a Congressional background. They cite examples such as Ron Ziegler, formerly Nixon's press secretary, who became the President of a truckers organisation. Others like Anne Wexler, who was assistant for public liaison for Carter, became 'for hire' lobbyists. They cite Gordon Adams book on the defence industry (*The Iron Triangle*,

1981) which says that 8 of the largest defence contractors hired 1,455 military and 186 former civilian government employees during the 1970s. In Britain in 1988 the Defence Committee of the Commons expressed concern at the ease with which British civil servants could join companies with which they had had contractual contacts.

The common image of American politics in 'sub system' terms stresses that policy is made by the relevant experts in and outside government. They develop their own appreciation of the problems, their own jargon, and their own attitude to solutions. Those in the community have much in common irrespective of their formal position in or outside of Government.

This description of the 'revolving door' which blurs the line between public and private is generally introduced as a feature of political life to be criticised rather than admired. The point of the criticism is sometimes that there is simply too much potential for corruption in these arrangements for us to be comfortable. However there is a worry that exists even when one has dismissed the thought of deliberate trading of jobs for favours. It is that the official who is in too close contact with particular interests loses his sense of a broader public interest. Responding to the daily and direct demands of his clients, he begins to see good public policy as public policy good for those with whom he has constant dealings.

Lobbying On What?

On the whole the industry likes to keep quiet about who works for whom. In part this is seen as discretion on behalf of clients, but it is also through an unwillingness to draw attention to the fact that influence is being exerted in a way that fits in uneasily with the picture book version of our democracy. The sorts of interests that have used commercial lobbyists are shown in the following list drawn up from press and other reports in recent years:

Lobbyist	Client or Topic
Charles Barker	abolition of on-course betting duty
GJW	GEC Marconi *re* torpedo contract
	Westland *re* the 'Heseltine' solution
	Sothebys *re* a hostile takeover bid
	GEC in their bid for Plessey
	Guinness
	Eurotunnel
	Scandinavian Air Services
	Chartered Consolidated *re* the takeover
	of Anderson Strathclyde
	for Sunday Shopping in 1988
	Minorco *re* Consolidated Gold Fields bid

Good Relations	International Paint on behalf of its anti fouling marine paint Music Copyright Reform GKN
Ian Greer and Associates	British Airways over route allocations City of Plymouth over dockyard privatisation British Airways over B Cal take-over Crown Life on 1981 *Finance Bill* Association of International Air Courier Services on 1981 *Telecommunications Bill* Birmingham International Airport Plessey in GEC takeover attempt
Lloyd-Hughes	against nationalisation of ship repair yards General Electric Ford
Countrywide Political Communications	for local authorities against nuclear dumping in their areas Kentucky Fried Chicken Bingo Association Singapore Airlines seeking to fly into Manchester
Profile Corporate and Political Relations	Bar Association Legal and General W.H. Smith Tottenham Hotspur
Sallingbury Casey	Massey-Ferguson against VAT on books and periodicals Lloyds Bank Boeing *re* decision to buy AWACs rather than the GEC Nimrod Electronic Data Systems *re* defence related contracts Consolidated Gold Fields against takeover proposal
Westminster Communications	Amusement Arcade Action Group Suzuki

This sort of activity need not be seen as *pressure* on Government. For one thing there is general belief that consultation with affected interests is a 'good thing'. If those consulted present their case through the intermediation of a professional consultant, it may be quite helpful for the department responsible to have the views presented in an effective manner. Thus the professional lobbyists are performing a useful service for the Departments in disciplining the representations from the outside in a way that makes them most useful for Whitehall. If consultation is a good thing, it seems odd to argue that those bodies that make best use of the opportunity are distorting the balance of the political system. Sometimes too by acting for a particular interest the lobbyist is making it easier for the Government to move in the particular direction it wished to go. For example, the efforts by Sallingbury Casey in favour of the Government's preference for Boeing AWACs rather than the home produced Nimrod (by emphasising the 'built in Britain' aspect of the AWAC) undoubtedly helped the Government gain some freedom from the GEC pro Nimrod pressure. (*Guardian*, 8th January, 1988).

In a point made by Professor Finer about the general 'lobby' as long ago as 1958, 'pressure' is the wrong kind of word to use about these relationships between Government and those attempting to influence Government decisions,

> ... 'pressure' implies that some kind of sanction will be applied if a demand is refused, and most groups, most of the time, simply make requests or put up a case; they reason and they argue.

And there are few groups with effective sanctions that make threats worthwhile.

Instead Jock Bruce-Gardyne (1986, pp.151-2) has noted:

> Like most of us, civil servants find it easier to bargain with denizens of a similar culture. When a departmental purpose, or the whim of politicians, decrees that "something must be done" about tobacco advertising the Whitehall mandarin ... gets into a huddle with his opposite numbers, the tobacco industry's own officialdom ... the tobacco industry's own civil service ... Then the horse trading begins. The usual result – desired by both sides – is a compromise which gives Whitehall just enough of what it is seeking, and the lobby something which it can sell to its employers.

Lobbying is a matter of staff on two sides of the fence attempting to deliver a deal to satisfy both sets of masters. The lobbyist and the civil servant recognise they have similar problems.

To comprehend how it can be that lobbying can produce results it is perhaps necessary to note that much legislation is not the implementation of major ideological commitments. Richard Rose (1984, p.71) has pointed out that:

> More than three-quarters of all the legislation that a government introduces is derived from the ongoing policy process in Whitehall. Whitehall departments

continually nag at problems, whatever the colour of the party in office, or the status of the parliamentary calendar. Civil servants consult with affected interests to see what can be done about problems of concern to departments ....

Finer (1958, p.22) noted:

A vast body of business – minor policy really – is transacted at this (civil servant/ lobby) level, never making a mark in the general press or in the proceedings of Parliament. Much of the greatest proportion of the Lobby's contact with government is of this uncontroversial and unheralded order. Nor is this relationship one of 'pressure', but rather it is 'mutual accommodation'.

The commercial lobbyist is thus not some kind of intruder into the private deliberations of the department. He is just another voice in the constant dialogue between the department, trade associations, companies, consumer groups etc. If we again look at the salmonella saga *The Observer* (18th December, 1988) described the routine way in which the draft notes leading up to the *1981 Animal Health Protein Processing Order* were altered in consultation. *The Observer* claimed that restrictions sought by the DHSS 'were watered down after protests from the industry'. They quote a Health Department source:

Before 1981 we wanted more thorough health testing ... because even then we were alarmed at the high level of salmonella in chicken flocks. But we were over-ruled by industry interests more concerned about costs, and the Ministry of Agriculture gave in ...

The Observer also quoted a MAFF reaction:

It is not unusual to have extensive redrafting of proposals after consultations – and it is no surprise that this Department would have differences of opinion with the Department of Health. This is a common occurrence.

This may appear a minor political issue but to the producer interests such a politics of detail is more important than the party political politics of *Hansard*.

Nor should we harbour the notion that the departments resist advice: the reverse is the case. The civil servant is on a constant scan for information that will improve the efficiency or at least the acceptability of his policy. Paul Pross writing (1986) on Canadian groups has made the point that for groups which have established their credentials with Government, 'Instead of clamouring to be consulted they are hounded for advice'. The virtue for the in-house or commercial lobbyist of action at this information-scanning stage is that they can help define the way in which the Government views the issue; they can get the item on the political agenda in terms that suit their client.

Another reason to qualify the image of a beleaguered Government under pressure is that there are also instances of the Government itself being the client seeking assistance in presenting its own views. Thus GJW have worked for the DTI, for the DOE and Department of Transport on issues like the controversial Okehampton by-pass. Sallingbury has acted for the MOD over privatisation.

The worry that the lobbyist is giving special access for his clients is thus countered by a view of Whitehall that sees collaboration between departments and groups as wholly normal. A civil servant quoted in *The Government Report* (1987, p.29) – a survey published by Public Policy Consultants – claimed:

> The staff in my Division make over 1300 visits a year to organisations. We would make even more if we were invited. There are very few civil servants nowadays who are not deeply concerned to establish two-way communication. Provided they have been properly thought through, officials are keen to hear any bright ideas an organisation may have on future public policy.

The CBI-produced book by Cyril Coffin *Working With Whitehall* notes that:

> The government relations staff of the major industrial groups have their counterpart in government in the shape of departmental units whose job it is to go halfway to meet industry and understand its problems. They are concerned with *sponsorship*. The most important relationship that the majority of businessmen will ever have with government is that of their sponsor department, and specifically with those officials who are responsible generally for communicating with, keeping an eye on, and looking after the well-being of – in the civil service jargon, for sponsoring – the sector or sectors of industry and commerce in which their business operates ... Everybody is loved ... by someone – or is at least regarded as an object of concern, and a possible partner. (1987, p.12).

Coffin noted that sponsorship had three main aspects – consultation, information, and problem-solving. Coffin indeed warns that there is a danger that the sponsoring civil servant can become too enthusiastic. The Minister or civil servant who has too obviously 'gone native',

> ... may find that his advocacy tends to be discounted by his colleagues, so that he loses much of his power to assist others who seek his intervention. (1987, p.23).

The arrival of Lord Young at the DTI in 1987 and his determination to replace the sponsorship system with a pattern befitting an enterprise culture may threaten this pattern of civil service/industry close cooperation – but the roots are so deep that the practices will not be eradicated instantly by ministerial edict.

Indeed the acceptability of lobbying from outside the Civil Service is no doubt increased by the fact that the Department is engaged in a constant battle *within* Whitehall. The contest is not between some homogeneous 'Government' and intruder groups, but between departments or between the Spending Department and the Treasury. In this world the outside group can be the ally rather than the nuisance. When an issue goes public the Sponsor Department can again be grateful that there is a supportive interest prepared to help shape the political climate by welcoming the initiative.

Lobbyists: Unfairly Useful or Fairly Useless?

The evidence to the Select Committee on Members' Interests in 1988/9 (*Parliamentary Lobbying*, HC 518) seemed to dwell on lobbying as a problem for the domestic arrangements of Parliament: there was a sense of intrusion by outsiders into the club. Cranley Onslow the Chairman of the Conservative Party 1922 Committee noted,

> ... penetration of this building by lobbyists ... more functions organised in the House, particularly under the auspices of our refreshment facilities ...

He also went on to note that there were more and more professional lobbyists in possession of Parliamentary passes. (At least 20 MPs have 'research assistants' who are in reality professional lobbyists) (*Observer*, 9th April, 1989). He drew attention to the Register of Members' Secretaries and Research Assistants and noted:

> ... I do not entirely understand and therefore will not pass judgement on the fact that page one reveals that the vice-chairman of the Hospital Doctors' Association is registered as either a Member's secretary or research assistant; the director of the Child Poverty Action Group is registered as a Member's Secretary or research assistant; that there is somebody from the Conservative Industrial Fund ... who is also working for a Member of Parliament ... why the Parliamentary Affairs Officer of the Institute of Directors holds a pass as a Member's secretary ...; why somebody who is employed by a firm of public relations' consultants specialising in Parliamentary matters is employed as a Member's secretary or research assistant.

Mr Onslow drew attention to the free facilities that such status provided:

> ... the possession of a pass enables these individuals to obtain pretty free access to this building and I estimate that it is possible whilst they are here they use the telephone, they acquire copies of documents from the Vote Office and other matters of this kind.

Evidence from the Society for the Protection of the Unborn Child confirmed that their Parliamentary officer, Christopher Whithouse, was employed as research assistant (with a pass) to Mr and Mrs Winterton (both Conservative MPs) and also did a degree of work for Michael Grylls.

Unfortunately for the lobbying cause, while the Select Committee on

Members' Interests was studying the issue of access in 1989, a media event took place over the activities of Pamella Bordes who secured a pass in the name of Henry Bellingham MP to work as a temporary and unpaid research assistant to David Shaw, Conservative MP for Dover. According to *The Sunday Times* (19th March, 1989) Ms Bordes had given the impression that she, 'wanted a career in public relations or parliamentary lobbying'. She worked for Shaw on his draft bill on the net book agreement. Association with this press disaster area was hardly likely to allow lobbyists continued easy access to passes.

There are two competing views. Firstly, there is the view that there is a possible if not actual abuse of the democratic system. Thus Ian Waller in *The Sunday Telegraph* on 17th March 1985 drew attention to the, 'lobbyists who hang like vultures around the Palace of Westminster.' He gave the work of the industry the half hearted endorsement that, 'Much of it is perfectly legitimate ...' This is as reassuring as a doctor saying that a large part of your leg doesn't have gangrene. An indication of the suspicion that this kind of activity can engender was given in a letter to the *Sunday Telegraph* in March 1985. It said,

> I was shocked by the revelations of Ian Waller's article on MP's consultancies ... I had thought that an MP represented only his constituents, and consider it improper in the extreme that, having reached parliament on their votes, he should spend his time there lining his pockets by serving interests of which they may know nothing and which may even be contrary to their own. Far from being accepted as a matter of course, this practice should be regarded as a public scandal.

Stephen Aris' piece in *Inter City* on Nov/Dec 1986 concluded that, 'If the lobbying business continues to grow ... (it) will cause great public disquiet and sooner or later it will have to be sorted out'. The Commons Committee on Members' Interests in their Report in 1985 (HC 408) claimed that while the principal of lobbying was not in question, '... we are aware at first hand that the professional element in parliamentary lobbying has increased, that it has become more organised and that some of its aspects occasion concern.' (para 3).

When Bob Cryer MP introduced a Bill to seek the registration of lobbyists in February 1982 he was able to quote with relish from an advertisement from Lloyd Hughes Associates. Even though marketing material may have to be read with scepticism this seemed to assert that clients were privileged in the policy process:

> Our success derives from confidence that we can match promises with performance. Notable specific successes have been achieved. Among them, we have saved the international motor car and motor cycle industries based in the United Kingdom millions of pounds by persuading the government to exempt them from provision of the *Trade Descriptions Act*, severely reduced demands

on an American company for the back payments of British excise duties, secured British government planning permission for an oil platform site.

An advertisement such as by Wedgwood Markham Associates Ltd, 'We can help you talk to the people who matter' and who advertise a Government Affairs and Government Intelligence Service or Identity Campaigns suggesting, 'Representation in the right place ensures that the effect of legislation is either minimised or turned to advantage', suggests to some critics that the clients of lobbyists are buying advantage. Advertising from the industry stresses that it can build a bridge to those who have the power:

> Your expert link to Westminster, Whitehall, Brussels and Fleet Street. (Westminster Strategy)
> Linking business and the policy makers. (Dewe Rogerson)
> Don't get stuck on the outside. (Political Communications)

In Dexter's phrase 'the squeaking wheel gets the grease': (1969, p.19). There is a danger that decisions are made on the basis of the skillful lobby rather than objective analysis.

Ironically one of the most critical sources of complaint is from within the industry. There is a repeated worry that some companies are letting the side down. Waller quoted Douglas Smith who was then the chairman of the Public Relations Consultants Association, who felt that some of the companies active in the field were 'cowboys'. He said:

> Large fees are being charged – running into six figures – based on false promises, and when the clients' funds or the hopes are exhausted, the cowboy consultants move on to fresh prey – they bring Parliament and public relations into disrepute ... Some of these companies are taking on every cause that moves, regardless of its chances of success. Companies and trade associations were being advised they had excellent prospects of influencing the Government when, in reality, there was not a chance in a thousand of doing so.

Smith asked for the wings of the vultures to be clipped.

The second perspective on the legitimacy of lobbying was given by Ian Greer in his book in 1985 in which he asserted that we have, 'not only the right but also a duty to inform our political representatives of our views ...' Though Greer claimed that vigorous and constructive lobbying has headed off legislation that would be disastrous for the industries concerned, he went on to say that the proposals would also have been disastrous for the country. He concluded however with the call that, '... unless action is taken swiftly to legitimise and regularise the activities of the lobbyist at Westminster, the suspicion and mistrust which is being built up by the unskilled operators will do irreparable damage ...'

The case for the lobbyist is made in the title of Greer's book – *The Right to Be Heard*. The underlying defence is that any interest has a right to 'fight its own corner'. As an extension to that there is the point picked up by Bernard Weatherhill in his preface to Greer's book – that a Member of Parliament is only as good as the information that he receives. Again the defence seems to be that the lobbyist is contributing to the democratic process by introducing information as to the impact of past and potential legislation. Another contributor to this book, Martin Smith, earlier (1986) made the related point that,

> Because the research facilities available to Parliamentarians are inadequate, the value of (the) communicative function cannot be overstressed. Politicians need to know by example how the broad sweep of national and international events turn into measurable consequences for the business, social and domestic life of their constituents.

The lobbyist can be the means by which the impact of departmental policy is 'tested' against the views of those who have most knowledge of their effects – the interested groups or associations.

Smith's point that the legislator requires assistance is confirmed by the active role that groups often take in assisting the Opposition in opposing legislation. Professor Griffith has commented,

> On important bills the affected interests outside Parliament will be anxious to help the Opposition in the hope of bringing further pressure to bear on the Government ... At times, this service by professionals and experts comes close in its drafting to the service provided for the Minister by his department. (In Walkland and Ryle, 1977, p.101).

However, there is a contrary view that more research assistance for Members would increase the need for outside advice, not diminish it; that the research service enjoyed by Congressmen only increases the market for information. (The research staff have to supply analyses as an exercise in self justification.)

On the whole though there is a strong argument that lobbying helps the law makers in Government and Parliament to discover how proposals would affect those most involved. (The 'only the wearer knows where the shoe pinches proposition'). In this light the professional consultant is merely aiding those with a legitimate right to play their part in the process. As Greenwald says (1977,p.80), 'the true currency of lobbying is information'. Miller (1987) has compared the process of deciding in Government to the process in a court; the decision cannot be made in a vacuum.

In their books both Greer (1986) and Miller (1987) go to some length to underline the ethical basis of the industry. Greer reckons that the consultant must sell his case on merit alone not by seeking 'favours' or pouring out the champagne. He also claims that the efforts of many lobbyists to 'eat their way out of trouble' has simply made MPs resentful – and in any case Miller claims that the status of the MP exceeds his influence – 'MPs continue to be feted as part of the system of government whereas ... they possess little power as individuals.' Martin Smith, in his article in 1986, has also warned against the danger of confusing a few illustrious handshakes at a luncheon with impact. He notes that lavish entertaining can actually have a negative effect. (For similar US view see Cates, 1988, p.244).

A desire for professional respectability is the obvious reason for this sort of noblest Roman approach by lobbyists but the tone does encourage the reader to keep counting the spoons. Undoubtedly hospitality *is* a part of the repertoire of the lobbyist; information is often communicated socially (Greenwald, 1977, p.80) and the social contacts can be used to establish the credibility of the lobbyist – that information from such sources would be respectable and reliable. Douglas Smith of Political Communications has quoted the example of a group faced with the problem of producing votes on a technical and 'non sexy' environment Bill. They organised a whisky-tasting party for MPs which ended just in time to steer the Members into the House. (*Observer*, 15th November, 1987). A nineteenth century lobbyist in the US had the motto 'the way to a man's "aye" is through his stomach.' This should not be dismissed too quickly. (cited in Scholzman and Tierney, 1986, p.294).

The ethical aspect of lobbying is touched in passing in most of the papers in this collection and is the main theme of the contributions by Charles Miller (in the second of his chapters) and by Alan Doig. The control of unwelcome lobbying is clearly difficult. This point was well made by E. Pendleton Herring in his book *Group Representation Before Congress* as long ago as 1929. He said,

> In attempting to regulate the lobby the inherent difficulty is finding some equitable rule which curbs the corrupt, the deceptive and the predatory and still leaves ample room for the legitimate spokesman ... To place obstacles in the way of the honest man does not prevent the thief from forcing his way through a rear entry.(1929, p.258)

In his evidence to the Select Committee on Members' Interests which reported in 1984 Sir Trevor Lloyd-Hughes was questioned about his use of the word 'inside information' in his advertising. The session went on with Mr Tony Durant MP asking,

> I was going to raise the same question ... I suppose there is another word that has the smell of something sinister about it and that is the word 'contacts' ... It has connotations of the smoke room.

In his response Sir Trevor acknowledged that, 'This goes back to Sydney Stanley ...' The reference here was to a detail in the early history of the trade that is usually, very deliberately, neglected. The Lynskey tribunal considered the activities of Sydney Stanley. In his opening to the proceedings the Attorney-General suggested that the enquiry was not simply discussing corruption in the sense of the Prevention of Corruption Acts, but corruption in the broader sense generally understood by the public.' (Rhodes, 1949).

It emerged that Stanley operated as a 'contact man' or 'fixer' between various commercial clients and the Board of Trade for items such as allocations of steel or paper. He pretended to clients that he had access and influence that did not exist on the scale claimed. He exploited his carefully cultivated contacts with a few to give the image of a key British player in financial matters. His activities eventually prompted the resignations of a Parliamentary Secretary at the Board of Trade and the Chairman of the Electricity Board.

Need for Registration?

Michael Burrell of Westminster Strategy has argued in favour of a register of lobbyists claiming that,

> At the moment lobbyists operate behind closed doors. A register of who's operating in the field for which clients would dispel the mystery and the myth that we are cloak and dagger merchants. (*Observer*, 15th November, 1987)

In the evidence to the Select Committee in 1988 the Public Relations Consultants Association reported on a survey of lobbyists (17 out of 24 responded). This produced a majority opinion that there is a need for the implementation of a registration system for paid lobbyists, seventy percent of their respondents wanted a Parliamentary Administered Register, and, failing the introduction of an 'official system', 80% wanted a voluntary Register. They advocated a system whereby all commercial lobbyists should declare:

> their name
> consultancy/firm name
> list of all Public Office holders who are employed or contracted,
> number of staff in the lobbying/government affairs area.

The lobbyists would agree to conform to certain standards of practice – list clients, refrain from inducements 'if such action is inconsistent with the public interest', not engage in any practice tending to corrupt the integrity of channels of public communication or legislation, nor propose action which would constitute improper influence on organs of government or legislation, not disseminate false or misleading information, not purport to serve some announced cause while actually serving an undisclosed special or private interest.

The registered lobbyist, according to the PRCA, should not abuse the booking of the facilities of the House, or obtain copies of Parliamentary papers without payment, but they would be given a 'lobbyist pass' to give them access to Westminster. (Miss Evie Soames pointed out in evidence that the pass was not to be for the purpose of using the library or the Members' lobby, but simply to avoid the public queues when seeking to attend Standing Committees.)

The criticism of this apparently altruistic recommendation for control of the profession was, of course, that it sought to give a privilege of 'Parliament approved' in terms of access and status to a limited number of consultancies. John Bowis, MP, queried the acceptability of a system developing whereby over, say hospital redevelopment, a firm of builders might afford the fee to employ registered lobbyists with their special access whereas the local league of friends of the hospital would not enjoy such facilities in their amateur lobbying.

The Memorandum for the Institute of Public Relations (which seeks to organise individuals rather than firms as in the case of the PRCA) also supported, 'moves to identify, for the benefit of the MPs and members of the public, professional lobbyists whether or not they are Members of the Institute ...' but this apparent support for a register was eroded by the caveats that they entered. They were worried about occasional lobbyists. One IPR representative gave the instance of when he worked for BOC. Only 3 times in his career there did he need to approach Members, but when he needed to do so he needed to do so instantly. Registration to allow such intermittent lobbying would produce a very cluttered register. Officers of trade associations, trade unionists etc would register 'just in case' they needed speedy access to members. The IPR also queried the position of single interest pressure groups such as Friends of the Earth, and the seeking of information from MPs in pursuit of a general public relations brief. Above all they seemed concerned at the possibility of 'preferential access' for registered lobbyists.

The professional generally, like the contributors to this collection, were divided on the need for a register. In the evidence to the Committee, Charles Miller and Patrick Nealon (for Public Policy Consultants) advised that registration was desirable – to prevent the emergence of a class of paid consultants many of whom may be of limited value to their clients and a hindrance to the work of members in the demands they may encourage their clients to make of the system and its time.

Charles Miller argued that he was happy to let the market decide who it should use, but that registration should require a listing of clients and the qualifications of staff. Potential customers and Members of Parliament could then decide who did possess worthwhile expertise.

GJW (Government Relations), in their memorandum, rejected the idea of registration on the grounds that it would give preferential status to a minority. However, they did suggest that as a means to avoid the abuse of free issue of parliamentary papers by pseudo research staff a sales point might be made available to give the earliest access to such documents. They suggested that an account at the sales point might be a *de facto* register.

In his evidence Ian Greer argued for a mandatory register of all who lobbied for commercial gain – not just a list of the 20 or so lobbying companies. It was conceded that this would be 'an immense administrative task'.

Michael Burrell and David Hall of Westminster Strategy used their opportunity to give evidence to the Select Committee to back registration.

Dorothy Drake and Charles St George of Profile Political Relations advocated a register and a code of practice. However, they did not favour a *Parliamentary* register but self regulation by the profession. They disagreed with Parliamentary registration partly because there was a need for control of non-Parliamentary activities and partly because they too were suspicious of the special status that the label 'Parliament approved' might confer.

Fred Silvester of Advocacy Partnership was suspicious of registration. He noted that in the USA registration had not inhibited the mushrooming of the level of lobbying activity. He thought that registration would be an advantage traded upon by established companies. He also noted the practical problems of identifying 'lobbying'. Is a telephone call a meeting? Is a chat at a dinner party? What about representations at constituency surgeries?

The controversy over the regulation of Parliamentary lobbying may be calmed by control of passes for 'researchers' and the provision of a sales point for HMSO publications outside Parliament (but releasing material as quickly as it is available within the Palace of Westminster). There is likely to be some continuing grumbles over the lack of a means to identify the shoddy operators – but it is the argument of the concluding chapter that it is operations *vis à vis* Whitehall and the civil service that should cause most concern and Parliamentary registration is perhaps peripheral.

Discussion of the regulation of lobbying inevitably turns into a discussion of US legislative attempts. The 1946 *Federal Regulation of Lobbying Act* required that any person hired for the *principal purpose* of influencing legislation had to register with the Secretary of the Senate and the Clerk of the House, and had to file quarterly reports, disclosing the amount of money received and spent for lobbying. The argument was that to prohibit lobbying would be to erode free-speech but 'identification, disclosure and publicity' would allow Congressmen to evaluate the representations made on them.

However, recent discussion by Scholzman and Tierney (1986, p.319) suggests that,

> ... the 1946 lobbying law is generally considered ineffective and limp. For example it is restricted in its scope. It applies only to lobbyist's efforts to influence Congress, not to their lobbying of the executive branch; only to contacts between lobbyists and legislators, not to contacts between lobbyists and congressional staff; and only to efforts to influence not to efforts to inform. Furthermore, in deference to the First Amendment, the law imposes virtually no restrictions. Instead, it merely asks for a modicum of information ...

The US law exempts a main focus of lobbying activity – congressional hearings and the preparation of testimony for hearings – and the officials who compile the register are not empowered to instigate the reports nor compel anyone to register. No agency was given the task of monitoring compliance. Scholzman and Tierney (1986, p.320) go on to point out that some heavily active bodies report on minimal expenditures on lobbying as they argue that most of their spending is for public information purposes, research, and the like. That the Justice Department initiated only 5 prosecutions from 1946 to 1979 appears to suggest the weakness of the regulatory regime rather than zealous compliance by lobbyists.

Taking evidence in the US persuaded the Canadian Committee investigating the need for registration (see Chapter 4) that there was nothing intrusive about the notion of enforcing disclosure of clients by consultancies. Sawatsky (1987, p.329) says of the Washington hearings:

> Unlike the Canadian practitioners, who seemed to lock their client lists in Chubb safes each night, the Americans paraded and even flaunted theirs, stopping just short of putting them on their business cards. The openness amazed the committee and destroyed the Canadian claims that the system would fall apart if clients were identified.

The hearings in California (where state law is more demanding) convinced the Canadians that broad registration was practical – but that even apparently rigorous criteria could be circumvented by the inventive industry.

Lobbying in Britain may be increasingly professional in that more and more decision making rests on complicated arguments about non-obvious impacts of policies on particular clienteles. But is it a profession? Clearly it is not a profession in the sense of law or medicine in which there is a restriction of a function to certain registered individuals. There is equally clearly a wish among some participants that it be so considered. The usual route advocated by those in neo-professions is (a) registration, (b) licensing, (c) graduate level entry. This was the method sought by reformers in the British engineering community in Britain in the 1970s: a call that saw eventually the creation of a British Engineering Council. A similar sort of campaign to introduce 'chartered managers' was advocated in 1988: the core idea was that the status of management as an activity would be enhanced by ensuring the quality of its practitioners. The argument in favour of restricting lobbying to registered lobbyists is, however, a case made difficult by the fact that it runs against the political fashion: it would smack too much of 'the closed shop'. Moreover it runs into the difficulty of seemingly restricting a basic democratic right. No-one would advocate a monopoly for the professional lobbyist and it is difficult to regulate to stop the bad lobbyist – while not also stopping the affected citizen.

Commercial Lobbying in a Political Context

The existence of the professional lobbyist should not be judged on the assumption that they are the only way for a company to ensure that it is best placed to make the right sort of noises in the right place at the right time. They are a means that can be used if other techniques fail, as a second string to the bow or by the *less* well connected companies. The outflow of politicians and civil servants to the business world can be reasonably assumed to be at least partly prompted by the belief that such people can be useful for the interests involved through their Whitehall expertise. This sort of British pantouflage is not difficult to discover. For example, advertising for seminars on 'Selling to the MOD' in May 1988 (held – at the Royal United Services Institute in Whitehall) made a point that one speaker, Tim Boyce, Contracts Manager at Plessey Defence systems was previously with the Procurement Executive of the MOD, Julian Forrester of the management consultants, Tidek, was formerly Financial and Policy Controller at the MOD. The sessions were chaired by Major General Geoffrey Burch, formerly Deputy Master General of the Ordnance and member of the Royal Ordnance Factories Board. By 1988 he was consultant to the Defence Manufacturers Association and adviser to the European Defence Manufacturers' Association Group.

The importance of relations with the MOD for defence contractors was made plain in the advertisement. Under a heading, 'a piece of the action', it stated,

> In 1988/9 the Ministry of Defence will spend some £8,250 million on equipment and some £3,500 million on support items (construction, transport, fuel, telecommunications, food, clothing, etc). This will involve placing about 40,000 new contracts within the next twelve months ... What do you need to get a piece of the action? ... or a bigger piece?

The seminar claimed that in getting contracts, 'an understanding of the culture, custom, practice and conventions is every bit as important as understanding the theory behind contracting with MOD.' If this is true it helps explain why MOD 'retreads' are thought to be so effective recruits by business.

Another impression of the co-habitation of the business and political worlds is gained almost incidentally in Linklater and Leigh's book *Not With Honour* (1986) on the Westland episode. As the authors introduce a rolling cast list of characters even a cursory read discovers the following:

Peter Levene, former head of United Scientific Holding to MOD as head of Procurement Executive (p.20).
Admiral Sir John Treacher, former allied Commander in Chief Channel and Eastern Atlantic, as Westland marketing chief (p.23).
Admiral Sir Raymond Lygo former Vice Chief of Naval staff, as Chief Executive at British Aerospace (p.27).
Lord Aldington, former junior minister at the Board of Trade and Deputy chairman Conservative Party Organisation. In the words of Linklater and Leigh, his 'connections in the pre-Thatcher Tory establishment were formidable.' Chairman of Westland Board (p.29).
Sir Ronald Melville, retired Permanent Secretary at Ministry of Aviation Supply, joined Westland Board 1974 (p.30).
Major General John Strawson, retired Chief of Staff UK Land Forces, joined Westland 1976 as Senior Military Adviser (p.30).

Sir Frank Cooper, retired MOD Permanent Under Secretary, temporarily joined Westland in 1982 (p.30).
Captain Bill Gueterbock, ex MOD, hired as a lobbyist by Treacher (p.40).
GEC headed by Jim Prior, former Thatcher Cabinet colleague (p.45).
Sir John Cuckney, chairman of Westland – ex Chief Executive Property Services Agency, ex chairman International Military Services, a MOD owned arms production and sales company (p.50).
Lazards recruited by Cuckney as merchant bankers, Chairman of Lazards, John Nott, immediate past Secretary of State of the MOD (p.51).
Bill Walker MP used by Sikorsky as an 'intermediary' (p.59).
Anthony Royle (Lord Fanshawe) appointed to Westland Board. Former MP for 24 years for Richmond. Gave up seat at previous election and place secured by Leon Brittan, Trade and Industry Secretary (p.60).
Sir Gordon Reece hired by Westland, Mrs. Thatcher's personal adviser (p.60).
Sir Peter Carey, retired Permanent Secretary at DTI, on board of Morgan Grenfell merchant bankers for Sikorsky (p.115).
Michael Marshall MP, former Junior Minister DTI, parliamentary adviser to British Aerospace (p.162).
Lord Hanson – recommended by Mrs. Thatcher for peerage. His company large contributor to Tory Party funds (p.180). Bought Westland shares and assisted rescue.
Cranley Onslow, MP Chairman of the Conservative Party 1922 Committee and adviser to Bristow Helicopters, (p.204).

In this milieu it was perhaps not of great significance that GJW was hired by Westland. The full cast list perhaps places the issues raised by commercial lobbying in some context.

The significance of the links between Westland and the political world lay in the dependent relationship that the nominally market sector Westland company enjoyed with Government. The essence of the lobbying was the attempt to create a public solution to a private issue. When business is not campaigning against Governmental interference it is campaigning for it.

Linklater and Leigh (1986, p.207) concluded:

> Finally, however, Westland is a story about political influence, it is worth making the point that although Mrs. Thatcher and her industry secretary were to become implacable in their conviction that Sikorsky must be given a free run at a British helicopter firm, they were relatively indifferent on the subject until Sir John Cuckney began to persuade them otherwise.
>
> It was his astute manipulation of the levers of power which succeeded in tilting the balance of the Government's opinion ... he established lines of communication to the very top via a civil service that is supposed to be famous for its unyielding discretion ... The way these events have occurred is instructive and worrying. Whether they amount to a corruption of the British political system is a question that needs to be confronted. Certainly the pattern of private

lobbying and influence revealed in the course of the Westland story is a disturbing one ...

It is not difficult to understand the frustration of the Defence Select Committee in 1988 (Defence Select Committee, 2nd Report, *Business Appointments*, HC 392) when they felt that the non cooperation of the Ministry of Defence was inhibiting their study of the movement of civil servants into the defence industry. Their request for information was turned down by the Ministry on the grounds that it would infringe the personal confidentiality of the ex-officials concerned. Naturally most of the drift of serving and retired officials is from less exalted levels than these picked up in the Westland saga. Rules were published in 1984 because,

> ... serving officers might be ready to bestow favours on firms in the hope of future benefits to come, they also seek to guard against the risk that a particular firm might be thought to be gaining an unfair advantage over its competitors by employing an officer who, during his service, had access to technical or other information which those competitors could legitimately regard as their own trade secrets.

Five hundred and sixty eight MOD officials left for industry in 1989, many with defence contractors. The *Independent on Sunday* (17th June, 1990) listed as examples:

Major-General Stephen Stopford	Director General of the MOD Fighting Vehicles and Engineer Equipment Division, 1985-1989, who moved to David Brown Vehicle Transmissions, makers of the Challenger tank gear box in May 1990.
Sir Colin Chandler	Head of Defence Export Services, 1985-1989, moved to be Managing Director of Vickers, 1990.
Sir James Blyth	Head of Defence Sales, MOD, 1981-1985, moved to be Managing Director of Plessey Electronic Systems, 1985-6.
Major-General John Sturge	Assistant Director of the Defence Staff in charge of signals, 1981, moved to Marconi Space and Defence Systems one week after leaving the MOD.
Sir Brian Tovey	Director of GCHQ, 1978-1983, moved to be Director of Plessey Systems two months after leaving MOD.

The Select Committee on Defence set up a research programme in 1989 to try to track, and quantify, the number of officials taking 'revolving door' jobs in private industry. One committee member, John Cartwright, told *The Observer* (12th March, 1989):

Increasingly, one finds that senior company executives on a defence contract were, as generals or whatever, the very officials who were dealing with it for the Ministry.

The Westland and defence examples demonstrate that the commercial lobbyists are in their way far less disturbing lobbying forces than the unofficial practitioners.

Michael Useem, after studying large corporations in the US and the UK, has argued that a politicised cadre in the leadership of major corporations has come to play a major role in defending the interests of business – 'Rooted in intercorporate networks through shared ownership and directorship of large companies in both countries, this politically active group of directors and top managers gives coherence to the politics of business.' (1984, p.3). To this group he attached the label *the inner circle*.

At least what the commercial lobbyist sells is openly available to all (who can pay) and is sufficiently open to be controllable should there be a political will. The other lobbyists perhaps even delude themselves that they are not in the lobbying game – and hence would be offended at the notion of control. The complexities of the relations between the defence industry and political administrators shows that commercial lobbying is part of a pattern of commercial and government influence and not its totality.

Writing on the John Tower affair in the USA, Martin Walker (*Guardian*, 8th March, 1989) noted that Tower was not unique in the way he had used his political position to secure consultancy fees. Walker said, of Tower's scale of operations, 'This is peanuts by the standard of the Beltway Bandits, as the tribe of consultants are often called (after the city's ring road where so many of them have their plush offices.)' Walker estimated that Kissinger Associates (including Lawrence Eagleburger nominated by President Bush as Under-Secretary of State) was grossing over $5 million per year. (General Brent Scrowcroft, appointed National Security Adviser was another member of Kissinger Associates).

Walker argued that the real issue over Tower was not his consumption of alcohol but 'the kind of sleazy city that Washington has become'. He noted,

> The walls of honour that ought to divide government and private industry, and the accountancy of conscience that should draw a clear line between public funds and private fee, have become dangerously, perhaps irretrievably, blurred.

No one would wish to directly equate British and American practice, but perhaps instead of being pushed to self congratulation in Britain by the comparison we should be spurred to attend to the barriers.

Contemplating the speculation over the share dealing of Ministers in November 1989, *The Observer* (5th November) noted that there were several other areas of concern over standards in public life. It noted that one in three MPs is a paid parliamentary consultant, yet (it said) the standards of disclosure of these interests were sloppy and, '...a number of senior Conservative MPs acknowledged that the borderline between the public and the private interest has begun to seem disturbingly uncertain'.

The Observer asked:

> Why should it be acceptable for an MP, but not for a local councillor, to speak and vote in a debate in which he has a direct financial interest? Why should MPs be allowed to use the Parliamentary order paper to further the interests of their clients in City takeover battles without disclosing on the order paper who their clients are? Finally ...why should MPs not be required to disclose ...How much, for what purpose and by whom they are being paid in addition to their Parliamentary salaries?

The issue refused to go away and in January 1990 (16th) an editorial in *The Independent* noted:

> There can be no objection to MPs with genuine professional skills – lawyers, business people, journalists or the like – marketing their talents. But the growth in lucrative 'consultancies' offered by companies and pressure groups which expect inside advice on activities within Whitehall and Westminster and the occasional speech on their behalf in the House of Commons is disturbing. Such relationships are inherently demeaning to both parties. Either the MP is tempted to deliver more than he ought or the organisation feels that it has been short changed. The gap between selling judgement and peddling influence is a narrow one and the suspicion, however ill founded, that MPs are sailing close to the wind, does damage to their reputation and to that of the House of Commons.

2 Lobbying:
The Development of the Consultation Culture

CHARLES MILLER

A British information officer lecturing in America in 1954 claimed that there was, '... a complete absence of pressure groups and lobbies in Britain.' This was quoted by the late Robert McKenzie (1958) who noted that such a remark was not a misguided effort in national propaganda but an honest expression of a widely accepted myth about the British political system. McKenzie went on to cite pre-war work by Sir Ivor Jennings who even then demonstrated the importance of pressure groups in the development of legislation. The British war-time experience of political cooperation – between parties and between Government and outside interests – reinforced the tendencies noted by Jennings. Government became more active and interventionist – and in extending its scope of action found it advisable to work with various sectional interests. If the description of Britain as a political system without interest groups was incomplete before the Second World War, it was positively misleading by the 1950s:

> Between 1942 and 1945 the coalition Government committed its successors ...to major initiatives in the fields of education, health, housing, employment, social security, industry and environmental planning... But more important still was the new structure of power, and the new structure of administration: the context within which policies were conceived. The Second World War gave rise to a revolution in government: not a social or an intellectual revolution, but an expansion in the role of government in society. By the end of the war a new administrative order was rapidly coming into existence.
>
> (Addison, 1987, pp.6-7)

Six years of war had softened up the nation to the idea of more pervasive government:

> The way in which an open society *voluntarily* transformed itself into first a resistance then a reconstruction machine is the most striking feature of the history of Britain from 1945 to 1950.
>
> (Hennessy, 1987,p.48)

By the end of the war the machinery required to process change was already in place. The legislation required to nationalise electricity, coal and gas, iron and steel, rail and waterways, long distance transport and Cable and Wireless as well as establish the National Health Service faced little parliamentary opposition. The balance of power within the Labour majority favoured Attlee. The financial independence still enjoyed in the early post-war years by many Tory MPs made the patronage power of the Whips a less influential force. Labour's back benchers, enjoying an outright Parliamentary majority for the first time in the Party's history, acquiesced in passing what were left of the reins to the Cabinet Committee system, exploited as never before by Attlee (he established 466, a total unapproached since) and a Civil Service made more dynamic by the responsibilities of wartime planning.

At the same time business and industry, which had accustomed itself to working with Government through the twin channels of its own representation on the back benches and the natural identity of its ruling class with that within Government, had to make accommodations. Firstly, the great social and economic reforms were being introduced by a Labour Government headed, as many have observed, by an almost infuriatingly immovable Prime Minister. If business and industry felt less able to exert leverage over Labour, immediate past history should have made it realise that its dealings with the coalition over the post-war structure were no more effective. What war did, however, was bring business and industry closer to Whitehall. Production and planning necessitated its cooperation and involvement at ministerial and official level. War had conditioned organisations to doing without Parliament. As a result, come 1945 it was Whitehall not Parliament, that increasingly provided the focus for business and industrial consultations on policy.

Check (1986, quoted in Addison 1987, p.17) claims that such consultations were of little consequence:

> While much of the secondary literature and the publications of the Federation of British Industry and the Trades Union Congress themselves indicate that there were numerous meetings and exchanges of opinion and information between government, industry and the trade unions, the archives of all three sides indicate that this high level of activity cannot be equated with a high level of achievement. The actual influence of the unions and industry on government economic policy was much less than has been claimed both by the representative organisations themselves and by some analysts of the political development of corporatist industrial society.

Addison (1987, p.18) nonetheless concludes from that analysis that,

> It may be more realistic to regard the employers and union associations as veto groups, with the power to prevent governments from acting when their vested interests were threatened, rather than as architects of policy. If so, the effect of the war must still be reckoned as far-reaching. The veto groups were now entrenched at the centre of power.

War had brought them closer to the official mind. They also came to realise the importance of those whose advice guides ministerial decision making. Before the war, the convention still prevailed that officials could only be contacted in writing. Personal meetings were frowned upon since they were deemed to circumvent the role of Parliament. Now civil servants were consistently accessible and the assistance of MPs was only needed where officials blocked a case, could not understand it, or where the decision was bound to contain a substantial political element.

The Executive had long since ceased to be regarded in a practical sense as a committee of Parliament. And extensions of the franchise, the proliferation of interest groups and a decline in their desire to be represented in, rather than by the House robbed Parliament of much of its consultative function. Ministers frequently felt that they needed to bypass MPs and consult on policy direct with interest groups.

The shift of focus and of the effective policy management power from Parliament to Whitehall fundamentally influenced post-war representations to Government. Business and industrial organisations could do what 'cause' pressure groups could not – lobby Whitehall, often by invitation. And they quickly came to realise it. Anthony Sampson (1971, p.16) noted:

> But most of the very biggest business interests do not bother much about parliament, and few of the big corporations now maintain their own members in the House. They have seen where decisive power lies, and so they now deal directly with cabinet ministers or civil servants ... 'It's so much easier here,' a senior manager in one big corporation once told me: 'We don't have to organise great formal expeditions as in Washington. Whitehall is only two tube stations away: we have a permanent secretary to lunch from time to time.' The chairmen of big companies do not need to stir up members of parliament; they are on speaking terms with people in the cabinet and senior civil servants, and can urge their view there. The more civil servants who go into industry, the closer the industry, the easier such informal pressure becomes: pressure to make someone do something they don't want to do becomes in the end a sort of like-mindedness in which it may not be clear who is the persuader and who the persuaded. The really important lobbying – about tax concessions, locations of industries, trade agreements or subsidies – takes place in the recesses of Whitehall long before any Bill reaches parliament. The member of parliament, however much he may resent – or be flattered by – the persistent attentions of the lobbyists, has the uneasy feeling that the real pressures are being exerted elsewhere.

The system of government was making it obvious to business and industry where the real power was held. It was wielded by quiet men working in dull offices furnished in the army camouflage style favoured by Whitehall in the 1970s.

Richard Crossman in a parliamentary debate in 1966 was even more despairing about the loss of power and influence by the House:

> Let me describe the central problem as I see it ... we still behave as though we were a sovereign which really shared with the Government the initiation of legislation, which exercised a real control not only of finance, but of the administration of the Departments. But, today, not only the House of Lords

has been shorn of most of its authority. The House of Commons too, has surrendered most of its effective powers to the Executive and has become in the main the passive forum in which the struggle is fought between the modern usurpers of parliamentary power, the great political machines...

...I know there are some of my hon. Friends who dream of a time when the secret negotiations of the Government with outside interests which precede all modern legislation and the secret decisions in the Committee Room upstairs which largely determine party attitudes will be rendered insignificant because the House of Commons will once again become sovereign and make decisions, for itself. I think they are crying for the moon. (*Hansard*, Vol.38, cols. s 479-80).

Though this accessibility of Whitehall seems to have initially developed for prestigious trade and professional bodies, the participatory mood of the 1970s came to see consultation with any group not directly challenging the authority of Government, or seeking demands which would produce heavy counter pressure, as a Whitehall norm.

A study by Political and Economic Planning in 1974 also claimed that the direct contact between civil servants and groups started between the wars, grew rapidly under the pressure of the wartime emergency and became established after 1945. Whereas once it was regarded as improper for civil servants to see pressure-group spokesmen and communication between officials and such people was by correspondence only, after the war, PEP states:

The official guide to civil servants' duties came to include a section on their obligation to consult all recognised interest groups. The criteria by which a group became accepted and put on the list of bodies to be consulted were fairly simple. The group had to represent the bulk of persons or companies or organisations in the area of activity and had to accept that all negotiations were to be confidential, even from its own members. In return, the leaders of these groups were consulted before any government plans were published and they could thus make their representation at a formative stage when plans were still open to argument and when no loss of face were involved in making changes. Those groups which wanted new laws ... would go to Whitehall if what was wanted arose out of existing policies: that is if the matter was not highly controversial. On the other hand, if the proposal was in this (controversial) category then the pressure group could not deal with government departments.... Those groups whose sole or main objective was a 'cause' requiring legislation clearly still had to try and influence Parliament.... But these groups constitute a small minority. The majority are interested in the development and execution of accepted policies and they are on the consultation list and deal directly with government.

Jock (now Lord) Bruce-Gardyne and Nigel Lawson (1976, p.114) claimed that failure of the lobby against the abolition of Retail Price Maintenance stemmed from a failure by the interests to note the changed role of

Westminster and a failure to secure consultative status from the relevant Department:

> In the fifties ... (it) maintained close links with the FBI.... This gave the RPM pressure group at least a proxy channel to power and a source of inside information on the current state of Whitehall thinking...This is in stark contast with the pressure group's behaviour in the sixties. It gave up the Board of Trade as a bad job...It neglected the FBI – an indirect route to the source of power which should have been cherished all the more in the absence of the direct route...All it did do, of any significance, was to build up still further its contacts with and support among Conservative back-benchers. Admittedly, this was where the soil was most fertile. But whereas in the fifties this parliamentary strength was cultivated as a means to an end, the purpose being to demonstrate to Whitehall that the pressure group was a force to be reckoned with, to be consulted rather than ignored, in the sixties it seemed to see backbench influence as constituting almost a veto (on adverse legislation) in itself. In any event, the upshot of the pressure group's unsophisticated strategy in the sixties was clear. It failed to keep itself informed about departmental thinking... As a result, it allowed itself to be taken wholly by surprise....

One MP has claimed that resort to using MPs as a means to attempt to attain influence is now an indication of weakness.

> MPs often dramatise issues. If people turn to MPs they are saying they cannot make any further progress within the system. (Public Policy Consultants, *The Government Report*, 1987, p.6)

As awareness of the existence of Government in our lives has increased, those who seek and are granted access to decision makers have proliferated. Thirty years ago, and perhaps up to the election of the Heath administration of the early 1970s, it was accurate to refer to the Establishment, a group of individuals united by common backgrounds and unspoken understandings. The privilege of corporate lobbying was largely granted to those who earned it by social affiliation – or by buying their way in through offering consultancies and board appointments to politicians. Words are still whispered into governmental ears over discreet luncheon tables, but social and administrative change has greatly diminished the influence of the Sloanes or working classes over parties or Governments. The rise of the lobbying consultancy was inevitable, the result of the lack of innate empathy between Government and the organisations dealing with it. People can no longer merely bank on the security of having been to the same school as the Ministers they seek to persuade. The tight and homogeneous social circle that decided things within and outside Government has disappeared. Politicians as a group are more socially diverse than they were, and the traditional concept of a ruling or managerial class has been largely bleached from our national character. Politics is now treated as a profession by most elected legislators.

The new politician is a more complex species than the duty-driven Knight of the Shires strain: closer in background, social and economic aspirations to those he represents, yet separated from it by his political outlook. As a cohesive Establishment has withered, those who can forge links, no matter how temporary or artificial, between Government and organisations needing to deal with it have become increasingly indispensable. Organisations are now more likely to employ a firm of consultants than take on an MP, although many Conservative and some Labour Members feature a range of retainers against their name in the Annual Register of Members' Interests. Whereas the Establishment was able to meet and influence Ministers through natural affinity, Government is now less likely to be swayed by personal contacts. In this account of a day in the lobbying life of another former Minister, Lord Jellicoe, what stands out is not his access to the system but the fact that he knows his way around. What you know is now at least as important as who you know, although it is still only a minority that realises it:

> On the morning of January 7, Lord Jellicoe, chairman of Davy Corporation, Britain's biggest process plant engineer, sent two telexes. One was to Sir Bryan Cartledge, ambassador to Moscow, regretting that he was unable to attend round-table discussions with the Russians on a weekend that coincided with a get-together of the Davy board. The other went to Sir Robert Wade-Gery, UK high commissioner in New Delhi. It confirmed that Jellicoe and British Steel chairman Bob Scholey would be there in 10 days' time for talks with the Indians about a proposed steel project. Jellicoe also dictated two confidential letters to officials with SW1 postcodes, then telephoned Kester George, assistant secretary in charge of East European affairs at the Department of Trade and Industry.
>
> After lunch, he drove from Davy's Portland Place office to the DTI in Victoria Street to meet Christopher Benjamin, head of a 62-strong team called the Projects and Export Policy (PEP) division.... The meeting completes Jellicoe's daily routine of at least half a dozen contacts with government.
>
> (*Business Magazine*, May, 1987)

So lobbying has become less personal, less a matter of decisions being taken and influenced by small and socially isolated cliques. Lobbying was less necessary when 'our interests' could be reconciled over a drink, during a house party, or at dinner in an age before the administrative complications of policy and the pressures on politicians to be publicly accountable, inhibited the power of Ministers and senior officials to make unreferenced decisions. Suddenly there were more people doing the lobbying and more people charged with responding to it. The power of access gave way to the need for technique. And the stage was also set for the rise of public relations as a lobbying tool. Unquestionably, there is today far more contact than ever before between Government at all levels and those it governs. It now seems difficult to believe that shortly before he became Labour leader, Hugh Gaitskell received only some twenty letters a month, a luxury for which even the most obscure Member in the most trouble-free seat can only pray today. Alf Dubs, a Labour MP until 1987 estimated that while in Opposition he received 20,000 letters a year and sent 10,000. A class of 1964 veteran, who has experienced corporate lobbying both as Minister and back bencher, highlighted its growth and the increasing breadth of Government's contact with the public:

> The most noticeable difference is the volume of issue-based lobbying and of attempts by commercial organisations outside my constituency to contact me, seek my support and influence me. Twenty years ago the bulk of my corporate lobbies were by those whom I knew or to whom I had been introduced through trusted friends. Nowadays, with more corporate activity directed at Government, I have to deal with a far wider range of people. It has meant a change of attitude and of approach to the way I consider corporate representations.

The workload of Ministers has mounted in line with that of MPs as a whole. With it has come even more delegation and reliance on policy advisers. Whitehall Ministers are supported by an average of 3,000 officials on a range of subjects of which they cannot hope even to gain a confident understanding, let alone any semblance of mastery. As a result, the more that organisations clamour for the ear of the Minister, the harder it is for him to make a decision that bucks the system. Christopher Chataway described the modern burdens of office:

> I always did my boxes in the early morning. I always got up at half past five and I really worked, worked hard against the clock till eight o'clock. Then throughout the day you're busy with Cabinet committee meetings or seeing delegations of one kind or another or in policy meetings when you're not at a dinner making a speech. So you do not get much time to question what you're doing or assess its importance.
>
> (in Mitchell, 1982, p.91)

That workload gives them less time for individual personal contact and forces them and the rest of the system to favour corporatism: giving preference to the views of major players or, regardless of their lowest common denominator quality, trade associations and other representative bodies. Departments are now too busy for the most senior officials to be involved in the bulk of the policy issues of concern to organisations. The Permanent Secretary meeting the blue chip corporate director is invariably doing so through no more than courtesy. His script is as prepared for him by those under his command as are Ministers' Cabinet Committee or Despatch Box briefs. A Deputy Secretary with several years experience as a journalist has advised:

> Your case will be probed at a lower level than you think. A telephone call or letter to a Permanent Secretary may gain you time or ensure that your concerns

receive faster attention but it is rare for senior officials to contradict the advice given to them by Principals or Assistant Secretaries. The level at which organisations contact Departments is largely geared to the vanity of the industrialist concerned. Many people think that two minutes with the Minister is worth a thousand with any official. There is, in fact, no reason why all representations, (other than the most political ones), should not be made at Principal and Assistant Secretary level. (*The Government Report*, 1987, p.16)

The Changing Face of Lobbying

To date the theme of this chapter has concerned the steady rise of negotiations between departments and business groups. In his 1983 Reith lectures the former Head of the Home Civil Service, Sir Douglas Wass, noted how far relations with outside interests had become institutionalised. He noted that there had been a bypassing of traditional party-based representative government and representation of the public had increasingly become a matter for interest groups.

> They have associated themselves with people of similar interests into trade unions, pressure groups and lobbies. They have sought to influence government decisions and primarily by the process of influencing their representatives, but by applying pressure at the very point where policy is made, in executive government. Departments 'mark' pressure groups and special interests.... Political decisions are reached with a view, in part at least, to satisfying these pressure groups and interests.... It is much easier politically for government to come to terms with some special interest than oppose it.
>
> (Wass, 1984, p.105).

Jordan and Richardson (1982) have presented this negotiative approach as 'the British style'. In their academic jargon they have included among the features of this dominant style aspects such as 'clientelism', 'consultation/ negotiation', 'the development of exchange relationships', and 'the institutionalisation and regularisation of compromise.'

They say (1982, p.81),

> In fact, there are considerable advantages in pursuing policy-making in relatively closed arrangements. There is a common language and understanding of what is at issue.... By developing understandings, uncertainty is reduced for both department and group.... The emphasis is on the integration and accommodation of groups at all stages in the policy process. The 'rule' is that affected interests have the right to be consulted.

They suggest that the integrated participation by outsiders in policy making is the norm – not some highly suspicious and exceptional role only open to commercial lobbyists:

Indeed, much of the most important pressure group activity is wielded by groups which do not need to conduct high-profile, public campaigns. Policies are developed in private arrangements between civil servants and their pressure group peers. Jordan and Richardson, (1987, p.6)

Wyn Grant (with Jane Sargent 1987, p.37) shares the rejection of an image of business and government as a political struggle between lobbyists and lobbied. Grant claims:

There is an exchange relationship from which government secures three types of benefit: information for policy design; consent for policy clearance; and co-operation for policy implementation.

On policy design he says:

Departments may be able to make use of information garnered from firms and business associations with whom they are in contact to press the departmental point of view with other parts of the machine.

With reference to 'policy clearance' he argues:

The notion of policy clearance refers to the securing of the consent, or at least the acquiesance, of affected publics to policy proposals ... Of course, there may be occasions when a government considers that it has to push ahead with a policy proposal in the face of organised opposition ... In such cases, the government can draw on its coercive powers, but these can be rapidly depleted and should not be used lightly. Moreover, the British system of government is one in which extensive and intensive consultation with affected interests ... is a basic operational principle.

If the key argument in the first part of this chapter was the opening of Whitehalls doors to outsiders, the theme of the second is the changing nature of the lobbying effort in the past few years.

The official of 1946, or even 1970, would be struck by the desire of today's corporate lobbyists to confuse administrative and political issues and direct their cases more towards Ministers and MPs even though the pressures induced by the sheer volume of work have almost entirely devolved the sifting and vetting function to departmental staff.

Although the effective focus of lobbying has moved to the Executive and Administration, the power of the media and of other new techniques of persuasion has attempted to divert the attention of business and industry back to the legislature. Those who were once insiders have been advised to reject their inheritance.

Commercial lobbying has exploded in scale, but in the main it has not acquired a corresponding technical precision and efficacy. Misdirection of effort has been prompted by an exaggerated media interest in Parliament (which is easy to report) compared with what is invariably the real policy making centre of Whitehall (which is far less accessible). Almost every analysis of pressure group and corporate lobbying activity has been conducted by those outside Government: by academics or journalists with no first hand experience and only rarely an understanding of its real workings. They see the Lords defeat the Government on an amendment and forget the other two hundred on that Bill that were meekly withdrawn. They see five Government backbenchers abstaining and call it a rebellion. They look at the apparent power of the Commons expressed on issues such as Sunday trading deregulation and forget about the hundreds of issues which the Whips ensure are voted through without demur. For politics, in their eyes, is about parties; and without party activity, they cannot recognise the submerged mass of the iceberg of politics.

Such accounts of the contact between organisations and Government as exist appear as unrepresentative to practitioners – whether lobbyists, officials or backbenchers – as dramatised trials and hospital sagas do to lawyers and doctors. Even the diaries and memoirs of Cabinet Ministers and senior mandarins are not entirely reliable as guides to the relationship between Government and interest groups. Their viewpoints are of those too mighty to be involved in the day to day work of government: board minutes rather than an accurate description of the workload of their company; recollections not unnaturally geared to the great events, overlooking the mass of representations and responses that comprise the backbone of the lobbying process.

The picture as seen by those outside Government circles is distorted by Government's enduring lack of keenness to allow the media to peer over the walls of Whitehall. As a result, organisations and the public know more than ever about the decisions of Government but are no wiser about the way in which they are reached. As the press and TV devote more and more space to politics from their vantage point in the Palace of Westminster, organisations may be forgiven for believing that the parliamentary and ministerial element in the decision making process is as strong, if not stronger than ever.

There is therefore surprisingly little background material on which a commentator can draw in assessing the development of post-war lobbying. Some trends are nonetheless clear. Most importantly, there is a greater willingness of those in Government to admit that power has moved from Parliament. As we have noted, Establishments no longer talk to each other; they have been replaced by two sides talking at each other. And we have seen the rise of a new class of 'barristers' (professional lobbyists), some of whom bridge the gap usefully and effectively; the rest merely serving to cloak the lobbying process in impenetrable smoke screen and confuse organisations further by misidentifying the point of power.

More money and time is devoted by organisations to lobbying today than at any time in the past. But it is as true today as it was when Attlee took power that for every instance in which Government is forced to maintain or amend policy through pressure, hype or parliamentary embarrassment, there are several hundred where decisions are made or influenced purely through the undramatic submission of a well researched, well argued and representative case. Although the commentators associate corporate lobbying with such campaigns as Mr. Cube, successfully created by Tate & Lyle to oppose sugar nationalisation in the late 1940s; with GEC's Nimrod being vanquished by Boeing's AWACS in the 1980s or with a rash of contested takeovers in which bidder and defender vie for the support of MPs whose opinions will, they assume, sway Ministers into referring or clearing the deal, in practice most lobbying is quiet and businesslike.

The greatest part of the time spent by organisations in dealing with Government is devoted to informing the system about their activities without necessarily seeking to influence policy or legislation. Those who have dealt with Government with consistent effectiveness over the years are those who have lobbied, in the pressure sense of the term, least. Witness the largely overlooked one and a half liner of Alan Lord, the former Treasury mandarin brought in by Lloyds, faced with the need to soften the impact of the 1987 Budget's threat to block the 'Reinsurance to Close' loophole protecting underwriters. He headed an organisation whose attitude to dealings with Government had for years been dominated by close Establishment connections with Ministers and senior officials, a confident reliance on the support of the many Conservative back-bench members of Lloyds and a supposition of natural identity between its members and those in the House. Its first reaction was to encourage its Names to lobby their MPs. Lord was cooler and more correct:

> We shall not start lobbying until there is no further scope for negotiation,
> (*Financial Times*, 15th April, 1987).

His tactics, executed with the understanding of a former insider, not only won the case for Lloyd's but recovered much lost respect for the Corporation within Whitehall. Lord proved the most fundamental maxim of successful post-war lobbying; the maxim that separates it from the more personal, almost cosy arrangements made between the Establishment within and outside Government in the hundreds of years prior to 1939: that friends in high places are no match for an understanding of the mechanics of the decision making-process, particularly in an age when the pervasive attentions of the media can demand that Government justifies every decision it makes and demonstrates that it has consulted widely in advance. If much organisational lobbying has not been more effective, it is because of a widespread failure to grasp this point.

Over the past ten years in particular, the blossoming of Communication as a corporate tool – or, more strictly, the business of adjusting the tone with which an organisation communicates with the outside world – has unfortunately drawn bodies away from a disciplined preparation of their case and towards the manner of its presentation. Form is taking over from content. That trend can be more easily comprehended when seen in parallel with the vigorously effective promotion by the public relations industry over the last thirty years of the concept that dealing with Government is no different from dealing with consumers, shareholders or a workforce. The concept suggests that they are all 'publics' and that devices more relevantly employed in the selling of baked beans or industrial machinery – use of the press, the glossy brochure, the lunch, the lobbying video or 'contact programme' to get to know MPs or inform them about an organisation or issue – can be a new and effective mechanism of convincing Government of that organisation's 'message'.

Virtually none of the advocates of this approach had active experience of work inside the system of Government other than an acquaintance with a few politicians. In the absence of an understanding of the mentality and processes at the heart of the machine, they concentrated on peripheral influences. The superficial attractiveness of mobilising such influences through the most visible element of that system was more alluring to many organisations than the prospect of detailed research into Government attitudes and the negotiation of a case with anonymous junior to middle ranking officials.

The real lobbying work continues in this style but the vagaries of events gave the communication-based lobbyists some justification for their arguments. The revival of interest in Parliament was partly a response to the circumstances of 1974-9, when the Government had at first a very small majority, then no majority at all and it was possible to defeat or amend legislation with comparative ease by securing the support of a few backbenchers.

The increased attractiveness of the PR approach to dealing with Government to organisations who knew no better in the 1970s and 1980s, meant that lobbying became regarded as synonymous with PR techniques. Many organisations devolved responsiblity for dealings with Government from senior management to PR or so-called public affairs or corporate communications managers, whose familiarity with traditional PR techniques was (and still is) somewhat stronger than their knowledge of Government. The doctrine entrenched itself and business and industry increasingly threw good money after bad in its quest to travel a path that only moved in parallel to that of Government, with only rare intersections.

The basis of the notion that to lobby is to communicate is the suggestion that the techniques of dealing with publics, as the PR industry terms them, are broadly similar regardless of the target. The industry, in debating definitions of its art in this field, has referred to 'Political Public Relations' thus:

> In fact, we are considering simply a specialist branch of public relations, using familiar communications techniques albeit in a different and often sensitive environment.
>
> (from Interact International, seminar brochure, 1987).

Organisations have often been so keen to communicate that they have forgotten to put together any case at all. In January 1985 an Assistant Secretary in Customs and Excise questioned Public Policy Consultants about a particular lobby against a provision in the 1984 *Finance Act*. The lobby had formed itself into an action group, mobilised its members at the grass roots and had used all the usual techniques: Parliamentary Questions, Early Day Motions, petitions and mass letters to constituency MPs. Its only weakness was that they equated power of delivery with strength of argument. 'If you see them', the Assistant Secretary asked of us, 'tell them that we aren't fools. We know they are lying and that their figures are grossly exaggerated. Ministers and the MPs they respect aren't going to consider an uncorroborated case. The lobby might as well save its money. We have done our homework and we see no evidence to prove that they have done theirs.'

Since 1979, attempts to sway Government through Parliament have multiplied. The Sotheby takeover battle can be taken as the start of that surge. There is now every indication that it has reached its zenith. The research in *The Government Report* (1987), revealed that many MPs and Ministers are now anaesthetised to much organisational lobbying, its effect diluted by over-use. The much vaunted British Airways parliamentary lobby has generated so much comment that Ministers expect it and it discount accordingly. An experienced Department of Transport official stated to us that since the BA/British Caledonian routes war in 1984, he did not feel any advice given to Ministers on civil aviation issues had been overturned or even amended as a result of lobbying by outside organisations.

Public Relations is about visibility, and it was at the visible manifestation of power that the new lobbying pundits aimed. They had not lived within the inner mechanism of the system but they had been to school where they had been taught, as all British children are taught, that Ministers make the decisions and MPs shape them. And it was easier to court Parliament than get to Ministers. Westminster was made the focus. The Public Relations Consultants Association published guidelines on lobbying in the British Parliament but could find no one to produce a companion tract for Whitehall. The CBI issued a manual on working with politicians but waited nearly three years before publishing a companion volume on the Civil Service.

Parliament, as far as business and industry were concerned, was back in the frame. MPs, the story ran, needed to be educated about companies and issues. Organisations became concerned that the attitude Parliament took to them would prejudice policy that might affect their interests and, more importantly, be noticed by a critical media. They began to feel once more that parliamentary pressure really could sway the Executive's decisions; that the perception by MPs was critical.

Although almost every public relations firm now claims to offer some version of a lobbying service, almost without exception such claims have been shown to be professionally bankrupt. They work through a network of introductions, usually to Conservative backbench MPs and Peers, and offer to help their clients get their 'message' over to a group they term 'opinion formers' – meaning anyone who ought to be regarded as important by their client. Distrusted by Government for their lack of intellectual discipline or procedural understanding, they remain outsiders despite their popularity with their market. The bulk of their success claims rarely stand up to experienced examination. Yet their greatest ally is Government itself. Officials and Ministers refuse to comment on the activities of the untrained PR communities. As a result it is impossible for a client to disprove the lobbyist's claim that he had a vital hand in the system's concessions to it; concessions that were probably granted more as a consequence of Whitehall's examination of the organisation's detailed submission, to which lobbyists will have had little input, than the form of its presentation to other 'opinion formers'. They are modern day Pardoners, taking full credit for their clients' miracle cures.

Word processors have facilitated the reproduction of representations and MPs predominantly bemoan that they are treated impersonally. Departments and MPs are under strain from the pure weight of lobbying, less and less of it being personally targeted. The best lobbyists are sparing in their demands on Government but nonetheless some senior MPs, such as former Minister Sir Hugh Rossi, believe that the weight of poor lobbying now swamps some good cases:

> The habit seems to have developed of organisations finding a tame MP to do whatever they ask. The growth in the number of EDMs tabled is the most irritating aspect of this phenomenon. Too many professional lobbyists have devalued the EDM by tapping compliant MPs to provide them with some manifestation of their work for their clients. Government takes no notice of them now – officials do not even draw their Ministers' attention to them.
>
> (Evidence cited in *The Government Report*, 1987).

Joel Barnett (1982, pp.28-9), when Chief Secretary to the Treasury, was struck with this campaign in 1974:

> This (clause to make US citizens resident in the UK subject to UK tax) was announced by Denis (Healey) in his Budget on 26 March, and immediately we began to be subjected to the US lobby in London. Now I understood the true meaning of the word 'lobby' and how it must work in Washington. It was quite incredible: wherever I went – speaking engagements, lunches, dinners and receptions – a friendly American would somehow contrive to refer to the issue, and put forward their case against the Chancellor's proposal. I was told that precisely the same was happening to Denis, to Douglas Wass, the Permanent Secretary, to top Inland Revenue officials, and even to the Prime Minister. The result of this most effective lobby was to convince us that it would be in our interests to revise our legislation, and on 9 May in opening the Second Reading debate on the *Finance Bill*, Denis announced that the test period would be altered to nine out of ten years, rather than five out of six.

Barnett described that campaign as, 'the most formidable lobby I have ever experienced'. But the effect of such techniques, based on persistence as well as a sound fiscal case, is exceptional. Three chapters on, he observes (1982, p.63) that:

On particular matters we were never short of representations, both from individuals and groups. The pressure groups for individual industries, such as drinks, tobacco and motoring, would always be politely received, but mainly ignored. We would either be convinced by the facts provided by our officials or not, as the case may be, but we were unlikely to be convinced by an obviously prejudiced group lobbying in their own interests. The same went for the CBI, although not to the same extent. But it was difficult to treat their representations too seriously when they invariably made such an unbalanced case.

What his first example describes, and what he would have seen in the equally successful campaign mounted ten years later to counter the threat of VAT being applied to books, was the face of good 'public lobbying'. Securing public and parliamentary support for lobbies not only broadens their base it diminishes allegations of special pleading: such peripheral work may also be regarded as their insurance policy. But what Ministers and senior officials rarely see is the hours put in by the most effective campaigners with their lawyers, economists and lobbying consultants to ensure that the case they submit to Whitehall is unimpeachable. The construction of a case is more often than not more important than its communication.

Ministers have over the years admitted that they can be influenced by representations from MPs they respect, but the occasions where Departments have gained a misleading impression of facts and are prepared to stand corrected as a result of political representations are comparatively few. The difference in the late 1970s and 1980s is that, instead of keeping MPs informed while negotiations take place 'over the road' and consulting them should the organisation's point not be accepted, MPs have become the *initial* point of contact for many organisations. But the lack of objectivity and preparation referred to above can embarrass and alienate parliamentarians in their dealings with Ministers on behalf of lobbies. Bruce George MP recounted an example (quoted in *The Government Report*) that was echoed by many of his colleagues:

> I took up an organisation's apparently persuasive case and met the Minister. He told me that I had only been given half the story. His officials had already been through all the facts with the organisation and the issue was clear as far as he was concerned. I felt as if I had been bounced, albeit innocently. I resolved to be far more careful in future.

Where organisations lobby wisely they invariably do so, as we observed earlier, in an undramatic way. Pilkington's 1987 parliamentary defence against BTR's bid was much praised by the communications pundits whereas, in our view, it was BTR's apparent inaction that evidenced the best grasp of the dynamics of decision making on the case. Pilkington threw every advert, article and compliant MP they could find at the Government to press home their virtues as an independent, innovative and socially conscious manufacturer and employer. Faced with such tactics a Sidney Treadgold or Michael

Howard (the current Under Secretary and Minister in charge of competition policy at the time), had they been sitting on the BTR board, might have briefed the chairman as follows:

1. BTR fully understands that current competition policy is, since the Tebbit doctrine, predominantly geared to references on commercial grounds.

2. We believe that Paul Channon, the Secretary of State for Trade and Industry, and Michael Howard, the competition Minister fully support this principle and are not easily swayed by social arguments. We know this because BTR has exercised the opportunity of meeting them and has consulted the departmental Special Advisers to confirm ministerial thinking.

3. We have some of the best lawyers in the country at our disposal. We believe we have made a convincing case to OFT to illustrate that the Competition Act is not applicable and that many Pilkington claims are exaggerated.

4. In short, we think we have Whitehall squared. Our assessment is that a political decision is unlikely. However, lots of MPs are being primed to support Pilkington and denounce us. The press is picking this up and thinks we are going to lose.

5. All experience (and our discussions with DTI PPSs) indicates that local MPs are obliged to support Pilkington. Their other supporters on the Government side are not going to take this so far as to defy the Whips should the crunch come – anyway, many are predictable dissidents and Ministers will discount their opposition regardless of whether they are former Prime Ministers.

6. Timing will be crucial. The Bank of England has just stated that it favours maintaining the independence of companies with a strong R & D base; and the post-Guinness atmosphere favours defenders over predators. If we lose, it will be as much because the timing of peripheral events is against us.

7. The bottom line is that these parliamentary and media spoilers will not, or are most unlikely, to influence Government; but they may well frighten City analysts who do not understand how Government works and jump at anything that looks important. Our parliamentary lobbying efforts must therefore be directed at them rather than at Ministers. Obviously, if the Conservative Trade and Industry Committee invites us to meet it, we should do so. But the battle will be decided elsewhere.

BTR withdrew because the Pilkington share price moved outside its range, not because of political or parliamentary pressure. Pilkington had to act as it did, and it did so as well as it could, but BTR correctly resisted the temptation to follow suit.

On the other hand, pressure as a technique can work on exceptional issues. And Ministers can be moved by imperfect cases. Sotheby's, attempting in 1983 to seek reference to the Monopolies Commission of a hostile bid, succeeded through an energetic massing of hordes of flag-waving MPs persuaded that a priceless national asset would be sold to foreigners. The fact that in the eyes of many, including the Secretary of State's advisers, Sotheby's was a very effective broker enabling our national assets to be sold to foreigners was overlooked. Lord Cockfield bowed to pressure. (See Hogrefe, 1986).

Obstruction has also on occasion proved successful, most memorably perhaps when Sir Anthony Kershaw, a consultant to BAT, was a party to 87 out of a total of 164 amendments to the 1981 *Zoo Licensing Bill* to prevent a Bill eliminating tobacco sponsorship of sport and the arts being reached. He later admitted to the BBC,' ...one of my interests in that particular Bill was to keep out the Bill banning smoking which came afterwards.' (Alderman, 1984, p.62)

The introduction of communication skills notwithstanding, the effective lobbying techniques used today are much the same as at any time in the postwar period. Indeed, the most effective technique is unchanged – the sound case that pre-empts all counter arguments.

Disregarding the lightweight element and their media orientated tactics, the balance of commercial lobbyists work in a manner more familiar to law firms, researching cases and working their way through the system in a careful and procedurally correct manner. The last ten years has seen a significant flow into the best firms of bright but frustrated Principals and Assistant Secretaries. In the financial sector, the flow has become nothing short of a torrent, with every major merchant bank raiding the Treasury and DTI for entrepreneurial economists and specialists able to guide them through the intricacies of competition, privatisation and fiscal policy. The 'turncoats' and their consultant employers have acted not just as a guide but also as a valve, helping organisations resist the now well-stimulated desire to throw themselves wholesale at Government.

Effectiveness

One of the problems of assessing the effectiveness of the lobbying techniques used, whether by organisations or their consultants, is that it is impossible in most cases to tell whether the tactics adopted make any difference. The 1950 lobby by the iron and steel industry against nationalisation centred around a deliberate refusal to nominate members for the new Iron and Steel Corporation, starving it of management skills. It appeared to be effective, but the 1951 Election ended Labour's tenure and the new Administration immediately introduced denationalisation legislation. Had the election not intervened, the Labour Government may well have held fast.

Luck plays a great part in determining the fate of any major lobby: the fortunes of the current campaign by manufacturers of recording tape to resist record industry pressure on Government to impose a tape levy as compensation against unauthorised copyright breach have changed with each new Secretary of State for Trade and Industry. Tebbitt opposed them, Brittan supported them, Channon opposed and, just in time to prevent a levy clause being included in the 1988 Copyright Bill, Lord Young again reversed DTI's position. If the visibility or irritation factor of an issue keeps it before Ministers rather than just officials, reshuffles can crucially affect their future.

Perhaps the best advice is that given by Bruce-Gardyne and Lawson (1976, pp.179-80), commenting in the 1970s on the lessons to be learnt from the lobbies of the 1950s and 1960s:

> There is no reliable general principle to the art of successful lobbying in the British system. Influencing policy in gestation is crucial; but while some lobbies consciously eschew appeals to the parliamentary dimension – the CBI, the textile lobby at most times, the TUC under George Woodcock's leadership – others have found it advisable to cultivate politicians to the point, if need be, of promoting backbench rebellion: the TUC under Vic Feather, for example, or the NFU at all times. The commonest line is to treat MPs as the last resort, to be appealed to only when the possibilities of negotiation with the civil servants has been exhausted. Yet on occasion the approach direct to the Minister can work wonders, as in the case of the launching of EFTA. It is a matter of horses for courses, at least where the politicians are concerned…In the words of the old military adage, 'time spent in reconnaisance is seldom wasted'.

But though it is difficult to generalise about what will bring success, we can be a little more positive about what brings failure. Over concentration on Westminster is less likely to bring rewards than the frequenting of the dull corridors of Whitehall.

3   Contract Lobbying in the USA

GRAHAM WILSON

Contract or 'for-hire' lobbying is the practice of an individual or company representing temporarily for a fee the views, attitudes or interests of a separate group or organisation external to government in the policymaking process. We do not have much firm evidence on who uses contract lobbyists, or how frequently. It seems probable, however, that most of the time contract lobbyists are employed by those groups best able to afford them, and obviously business organisations and corporations are better able than most to pay for their services. Although to some degree constituting an alternative or even rival form of interest articulation to the use of permanent interest group representatives, contract lobbying has become a central, if controversial feature of the American interest group system.

The reasons for the considerable and increased importance of contract lobbying tell us much about the current interest group system. There have probably always been Washington 'insiders' who have helped clients resolve difficulties with government. Traditionally these insiders have been of two types. First, there is the former government official who knows and is known by 'everybody', or rather by enough people in a particular policy community to be able to offer clients unusual access to decisionmakers. Clark Clifford and Tommy Corcoran are notable examples of insiders who stayed on after service in the Truman and Roosevelt Administrations to become highly paid and regarded contract lobbyists. The second type of long established contract lobbyist is the Washington lawyer or 'superlawyer' who rarely goes to court but like the former government official specialises in lobbying government (Goulden, 1973). A well known example of such law firms is Arnold and Porter. Both these types of lobbying have probably been growing rapidly in the last twenty years; it is certainly the case that the number of lawyers in Washington has increased dramatically, and at a pace which cannot be explained by the growth of litigation.

Though various figures for the growth of registered lobbyists are reported the scale of increase is not in doubt. Hedrick Smith, author of *The Power Game* claimed in 1988 that there were only 365 lobbyists registered in 1961 but 23,011 by mid 1987. This has had an impact on techniques. Smith claimed that one Senator told him that there were 200 lobbyists pressing to talk to him on one key tax bill. (*Sunday Times*, 6th November, 1988).

Of late, however, the former government officials operating on a relatively small scale and the superlawyers have been joined by firms providing contract lobbying alone. The best known example of this type of lobbyist is Charls [sic] Walker Associates, led by Charls Walker, one of the most famous of all the Washington super lobbyists (see Drew, 1983). Other prominent individuals include Bob Gray, Thomas Boggs and Jack Bonner. Although it might be convenient to see the superlobbyist firm as merely the former government officials working as lobbyists writ large, the fact remains that contract lobbying is now practiced on a greater scale and has reached a level at which it is possible to establish contract lobbying as a business or profession in its own right.

At first glance this development might seem surprising. For one of the general features of American interest group politics in the last twenty years (and in line with Wyn Grant's chapter here) has been the growth of both in-house lobbying capability in corporations, and the expansion and improvement of interest group organisations themselves. As many political scientists have emphasised (see Wilson, 1981, 1985; Vogel, 1983; Berry, 1984), the 1970s witnessed a major mobilisation by business to defend its interests against the onslaught from environmentalists, consumer protection groups, and similar organisations which achieved major political successes against business in the late 1960s and early 1970s. Business fought back in a variety of ways. Existing umbrella groups such as the Chamber of Commerce modernised and improved their operations. Trade associations such as the American Petroleum Institute or the Chemical Manufacturers' Association increased staff and resources. An entirely new business umbrella organisation, the Business Roundtable was created to represent the interests of the very largest corporations in the United States; it was thought that existing business umbrella groups were both too focused on smaller businesses and too ideological in their attitudes. Simultaneously, individual corporations substantially upgraded their political capabilities. The number of corporations with representation in Washington increased substantially, and it was generally thought that the calibre of lobbyists employed by business was high. In terms of the number and quality of its representatives, business was much better represented in the mid 1980s than in the early 1960s when a definitive study of business and politics had concluded that business lobbyists were low quality, fragmented and under-financed.

Why, then, if many corporations which used not to have their own 'in-house' lobbyists now do, and if the business interest groups are also much improved, should there be scope for contract lobbying to grow? It could easily be imagined that the growth of 'in-house' lobbying and the improvement in the quality of business interest groups would have taken away the potential market for contract lobbyists. In practice, however, contract lobbying and more direct forms of corporate political involvement have grown simultaneously. There are a number of reasons for this.

First, the dramatic growth in business political activity has perhaps obscured the fact that not all corporations, indeed not even all very large corporations, have a significant independent political capability. The majority of the *Fortune 500* corporations in the mid 1980s did *not* have a political action committee (PAC) which would allow them to make political contributions from shareholders or executives to candidates for Congress; yet most Washington lobbyists now regard PAC contributions as a necessity for obtaining access to legislators. Exactly why some corporations are more politically active than others is a matter for some debate. The explanation favoured by most political scientists is that, as David Truman (1971 ed) would have predicted, those corporations which have been mobilised politically are those which have been challenged the most by the rise and success of the public interest movement and the consequent adoption of regulations to the disadvantage of business. Regulations designed to protect the environment or consumers bear more heavily on some corporations than on others; it is those corporations most seriously affected which will be the most active politically. Clearly this is a plausible interpretation. Yet in an earlier paper, I have argued that there is a much stronger relationship between the political activism of a corporation and the scale of the contracts it obtains from federal government than between the scale of corporate political activity and perceptions of how serious a problem regulation poses for the company (Wilson, 1987). In either case, we might accept that many corporations have not been mobilised fully politically and remain as potential customers for contract lobbyists. Indeed, one very simple reason why contract lobbyists are employed is that not only individual corporations but established interest groups such as the Business Roundtable do not have enough permanent staff to cope with the crises which arise from time to time for most groups.

Similarly, the mobilisation of business has not ended that political naivety which has so often been the characteristic of the top American executive. For reasons that David Vogel has explored (Vogel, 1978), many business executives in the United States have sought to ignore as much as possible the growth of government in domestic life, the legitimacy of which they do not accept. Many otherwise sophisticated executives are isolated from politics or government, and lack a comprehension of it that would be second naure to a Japanese or French executive who might well have been educated with top civil servants or even have been a high level civil servant earlier in his career. The less scrupulous contract lobbyist can exploit this naivety among top business executives by offering a simple solution to a complex problem. Thus Michael Deaver made a telephone call on behalf of TWA to Elizabeth Dole, the Secretary of Transportation, asking her not to act against TWA's policy in a takeover battle. The telephone call had predictably little affect; Dole was too astute to respond to such a crude approach by the former member of the White House staff and had inumerable ways open to her of deflecting any pressure Deaver might exert. The management of TWA thus paid Deaver $250,000 for a single phone call which was unlikely to have the desired effect. This was a classic example of management naivety about how the political system works, a reflection of the belief that decisive action by the right person gets results.

Yet American contract lobbyists do not obtain fees only from the relatively inactive or naive corporation. On the contrary, the American contract lobbyist is frequently employed by the politically active and influential, including not only corporations but interest groups such as trade associations which themselves have offices in Washington. The reasons for this are particularly interesting. Why should organisations with their own lobbyists and political contacts none the less employ contract lobbyists? There are again a variety of reasons.

First, as we have noted above, interest groups sometimes turn to contract lobbyists when the interest group is temporarily short of staff, perhaps because it is in the midst of an unusual crisis or busy period. Contract lobbyists are hired when the work load is heavy, just as extra secretarial staff from a secretarial agency might be brought in during a busy period. Yet although this practice makes sense economically, it is clear that organisations with the ability to pay their own lobbyists if they wished to (such as the Business Roundtable) employ contract lobbyists so regularly that something other than keeping costs down must be involved.

Second, some contract lobbyists are renowned for their expertise or contacts (or both contacts and expertise) in a particular policy field. Charls Walker, for example, has a reputation for knowing more people involved in making tax policy and more about the problems of tax policy than most people in Washington. An industry's trade association or a single corporation anxious to secure a tax break would be well advised, therefore, to employ Walker even though they have their own 'in-house' lobbyists. It is perhaps as well to dispel at this juncture the notion that contract lobbyists as 'hired guns' have less standing with politicians and their staffs than those employed directly by interest groups. On the contrary, the contract lobbyist is often regarded as particularly trustworthy on the grounds that were the contract lobbyist to supply misleading information or otherwise antagonise politicians, their future access could be destroyed; credibility for a contract lobbyist, once lost, could not be regained. For that reason, and in line with Charles Miller's proposition earlier in this book, legislators and their staffs actually prefer dealing with contract lobbyists, believing that the penalties for misleading information are so great as to deter the contract lobbyist from telling untruths or half truths.

A third reason why politically active interests turn to contract lobbyists is that the issues of the day may have immobilised trade associations of umbrella groups because the interests of members diverge. This has been a particular problem in the 1980s for the business community. In the 1970s, issues such as consumer or environmental protection tended to unite different industries and the corporations within them. In the 1980s, issues such as tax reform have affected different industries and corporations very differently; in consequence, trade associations or business umbrella groups have been unable to attain the degree of consensus needed to act politically. Corporations supporting or opposing tax reform have been driven to use either their own lobbyists or consultants because the trade association for the industry has been immobilised by disagreements among member corporations.

A fourth and related reason for turning to contract lobbyists has been the need to form coalitions. Coalitions have always been a feature of American, and other, interest group politics; their importance again has increased in the 1980s as broad blocks such as automobile manufacturers or the chemical industry have been fragmented in their reactions to issues such as tax reform or foreign trade issues. Coalitions are now often created by a group of interests to support or oppose a single bill, and disappear as expected when the bill is enacted or defeated. It is the job of the contract lobbyist not only to represent but to forge such coalitions. In effect, the contract lobbyist becomes the centre of what is, and is intended to be, a very temporary interest group. Thus the contract lobbyist benefits from the very temporary, fluid nature of current American interest group politics.

To some extent, the fluidity of American interest group politics reflects the current, probably temporary nature of American politics. A revival of conflict on issues such as environmental protection between the public interest groups and business would no doubt prompt a renewal of the trends towards stronger organisations to protect general business interests which were evident in the 1970s with the creation of the Business Roundtable and rejuvenation of the Chamber of Commerce. In contrast, in the absence of any threat during the Reagan years to the *collective* interests of business, issues affecting the interests of individual corporations have taken on a greater significance. Opposition to what is seen as excessive regulation by the federal government to reduce hazards in the workplace is likely to produce permanent coalitions; proposals for tax reform generally produce relatively transient coalitions as some firms are helped and others hurt by particular proposals.

Most of these factors apply both to Britain and the USA. Yet there are also long standing features of the American interest group system which contrast vividly with the more institutionalised interest group systems of Japan, France or the neocorporatist countries and which create more room for the political consultant to create temporary coalitions. In countries with more institutionalised interest group systems, there is usually an established way of handling issues. Problems are passed up from corporation to trade association to be discussed with the corresponding section of the relevant government department, or, if the issue is of sufficient importance or general interest, it is passed on to the business umbrella group to which associations will invariable be affiliated.

In contrast, in the United States, the interest group system is untidy and ill co-ordinated. There is no single business umbrella group, and even trade associations enjoy only limited support from corporations. Indeed, this untidiness is paralleled in other economic sectors. There is no single farmers' organisation which enjoys the status of being labelled as the voice of agriculture; three organisations compete as representatives of agriculture in general, while dozens of commodity organisations are regarded by some commentators as more imporant than any of the general farm organisations. Only the precipitous decline of unions in the United States has united them. Until recently, three of the largest unions, – the Teamsters, the Mineworkers and the Auto Workers – were not affiliated to the unions' umbrella organisation, the American Federation of Labor-Congress of Industrial Organisations (AFL-CIO). In this untidy or decentralised setting, there is more scope for the individual political consultant to form coalitions than in countries in which such coalition formation would cut across the established and accepted way of doing things. Nor are potential coalition partners in the United States as encumbered by ideological limitations on with whom it is permissible and impermissible to form coalitions as in Britain. Alliances composed of both employers' organisations and unions are commonplace; even the most liberal unions such as the United Auto Workers have become used to collaborating with their employers on a variety of issues on which they feel that their interests coincide.

Thus the contract lobbyist in the United States has more space to operate in than in many other systems. The formation of temporary *ad hoc* coalitions whose centre is the contract lobbyist is less likely to conflict with institutionalised patterns of interest group activity than in other countries. The decentralised, competitive nature of the American interest group system naturally offers little obstacle to the contract lobbyist forming new, temporary coalitions to a degree almost unimaginable elsewhere. The rise of the contract lobbyist reflects not only the possibly temporary conservative mood of American politics but also deeper, more permanent features of the political system.

To all of these factors we must add the growth of government. Government affects more interests – especially more corporations – more significantly than in the past. People are so used to hearing that government is smaller in the USA than in other liberal democracies that they can forget that government has grown significantly in the USA, and has grown to the point where it is as 'big' today as was government in other OECD countries in the very recent past. The proportion of GNP spent by governments (state and federal) in the USA today has more in common with France and Germany in the early 1970s than with the USA described by writers such as Louis Hartz in his explanation of the liberal tradition of limited government. Nor is expenditure a sufficient measure of the extent of government. Government in the United States has long pursued through extensive regulation, goals sought by more direct means in other western countries. Both the growth of government expenditure and the growth of regulation have made government matter more – and have made the details of government policy matter to more people and interests than ever before. This again is a long term change producing work for the contract lobbyist.

If government has grown considerably in the past, political activity continues at a considerable pace in the present. Whether liberals or conservatives dominate American politics, today's professional politician or, as he or she often aspires to be, *policy entrepreneur* is less likely than in the past to be able to afford to be inactive. Legislators must produce new policies to make their mark. In consequence, the flow of new policy proposals continues even in supposedly conservative times, and with it the flow of work for both established interest groups and the contract lobbyist.

If the rise of the contract lobbyist was due only to the increase in degree to which government affects interests in society, little more need be said. Yet the fact is that there is a widespread perception that contract lobbying has become relatively more important of late, gaining ground at the expense of interest groups themselves. Why should this be? After all, an increase in the need for governments to consult interests or in the need of interests to try to influence government could in principle be met by expanding interest groups. We need to ask therefore not only why there has been an increase in the demand for representation but why that demand has not been met by established interest groups alone.

In the first place, established interest groups have often been perceived as suffering from real weaknesses. The Chamber of Commerce, for example, has generally been seen as a highly ideological organisation representing the general prejudices of small scale business rather than the practical needs of corporations. Attempts to change the image of the Chamber in this respect in the late 1970s seem to have run out of steam, even though the Chamber is generally regarded as a much more politically effective organisation than it once was. The National Association of Manufacturers, like many trade associations are generally acknowledged to be weaker than their equivalents in countries such as Japan, in part because of the effects of American anti-monopoly law. (See Lynn and McKeon, 1988). Thus, contrary to the popular wisdom, interest groups are not sufficiently entrenched in the United States to discourage use of contract lobbyists. Furthermore, the American interest groups, like their British counterparts, suffer from the fact that they generally operate by consensus so that the absence of unity prevents the organisation from taking a clear position on the issues. Although refusing to take a clear position avoids the loss of members through resignations, it can also lower the standing of the organisation as policymakers perceive it as having nothing, or nothing of value, to say.

Many of these weaknesses are less apparent when the collective interests of business seem to be under attack. Achieving unity against the Environmental Protection Agency or the Occupational Safety and Health Agency in the 1970s was not difficult; most business executives resented not only the costs imposed by those agencies but also the 'interference' they embody in the traditional autonomy of management from government. In the 1980s, the challenge for business groups has been much harder. The triumph of the right in the 1980 elections brought to power such a pro-business administration that at least initially business interest groups were so delighted that in the words of one business interest group official, they thought they had 'died and gone to heaven'. Whether this euphoria was entirely justified can be debated. However, it was indubitably the case that freed from the dangers posed by liberals, environmentalists and other sundry villains, business unity fragmented. The conservative agenda included items such as tax reform which in practice benefited not only some industries much more than others, but in practice affected some companies favourably and others adversely. Established interest groups could never cope with a situation in which their members' interests were affected so differently. Instead, interests would attempt to make their views known through the deliberately temporary coalitions created around contract lobbyists described above.

The Effectiveness of Contract Lobbying

The large sums paid to contract lobbyists can give the impression of great power. If it is reasonable to pay Charls Walker so much, he must be able to accomplish a great deal. Yet in fact it is not clear that contract lobbyists are highly effective. The traditional view taken by political scientists, as opposed to journalists, has been that the power of lobbyists is limited. (The classic statement of this is Bauer, Dexter and de Sola Poole, 1968. For a more sympathetic view, see Milbrath, 1963.) Lobbyists possess few sanctions, such as the ability to deliver votes for or against a politician, and know that the politician who is a great disappointment on a vote today may be needed as a supporter tomorrow. Therefore lobbyists are generally better seen as unpaid staff assistants helping friendly legislators than coercers of reluctant politicians.

Admittedly, a number of developments may have changed this picture somewhat since it was painted in the 1960s. The decline in the proportion of the electorate with a strong party identification has increased the opportunities for interest groups to steer their members' votes towards friendly candidates. The improvements in the technology of communication has opened up new opportunities for interest groups to mobilise members rapidly. The dependency of candidates for Congress on interest groups for electoral support has indubitably increased. The greater openness and the 'Sub-Committee Bill of Rights' in Congress has increased opportunities for lobbyists to monitor the work of legislators; committee mark-up sessions, when legislation is written or re-drafted, once held in secret are now generally held in public session.

Yet for all these changes, constraints on the lobbyist remain. Although, as critics of the pluralists have contended (and pluralists long admitted), not all interests in society are organised or have equal strength. The variety of groups and interests effectively represented in Washington is considerable. It is unlikely that the absence of support from interest groups significantly changes the balance of political power in Washington; both liberal and conservative legislators obtain support from sympathetic interest groups. A politician refused support from one political action committee is likely to gain support from another. Most interest groups know that their ability to punish their enemies is extremely limited (so that unions, for example, can do little to hurt hostile sunbelt politicians) while the politician who disappoints on one vote remains a potential supporter in the future. Above all, in an era when the value of incumbency is so great that the proportion of incumbents successfully seeking re-election to the House of Representatives recently reached a Soviet level of 98%, threats from interest groups have limited impact even on the highly insecure legislators.

Contract lobbyists have even more limited ability than most to threaten reprisals for an 'incorrect' vote. Their stock in trade is to be the ultimate insiders, reaching those parts of the decision making process an ordinary lobbyist cannot reach. Contacts and friendships necessary for this would be destroyed by threatening behaviour. It is interesting to note that in a recent survey I conducted of corporate Vice Presidents responsible for political activity, contract lobbyists were given relatively poor grades for their effectiveness. Only 29% of corporations regarded consultants as important or extremely important in communicating their views to government (See Wilson, 1987). Such views should be treated with caution. Corporations may turn to contract lobbyists when other approaches to their problem have failed, and their cause is almost lost. Moreover, generalising across policy areas can produce misleading conclusions about the effectiveness of interest groups. Expertise and friendship can produce results, particularly on issues which are technical, and as far as most people are concerned, obscure. Tax policy, Charls Walker's area of expertise, has been renowned as an area in which the contract lobbyist can have an impact. Decisionmaking on tax policy has traditionally been relatively concentrated (by the standards of the American political system) even in Congress. Tax issues are also highly technical, and yet of considerable importance to those affected by the details of tax legislation. A few words, not noticed let alone understood by legislators (and more so the general public), can save a corporation millions of dollars.

Yet tax policy also shows the limitations of the power of contract lobbyists. As a recent account shows (Birnbaum and Murray, 1988), the dozens of contract lobbyists hired by corporations to defend their interests were unable to prevent a significant alteration in the tax laws in 1986 to the disadvantage of their clients. Of course the blow was softened by the simultaneous changes in tax law saving corporate executives as individuals vast amounts in taxation. Yet all in all the tax reform legislation did show that well represented lobbies were unable to prevent changes supported by politicians for reasons of both liberal and conservative principle, even though the public remained indifferent and even sceptical about tax reform. As the authors of the account of the adoption of tax reform make clear, if any issue should have been susceptible to the influence of well connected lobbyists, it was tax reform. In the event, in the 'showdown at Gucci gulch' the lobbyists met their Waterloo (though again, one must emphasise that they like their business executive clients benefited *personally* enormously from the legislation).

The introduction of even such a major change as the 1986 tax reform legislation should not necessarily lead to a fundamental re-appraisal of the entire political system. The passage of time will probably lead to a gradual re-steering in the tax system to the advantage of those who can employ lobbyists to represent their interests. Yet a number of factors which help explain the adoption of tax reform also had been emphasised by those taking a more sceptical view of the power of lobbyists in the past. First, a number of political scientists have argued that in contrast to a popular view of American politics, politicians themselves are important sources of policy ideas. (See Nordlinger, 1981; and Skocpol, 1985). Politicians and administrators do actually have views which they act on, and, as noted earlier, it is possible that the need to be a policy entrepreneur today is greater than in the past, forcing more politicians than ever to try to shape policy as opposed to quietly serving out terms in Congress or discretely seeking membership in an 'inner club'. Tax reform was very much the product of the thinking of politicians, not popular pressure or interest group politics. Second, as much of the interest group literature had suggested, interest groups were deeply divided by proposals for tax reform. The mobilisation of some corporations in favour of tax reform and others against created more freedom for the politicians to act. Third, the lobbyists representing clients threatened by tax reform had no sanctions to use against advocates of tax reform without doing themselves great damage. In particular, consultants were not about to destroy their own businesses by making threats against politicians whom they had cultivated for years. While it is possible that in the future, as tax issues return to their usual obscurity, contract lobbyists will succeed in securing the adoption of loop holes designed to benefit their clients, the adoption of tax reform may finally popularise the sceptical view of the power of lobbyists long current in political science.

The fact that even the best financed lobbies can lose in Washington may encourage a degree of complacency about contract lobbying. If important changes in public policy can be made in the face of the opposition of interests represented by the best, and best known lobbyists in Washington, the concern that the political system can be 'bought' is reduced. Moreover, as we have seen, contract lobbyists might need to be even more careful than other lobbyists to avoid compromising their reputations on which their handsome livelihoods depend. The view of Congressional staffers that contract lobbyists gave more honest information than ordinary lobbyists for that reason has been noted above. We might also praise the role of the contract lobbyist in constructing coalitions which might otherwise not emerge. Finding political partners for those who lack them may be regarded, like running a computer dating service, as a useful if unglamorous occupation.

Yet the contract lobbying system also has a number of serious disadvantages. The most obvious is that contract lobbying requires that interests pay a substantial fee to enter their views into the policymaking process. Contract lobbyists are not in general available to food stamp recipients or even environmental groups; it will be interesting to see whether the political consultants develop any tradition comparable to the law firm's *pro bono* work for deserving interests which cannot afford the regular fee. But *pro bono* work does not solve the problem of differential access to the courts based on income, but merely ameliorates it. Contract lobbying at its simplest involves paying large fees to someone with connections to policymakers to put across your point of view. Arguably, it is quite simply unfair that this sort of access should depend on wealth. Contract lobbying though is not the only example of the biasing of the interest group system to the wealthier: it is a symptom of a wider imbalance. Defenders of political action committees have argued that their contributions to political campaigns do not buy votes, but merely purchase 'access'. The contradictions between this defence and standard principles of liberal democratic theory are scarcely emphasised. Yet, one does not have to be a very strong liberal or democrat to object to 'access' being dependent on the ability to hire a contract lobbyist or operate an effective political action committee. The American political system strays from its own ideals in accepting that access should be purchased.

Of course, this departure from liberal democratic ideals is by no means limited to the USA. The well connected former civil servant in Japan or France may provide the same sort of linkage between powerful interests such as business and government as does the American contract lobbyist. Environmentalists and even unions have fewer such links. The British interest group system has always given some interests much more access to government than others, and the growth of contract lobbying in Britain raises here the same normative concerns as it does in the USA.

The second disadvantage of contract lobbying in the American context is that it reinforces the tendency for interest groups and politicians to interact only intermittently. The interest group concerned about a policy proposal hires a contract lobbyist to try to defeat or change it; the interest group in question does not take a continuing responsibility for helping to solve or manage the problem which has given rise to the proposal in the first place. Contract lobbying therefore increases the risk of irresponsibility in interest groups. Why is this particularly a problem in the USA? As Olson (1982) has argued, the more encompassing are interest groups, the more responsible they can be. A union federation speaking for all workers can accept an economically necessary pay freeze in order to promote the long term prosperity of members; competing unions cannot be sure that a sacrifice made by any one of them will be matched by all. The interest group system of the USA is very low on any scale of 'encompassingness'. Numerous groups typically compete for the support of sectors of society (e.g. farmers or corporation). 'Umbrella' groups such as the AFL-CIO have little authority over members. Fragmented American interest groups are less able to show statesmanlike restraint than are more encompassing groups in other countries. Fragmented interest groups in the USA are also less able to function as partners of government in the same way as can more encompassing groups in neocorporatist countries because they lack the authority with both policymakers and members which neocorporatist groups possess. The American interest group system therefore tends towards irresponsibility rather than sharing problem solving between interest groups and government. Contract lobbying reinforces the factors producing these dangers. Contract lobbyists can be hired by very narrow interests; their contact with an issue and responsibility for solving problems associated with it is episodic.

American politics has often been criticised as being even more biased to the wealthy than politics in other democracies. The rise of contract lobbying strengthens this criticism as contract lobbyists are necessarily more available to those with the money to pay them. In addition to this concern, contract lobbying may cause technocratic concerns in that it makes it even harder to achieve permanent partnership between government and major societal interests in addressing the problems facing American society.

4 The Rise of the Lobbying Issue in Canada: 'The Business Card Bill'

PROFESSOR A. PAUL PROSS

The practice of lobbying has not, until very recently, been much discussed in Canada. Perhaps this is because, despite much evidence to the contrary, Canadian political mythology has traditionally held that lobbying is rarely found in this country. As in Britain, for many years it was considered an unbecoming political activity imported from the United States. The realisation that lobbying thrives in our federal and provincial capitals, and is a necessary part of modern policy-making, has taken hold slowly and has precipitated a confused and uncertain response.

Perhaps the myth derived from the fact that Canadians were less aware than Americans of the extent of lobbying activity. (Presthus, 1984, pp.44-57) The Canadian Parliamentary system is not as open as the Congressional and, again like Britain, a great deal of lobbying takes place at the bureaucratic level where, until recently, administrative secrecy and a moribund press combined to ensure that it received very little publicity. This was particularly true during the years between the beginning of the Second World War and the late 1960s when a cohesive and formidably intelligent 'mandarinate' exercised immense influence in Ottawa. (See Granatstein, 1982; Pross, 1986) During those years it was an article of faith with successful lobbyists that the Canadian Parliamentary system rendered it, 'inevitable that Canadian organizations find it essential to influence policy and legislation before the Parliamentary stage is reached.' (Dawson, 1967)

The conditions that kept lobbying in obscurity changed during the late 1960s and the 1970s. The consensus of the 1950s evaporated and public opinion became more turbulent. The mass movements of the 1960s led to attempts to create more open government. Administrative reform – particularly the growth of central agencies – disrupted familiar patterns of communication between agencies and their policy communities and forced established client groups to debate rivals in public. (See Aucoin in Pross, 1975) Growing government complexity led to a diffusion of power and a decline in the legitimacy of the bureaucracy. Interests organised themselves at a startling rate. Numbers alone forced more open competition for access to policy-makers, but in any case many of the newer breed of lobbyists were quite prepared to exert public pressure on officials and politicians. Finally a significant factor was the reform of Parliament. As early as 1971 Robert Presthus noted that backbenchers were being lobbied more frequently than conventional wisdom suggested. Since then parliamentary committees have become more active and independent, creating useful forums for groups interested in securing last minute changes in legislation, stalling bills or laying the groundwork for future policies. (See Franks, 1987; Pross, 1986; Nord in Clarke et al, 1980).

Proliferation of interest groups and a more open style of lobbying was bound to excite discussion. Commentaries on interest group activity and lobbying appeared more frequently in the press and an academic literature developed. Newspaper and newsmagazine articles tended to stress the similarities to American-style lobbying – particularly its more spectacularly venal aspects – but also drew attention to the Canadian tendency to lobby the bureaucracy in preference to the legislature. Initially neither journalists nor academics took a critical view of the growth of lobbying. Many welcomed it as a sign of a more open and dynamic polity. When concern did surface it focused on four different, but related, issues: the inequalities among interests; the problem of the special interest state; the attempts of some groups to influence the election of certain MPs; and the effects of influence peddling. (For example see Shackleton, 1977; Malvern, 1985; Sawatsky, 1987)

To the extent that these concerns can be disentangled, it is the last that has done the most to precipitate interest in the regulation of lobbying. During the 1970s a series of incidents drew attention to the questionable aspects of lobbying at all levels of government, but at the federal level in particular. In 1976, for example, two major lobbying scandals caught national attention. The Skyshops affair saw a prominent Liberal accused of using his association with the government to secure airport retail concessions from the Department of Transport, and the Canadian version of the Lockheed scandal revealed that two prominent former civil servants had advised the company in its negotiations with the Department of Defence (See Shackleton, 1977, p.144). A year later the activities of the gun lobby attracted national attention as it worked to discourage the introduction of rigorous gun control legislation (Lewis, 1977). During the next few years other scandals appeared regularly in the news, culminating in 1983 with accusations – later dismissed – that a former member of the Trudeau cabinet had himself engaged in influence peddling. In 1984 Brian Mulroney made the patronage issue an important part of the Conservative election campaign.

These episodes precipitated a discussion of public morality and led to the incremental development of conflict of interest guidelines, but not the regulation of lobbying itself. Rather, attention was focused on persuading public office holders to accept a code of conduct that, in effect, sanitized them.

In Parliament, however, a number of private members were interested in regulating lobbyists. Between 1969 and 1985 twenty private members' bills were presented to the House, and from time to time the issue was raised in question period. Three members Barry Mather (NDP, Surrey); Kenneth Robinson (Liberal, Toronto-Lakeshore), and the late Walter Baker (PC, Carleton-Grenville) secured second reading for their bills providing for the registration of lobbyists and the latter's bill was introduced again after Baker's death by James McGrath in 1985 as a memorial gesture. Though numerous, these bills frequently replicated one another. Walter Baker's description of his own bill fits most others, 'It defines lobbying ... as the actions of any person or any group attempting to influence the course of either legislative or executive action. It establishes a register of lobbyists to be administered jointly by the Clerks of the two Chambers. Lobbyists must set down their names, the person or group on whose behalf they are acting, and the duration of any contact...' (House of Commons, *Debates*, 28th January, 1977, col. 2516).

In promoting registration these members argued that the public at large ought to know more about who is making representations to government about public decisions and what their interest is. This aspect of the debate is often referred to as the *'transparency'* issue. Second, they were concerned for openness in government, arguing that dissemination of knowledge about the representations being made to government would encourage related interests to participate in public policy debate. By working towards transparency and openness they challenged what they saw as a distressing tendency toward the growth of secret, behind-the-scenes dealing in public policy. Of less significance was a desire to use registration to facilitate communication between parliament and special publics and a concern, shared by public servants, to establish the *bona fides* of those seeking to influence government.

Personal experience of the policy process also led at least one member to tackle the registration issue. John Rodriquez, after more than a decade in the House, felt 'frustration and anger ... at seeing power wielded by certain individuals' and watching certain groups 'influencing decisions through their connections.' Rodriquez felt 'outrage at how highly placed party people slip into lobbying firms.' (Interview, 1986) Walter Baker expressed his concern in institutional terms:

> All our instruments are becoming suspect. This Parliament is becoming suspect. Members of Parliament are becoming suspect. The Public Service is becoming suspect. Those who talk and push for a point of view, even legitimately, are becoming suspect. The trust which heretofore existed pretty well throughout the country with respect to all kinds of institutions, is breaking down. People are questioning. The purpose of this bill is not a negative thrust as I understand the Hon. Member. It is very positive. It says, 'Let us recognize the legitimacy of (lobbying) but let us ensure not only that right is done, or that justice is done, but that it appears to be done.' And what better way is there, or has there been since time immemorial, than full disclosure? (*Debates*, 19th January, 1983, col.22012)

The members who supported registration came from the three major parties, but they did not act in concert. According to John Rodriquez there is no distinct group in the House interested in this issue and pursuing it collectively across party lines. The fact that some MPs have presented identical legislation and spoken in similar terms is 'accidental'. They have simply reached similar conclusions. He estimates that no more than 10% of the Members are interested in the issue.

It is, however, interesting to note that many of the MPs who promoted registration were also involved in the campaign to introduce freedom of information legislation and the campaign to reform Parliament, suggesting that there is a group of private members on both sides of the House, most of them veteran MPs, who interest themselves in issues relating to the advancement of democratic institutions and – informally or not – aid and abet one another in campaigns directed to that end.

From 1969, when the Mather bill was first proposed, until 1985 when Prime Minister Mulroney endorsed the concept, the idea of regulating lobbyists through registration was very much a private members' scheme. The Liberal government of Pierre Elliott Trudeau did not adopt the issue. When the Mather, Baker and Robinson bills reached second reading it ensured that they were talked out and it gave perfunctory and unhelpful responses to questions on the subject. (See *Debates*, 28th July, 1975 and 16th December, 1976) Some senior officials were concerned by the rise in lobbying activity, but did not bring their concerns to the point of defining a policy issue or even of initiating analysis. Nor were the press and general public vocal. An article in the *Vancouver Sun* in January 1977 reviewed the proliferation of lobbying activity and suggested that, 'there is a reluctance on the part of the (Trudeau) government to concede that Ottawa has a lobby industry and that, given the influence over the operation of government by these lobbies, perhaps some effort should be made to identify them.' But such comments were rare and little was said outside Parliament about lobbying during the 1960s and 1970s. Interest picked up a little in 1981 with the publication by the Conference Board of Canada of the report of a conference on the subject, entitled *Lobbying: A Right? A Necessity? A Danger?*, in which Walter Baker's views were given some exposure. In 1982 the Canadian Bar Association issued an important report on Parliamentary reform in which the lobbying issue was discussed briefly and a system of registration endorsed. For the most part, however, the issue remained in the back benches and on the back boiler.

On 9th September, 1985, therefore, Prime Minister Mulroney surprised his colleages, the media and officials when he moved the registration question to the national public agenda. In an 'Open Letter' to Members of Parliament and Senators he undertook to introduce legislation to '... monitor lobbying activity and to control the lobbying process by providing a reliable and accurate source of information on the activities of lobbyists.' He promised to ensure that paid lobbyists would register and identify their clients. This would, '... enable persons who are approached by lobbyists for Canadian corporations, associations and unions, and by agents on behalf of foreign governments and other foreign interests, to be clearly aware of who is behind the representations.'

Although the Prime Minister's statement was part of an expected package of measures dealing with public sector ethics, the reference to lobbying caught both Parliament and officials by surprise. No previous government had linked lobby regulation to the growing body of rules governing the behaviour of public office-holders. In fact, a major task force on conflict of interest (1984) had explicitly avoided dealing with the question of lobbying, saying that 'uncertainty as to the commonly used meaning of the word "lobby",' suggested it 'not be used in any rules governing ethical conduct at the federal level in Canada.'

The reasons for Mr. Mulroney's announcement are unclear. Later events tarnished the image of the Conservative government and trick us into investing the late summer and early fall of 1985 with an atmosphere that did not exist. The Stevens inquiry, the Oerlikon affair, the fall of Roche LaSalle and other embarrassments were not to begin to seize the headlines for another six months. There had been minor incidents. A lobbying firm, Government Consultants International, headed by a former Conservative Premier and by the brother of one of the Prime Minister's principal advisors was discovered to have charged a surprisingly high fee to secure an interview between the Minister of Fisheries and a fisherman anxious to obtain a fishing license. The Minister of Justice was accused of passing work to a law firm employing his sons. The firm, highly regarded and frequently employed by earlier governments, announced that it would abstain from doing government work. The public was beginning to recall that though the Prime Minister had made patronage an election issue, he had, as a candidate for the leadership of his party, promised that his government would be willing to help its friends. At the time of the Prime Minister's 'Open Letter' on public sector ethics, however, these difficulties were still being treated as the consequences of inexperience.

Among those who have speculated on the reasons for the Prime Minister's action, two theories prevail. The first holds that Mr. Mulroney was genuinely upset by the incident involving Government Consultants International, and was anxious to find a means of distancing his ministry from overeager friends; that he was driven by a desire to preserve a 'squeaky clean' image for his administration and was anxious to avoid the taint of influence peddling that affected the previous Liberal regime. The second harks back to the 1984 election campaign and suggests that the Prime Minister was personally convinced that a system of lobby registration should be introduced as part of a package of measures intended to improve public sector ethics in general. Perhaps there is some truth in both of these theories, and perhaps, too, chance was involved. Walter Baker had died not long before and James McGrath had re-introduced his lobby registration bill as a tribute to a Parliamentarian who was warmly and highly regarded by his colleagues. It may have been that McGrath's gesture caught the Prime Minister's eye and suggested an addition to his public sector ethics package. Whatever the Prime Minister's motives, there is general agreement that he himself decided that the registration issue should be addressed and that, despite opposition from lobbyists, he was responsible for ensuring that it did not die on the order paper when parliament was prorogued in the summer of 1986.

Developing Concepts of Regulation

The debate over lobbying progressed through four stages, beginning with the private members bills and proceeding through the preparation of a government discussion paper in 1985; its review by a Parliamentary committee, and finally the presentation and passage of legislation.

Because private member's bills rarely become law, and because there are important restrictions on their scope, they seldom present a full-fledged policy proposal. Nevertheless, the private member's debates helped to define the major issues surrounding the lobbying question and articulated an approach to the regulation of lobbyists that influenced subsequent action. It identified four major issues: (1) the need for transparency in government; (2) the need to foster openness; (3) a perception that registration could be used to facilitate communication between Parliament and special publics, and (4) a concern lest measures taken to regulate lobbying should impede citizens' access to government. These were parliamentarians' issues, related to the maintenance of democratic institutions, access to Parliament and the safe guarding of fundamental rights. Administrative issues received little attention, apart from a determination to ensure that red tape did not impede public access to government. The relationship between lobbyists and their clients and other professional issues were scarcely noticed by the private members and emerged at later stages of the debate.

Baker best expressed the transparency issue and the need for openness when he introduced his bill in 1977:

> Naturally, pressure can take illegitimate and illegal forms and have unfortunate consequences, and these dangers bring me to suggest registration of lobbyists. There is, of course, the possibility of bribery, blackmail or other questionable practices. It is the hope that contacts, which must be made with the knowledge of anyone who cares to examine a register, would be less likely to have a shady dimension. There is an even greater danger that if pressure is carried on secretively or unobtrusively, all sides of a debate will not be heard and legitimate points of view or bodies of information will be excluded until a stage in the debate when decisions have been irrevocably taken.

Baker was also a strong advocate of Parliamentary reform and very much alert to the consequences, undesirable as well as desirable, of reform. Registration, he believed, would permit parliamentarians to cope with the increased attention they were bound to receive from lobbyists:

> I believe we are moving in a number of ways, or at least we should be moving, towards more open government. This will create both opportunities and dangers. To date lobbyists have dealt principally through public service channels, and in theory at least these contacts have a minimum of danger because the interests and motivations of those concerned are clearly defined and established within an administrative framework. If legislators become more promi-

nent in policy formation, I believe lobbying activity will increase and should be open, because in the political process motivations and interests are not so easily defined and traced. (*Debates*, 28th January, 1977, col 2516)

When Baker spoke in support of the Robinson bill in 1983, Parliamentary reform had just moved another step forward with the allocation to committees of increased powers to initiate and conduct inquiries, and he warned again that Members would be pressed to make representations on behalf of groups and that registration would help them establish the interests and objectives of those attempting to influence them. He was also, however, aware of the role of lobbyists and interest groups as alternative sources of information about public policy that would be increasingly valuable as the reformed committee system gave members the oppportunity to contribute meaningfully to policy debate. In this context, Baker saw registration as a useful tool for identifying interests and inviting them to share their expertise with policy-makers.

Most who spoke in these short debates expressed views similar to Baker's, but neither he nor they were oblivious of the problems associated with registration. They were conscious that registration might impede the private citizen's right of petition. In Ian Dean's words:

> I think we must never be seen as trying to subvert or discourage public input. That is to be encouraged. It is essential that the public at large feel free to contact Members of parliament whether they be in the Senate, the House, in Opposition in the backbenches or in Cabinet. Members of the public must know that we want this input, but we must make it easier for them to participate. (*Debates*, 19th January, 1983, col.22013)

For this reason they found the problem of defining 'lobbying' and the 'lobbyist' especially difficult. Kenneth Robinson, for example, wondered whether Baker's 1977 Bill would extend to anyone who discussed a public policy issue with a public servant, or 'if a chat between a constituent and his member of parliament that touched on some current legislative matter could be construed as lobbying.' Robinson's own 1983 Bill did not resolve the problem. It defined a lobbyist as...

> ...any person who attempts to influence, directly or indirectly
> (a) the introduction, passage, defeat or amendment of any legislation or budgetary estimates before either House of parliament, or
> (b) a decision to be taken on any matter coming within the administrative jurisdiction of a Minister of the Crown, whether or not that matter has come or may come before either House of Parliament for legislative action.
> (*Debates*, 19th January, 1983, col.22010)

In 1977 Baker wanted to regulate 'those whose principal function is to lobby on behalf of others... not who occasionally must defend their interest by contact with politicians or officials.' In Baker's posthumous 1985 bill, this was expressed in a slight, but significant, modification of the definition so that a 'lobbyist' is '...any person who, *for payment*, attempts to influence, directly or indirectly' the passage of legislation or the taking of public policy decisions. Here the traditional definition of lobbying – which covers both those who lobby on their own behalf and those working for third parties – is revised in the interests of a formulation suited to the needs of regulation. This perception of the lobbyist as an individual working for compensation has been maintained in all subsequent phases of the debate.

However, each successive phase of the debate has introduced new limitations to its scope. The 1985 discussion paper from Consumer and Corporate Affairs (discussed more fully below) specified that lobbyists for foreign governments, corporations and individuals should register, but went on to introduce a distinction that later significantly influenced the 1987 *Lobbyists Registration Bill*:

> It is likely that the definition of a lobbyist would not include religious or educational institutions, public interest groups of a local character, or other temporary grass-roots organizations, on the grounds that their lobbying interests, usually on broad social or economic issues, are a matter of public record. In other words, they already fully meet the important objective of openness.
>
> (*Lobbying and the Registration of Paid Lobbyists*, 1985)

It left open the question of whether or not officers or employees of trade unions, professional associations, national interest groups, and corporation employees should be registered. However, it introduced the view that the interests of some lobbyists are self evident whilst those of others are not, and so inspired the controversial two tiered approach to registration that was incorporated in the bill.

The parliamentary debate also produced a distinctive regulatory approach that had its genesis in the backbenchers' own experience. For example, their knowledge of the Canadian policy process encouraged them to avoid the approach of the US *Federal Regulation of Lobbying Act* (1946) with its emphasis on detailed reporting of lobbyists' expenditures and its insistence that lobbying applies only to attempts to influence the passage or defeat of legislation in Congress. Instead they defined lobbying broadly to include both legislative and administrative lobbying and they kept reporting requirements to a minimum. Thus paid lobbyists were to register with the Clerks of the Senate and the House their names, the names of their clients and the duration of their contract. The registration would be up-dated at least annually but also whenever a new client was acquired, and the register would be open to the public. Penalties were stiff, a fine of $5,000 for each month in violation and prohibition from acting as a lobbyist for three years.

Once registration became government policy the development of a regulatory framework was referred to the Department of Consumer and Corporate Affairs, presumably selected because it acts as a registry under the conflict of interest guidelines and therefore could be expected to design and administer what was seen as a component of the public sector ethics package.

The officials hesitated to draft legislation. They were surprised to find that there had been virtually no academic discussion of lobbying in Canada and therefore no intellectual framework within which legislation could be developed. The research that did exist suggested that a system of registration might either be ineffectual or create more problems than it could resolve, or both. For example, inhibiting citizens' access to government, or, as the lobbying community was quick to point out, intruding into the confidential relationship of a professional and his or her client. Such considerations led the department to recommend against preparing legislation and in favour of developing a discussion paper which would encourage a public debate that could, in turn, guide the drafting of legislation. This advice was accepted, though it later led to suggestions that the thrust of legislative reform had been hobbled by the lobbyists' lobby. In actual fact, despite occasional media suggestions that the issue was the subject of 'intense lobbying', opposition to the concept of registration seems to have been quite muted. The discussion paper was prepared in the policy analysis section of the department with very little outside assistance and, according to officials, few representations from lobbyists themselves.

Lobbying and the Registration of Paid Lobbyists, was released in December, 1985. It reviewed the private members' debate; identified central issues; discussed practice in other countries; set out a possible registration system, and presented questions for debate. These included: Do the objectives of registration warrant overriding democratic freedom of access to government? If registration is necessary, what constitutes lobbying, and, therefore who should be registered? How is 'lobbying' defined? How much should the lobbyist be required to disclose about his or her business and about the client? Does such disclosure violate the provisions of the Charter of Rights? Nor were the relevant administrative issues insignificant. Many believed, for example, that administrative red tape should be kept to a minimum lest it render regulation ineffective or choke off private citizens' access to government. 'How much red tape?' therefore became an important question. Asking it prompted some to raise the further question: Is self-regulation possible? Similarly the way in which registration would be enforced and even the administrative location of the registry were matters of some significance.

The paper took no position on the central question of whether registration is necessary, though its tone favoured it. As one official put it, 'the lobbying issue won't go away. If we deal with it now, we can maximize the degrees of freedom for all parties, but if we have to draft regulations in response to a major scandal we may not be able to do that.' By the time the paper was presented formally to the Commons committee reviewing it, this position had solidified and the minister, the Hon. Michel Côté, was prepared to say that because lobbying has become an increasingly pervasive method of influencing public policy, the government needs 'a reliable and accurate source of information on who the paid lobbyists are and who they represent.' (Standing Committee, *Proceedings 1:13*)

Nevertheless the Department was ambivalent about the need for registration, at pains to point out that the 'basic right' to lobby should be treated as a 'legitimate activity' while at the same time acknowledging that both the public and officials need to know more about individuals and groups attempting to influence public policy. This ambivalence may be responsible for the fact that the discussion paper makes few explicit references to the objectives of regulation. At the hearings, although the Department acknowledged the public's need to know, Mr. Côté and his officials suggested that the central object of registration from the government's point of view is to permit policy makers to know who they are dealing with. The democratic concerns of the backbenchers receded in importance.

Nevertheless, the discussion paper defined registrable lobbying activities in a fashion that was consistent with the earlier debate, treating lobbying as...

> any direct or indirect representation made by a paid lobbyist to a Public Office Holder... (i) to make or amend federal legislation or regulations; (ii) to make or change federal policies or programs; (iii) to influence federal decisions on the awarding of contracts, grants, and contributions; or (iv) to influence federal appointments to public office.' Registrable activity could also include 'the gathering and sale of information with a view to assisting in or advising about clients' lobbying activities as defined in (i) or (iv) above. Clients may obtain access to such information in a variety of ways including subscriptions to special publications with limited circulation; and (v) the arranging of contacts and meetings for clients by intermediaries who do not themselves make direct representations on the issues or attend the meetings.

Exceptions could include appearances before boards, commissions tribunals, and committees of Parliament, and lobbying representation made on a voluntary, unpaid basis, as well as communications with officials about the normal administrative machinery of government operations.

A new issue introduced by the paper was the argument that registration could threaten the 'privileged nature' of certain professional relationships. For example, 'the privileged nature of the solicitor-client relationship' might be affected in a manner that could arouse 'legitimate concern'. The accountant-client relationship might be similarly affected. Thus, 'due regard' would have to be taken to ensure that 'no special professional or legal relationships are unintentionally compromised by a general registration system.' The paper also pointed out that a further body of information that could be requested, such as lists of clients and some financial data might be 'commercially confidential' under the *Access to Information Act* and therefore 'not available to the public unless contrary legislative provision is made.'

In contrast to the backbenchers' concern for transparency, openness, ease of communication and access, the Department suggested four principles that should guide the development of a registration system: First the object of regulation should be to enhance openness in government, helping to remove 'the shroud of mystery from this important activity' and demonstrating 'the Government's commitment to transparency and integrity in its relations with the public.' Second, there should be 'no doubt as to who should register and who should not,' and therefore regulations should be expressed clearly and concisely. Third, there should be no undue impediment to obtaining access to public office holders and, fourth, 'administrative requirements should be kept to a minimum'. Otherwise registration might become 'so onerous as to discourage lobbying by anyone with modest means or create a bureaucratic system requiring substantial resources.'

The discussion paper was released in December 1985, receiving only limited publicity, and was forwarded to the House of Commons Standing Committee on Elections, Privileges and Procedure, which opened its hearings on the registration issue on Monday, April 14, 1985. Representatives of seven consulting firms, three interest groups and one corporation appeared before it, in addition to two MPs – John Rodriquez and James McGrath – and the Minister of Consumer and Corporate Affairs. As well, sixteen groups, four individuals and one corporation and the Women's Bureau of the Progressive Conservative Party, submitted written comments on the discussion paper. Following its public hearings the committee visited Washington and Sacramento where it discussed US federal and Californian regulation of lobbyists with federal and state officials and with lobbyists and legislators. (Standing Committee on Elections, Privileges and Procedures, *First Report to the House re Lobbyists and Registration of Paid Lobbyists*; 2/ 33 1986-7)

The majority of those testifying or submitting written comments on the proposal tended to oppose it, but there were important divisions within the lobbying community where some felt that regulation could be used to cleanse lobbying of its venal reputation. Opponents attacked registration as unnecessary, undesirable, unworkable and ineffectual. The Institute of Association Executives, a national association of professional heads of interest groups, was not 'aware of any great history of abuse of lobbying in this country', and was 'not really convinced that there is a need for some sort of even a simple system of registration of lobbyists.' The Canadian Chamber of Commerce also saw no evidence to suggest the public needed the protection of a lobby registration system. The Canadian Manufacturers Association expressed 'some surprise' that the government had treated registration as a priority when it had a 'limited amount of time ... to address many other pressing matters that affect social and economic issues so critical to Canada's economy.' 'If it ain't broke, don't fix it', was a common quip. This approach antagonised several committee members. Brandishing newspaper clippings and citing notorious episodes in the past they would challenge witnesses to prove that lobbying was not a problem in Canada, only to meet the bland reply that 'one or two incidents over a period of many years' did not warrant imposing a regulatory system.

Briefs attacking registration as undesirable frequently appealed to the ideological bent of the Conservative government. Several reminded government members of the committee that their party had committed itself not to use regulation, '... unless it has clear evidence that a problem exists, that government intervention is justified and that regulation is the best alternative open to the government.' In addition, registration was represented as an invasion of privacy undermining business norms of confidentiality, some of which are embodied in law. The thrust of this argument was blunted by the position taken by the Canadian Cable Television Association which suggested that reporting requirements applied to associations be limited to the items of information normally filed with the Department of Consumer and Corporate Affairs as part of an association's obligations under its articles of incorporation. This information would include the constitution and by-laws of the association membership figures, audited financial statements and staff complement. However, the suggestion that fees or actual charges be made public was attacked more effectively, either as an invasion of corporate privacy – for David MacNaughton of Public Affairs International it was equivalent to asking a manufacturer for data on products and pricing – or as a violation of the firm's relationship with its clients.

Most opponents of registration concentrated on trying to convince the Committee that the scheme would create a bureaucratic monster that would not only fail to achieve openness and transparency but would also limit access to government. Thus, a number of briefs emphasised the need for administrative simplicity and warned that the benefits to be derived from registration could easily 'be outweighed by the required bureaucracy.'

Two aspects of registration were likely to foster bureaucratic complexity. First, an inclusive definition of lobbyists would be hard to administer efficiently. According to the Canadian Manufacturers' Association, it would be 'hard to imagine who isn't caught' by the definition evolved during the private members' debate. The second factor likely to promote a highly bureaucratic regime was the insistence on the part of some proponents of registration that lobbyists should disclose considerable information concerning their clients, their lobbying activities and the costs of lobbying. Here there was consensus: it would be extremely difficult to define what costs should be directly associated with lobbying in general or even with specific campaigns. In a letter to the chairman of the Standing Committee, the Canadian Medical Association argued, typically:

> The CMA would find it very difficult to accurately report on the amount spent on lobbying unless the term was more specifically defined. We could report on the costs of *CMA only activities* where they have a direct, vested interest for the Association or its members – for example, the Association's lobby activities for increased tax deductible registered retirement saving plan contributions. But, we could not accurately report on the cost of: activities of local branches of the Association, provincial divisions, speciality bodies, CMA Councils and Committees, staff, etc., that have bearing on CMA advice and input to government

on a myriad of activities such as the control of the medical manpower supply or the Medical and Health Advisory Committee of the Correctional Service of Canada.

Furthermore, as Bill Neville, of Public Affairs International, pointed out to the Standing Committee, the amount of money spent on a campaign was no guide to its effectiveness. Some of the most expensive campaigns are, 'inept and ineffective whilst some of the most successful have cost very little'. Even the Coalition on Acid Rain, which advocated more financial disclosure than most other witnesses, warned the Committee against creating a burdensome reporting process. The coalition reviewed for the Committee the various forms required by the US registration process and demonstrated the financial and other burdens imposed by that system.

Opponents also argued that the most elaborate reporting system would fail to secure the integrity of the policy process or even to identify those actively working to influence it. Again, American experience was held up as an example. As Bill Neville asked, 'Does the registration of lobbyists address the problem of the political fix?' Those who believe that decisions can be bought 'are not going to be dissuaded from trying by a lobbying registration bill.' When coupled with a fear that red tape, however ineffectual, might also stifle citizens' access to government, the lobbyists' argument that a registry would be unworkable and ineffective carried far more weight than their assertions that registration was unnecessary or undesirable.

For some 'avoidance' was a more useful strategy than outright opposition. They argued that a registration scheme should not apply to their type of organisation. Those taking this approach came from each type of lobbying organisation – interest groups, corporations and independent firms – and they based their position on the government's claim that a primary objective of registration would be the identification of interests. Thus corporations like Imperial Oil and interest groups like the Canadian Manufacturers' Association, the Canadian Jewish Congress, the Chamber of Commerce, and the Canadian Cable Television Association argued that '... consultations are expected, invited and beneficial.' Nor, in these circumstances, is there doubt about whose interests are being represented.

This position was countered differently in the case of interest groups and corporations. As far as corporations and trade unions were concerned, at least one member of the Standing Committee, John Rodriguez, argued that while a corporate representative is indeed, by the nature of his employment, identified with a particular interest, 'it is extremely important ... that the people who elect ... Members of Parliament are (able) to know who comes to the Hill on (for example) Inco's behalf and who sees Royal Canadian Mint personnel, who sees the Supply and Services Minister and bureaucrats, and who sees the MPs on all sides of the House ... In an open kind of government ... there is a need for that kind of transparency.' As far as interest groups were concerned, in a brief to the Minister the Institute of Association Executives summed up the dilemma facing its members:

We have considered the alternative of exemption of association executives from any registration requirement but have dropped it in the realization that exemption would create a loophole for certain entities to claim association standing in order to avoid registration, whereas in reality their motives would be dubious at best. We would not wish to see the good record of association executives jeopardized by an illegitimate connection, in the eyes of the public and government, between our members and those who seek refuge for questionable motives.

One lobbying firm argued that it could be excluded. Public Affairs International suggested that the lobbyist's knowledge is brought to bear in one or other of three ways: by representing interests to government; by providing a 'dating' service, or by 'mapping' decision processes for clients. Representation is the best known of these activities and involves articulating to officials, politicians and sometimes the general public the needs and views of particular interests. The dating service puts clients in touch with appropriate officials and advises them on how best to present their case. Mapping services help clients develop a strategy for taking the proposal through the entire decision process, basing their advice on their familiarity with the structure and personnel of agencies and their ability to keep abreast of changes in decision making processes and regulatory procedures. In an argument that seemed later to carry weight with the government, though not with the Committee, PAI suggested that only firms engaged in representation and dating ought to register. 'The central concept of any definition of lobbying,' PAI argued, 'is the act of representing an interest to and before Parliament and the government ... to go beyond the core definition and to seek to draw the defining line at activities other than representation is to fail the critical test of clarity and to create impossible administrative difficulties. A firm that is "merely providing information, analysis, and advice" would not be engaged in "lobbying" as defined by the government's discussion paper.'

This view won some sympathy in the bureaucracy, but the members of the Standing Committee tended to agree with Dominique Boivin of Les Partenaires when he suggested that 'A lobbyist is a lobbyist is a lobbyist', and with the testimony of Gordon S. Floyd who held that

> public servants and politicians who are interviewed in the course of (mapping) activities ... should know the interest that is truly being served. In our view, openness is an essential part of our democratic system, and should be required of all of those who want to play a role in the political or governmental process.

As in Britain a number of lobbyists favoured registration. For Donald Thom, a former public servant who is now president of an Ottawa lobbying firm, 'the central problem ... is the identification of ... the players.' Some lobbyists – government relations specialists in corporations and employees of interest groups, for example – are readily identified with specific interests, but the paid consultant may have several clients. These lobbyists were also motivated by a desire to professionalise lobbying. As Gordon S. Floyd put it to the Standing Committee:

> Ultimately ... what is needed is a code of behaviour, one that we would like to see developed and administered by firms in the business, imposing strict standards of behaviour on public affairs specialists. We think adherence to such a code should be a condition of registration with the government and that registration should be a condition of conducting business on behalf of third parties with government officials.

This approach interested several members of the Committee, though they were sceptical of the ability of lobbyists to establish an association able to develop appropriate codes and to enforce them.

Representatives of interest groups tended to adopt an avoidance strategy, though the National Farmers' Union and the Canadian Association of University Teachers, as well as the Coalition on Acid Rain submitted letters explicitly calling for registration.

The sessions in Washington and Sacramento reinforced the members growing conviction that some form of registration was desirable, though they felt that the US systems were overloaded by detailed reporting requirements.

However, not long after the Committee's return to Ottawa the government decided to prorogue Parliament and thus suspended all matters still outstanding on the Order Paper. Until November it was not certain whether the Committee would be invited to continue its work, but its order of reference was renewed, permitting it to meet again four more times, largely *in camera* to complete drafting its report which was presented to the House on 27th January, 1987.

The Committee endorsed the concept of registration, finding that 'while few witnesses advocated registration,' those who did 'advanced reasons which we consider to be compelling.' It would permit the public and officials to hear and consider rival positions and it would remove some of the mystery surrounding lobbying activity, perhaps even bringing legitimacy to it. However,

> ... the strongest argument we heard in favour of registration is that disclosure of information in this area is vital if we are to have an informed public. An informed public is vital for the survival of democracy. Information provided through a register is a tool which can be used by the general public to evaluate the pressures which are brought to bear on government.

It prescribed a broad definition of lobbying and lobbyists, going beyond the definitions that had been put before it and extending registration to include 'indirect lobbying' and those who 'initiate and those who are paid to organize mass mailings or advertising campaigns to disseminate material designed to influence government through public opinion.'

On the key issues of registration and definition, then, the lobbyists failed to convince the Committee. In other respects, however, they were more successful. There was apparently a good deal of internal debate, but the Committee did accept the argument that only limited disclosure should be required. It rested its argument for disclosure on a public interest position – 'confidentiality in these areas is deemed to be waived when the parties are dealing with matters of public policy' – and on the advice of California lobbyists that disclosure did not create an excessive burden for them. On the other hand, it accepted the lobbyists argument that:

> Entering any new field, especially one which poses as many difficulties as this, should be done with caution. If the lobbyist or the lobbyist's employer is required to furnish copious amounts of information we could create a situation similar to that found in some states in the United States where disclosure has been unmanageable both for the lobbyist and the state. However, enough information should be required to make registration a meaningful exercise.

Perhaps most important, from the lobbyists' perspective, it cautiously accepted the view that though self-regulation without registration could not be counted upon to secure appropriate regulation of lobbying, self-regulation with registration might effectively integrate lobbying in the policy process.

> We are not convinced that self-regulation even with some governmental involvement would be able to attract a large membership and be able to perform the types of disciplinary tasks which have been described to us. We are also somewhat concerned that suggestions to form such an organization only arose as a result of the release of the government's discussion paper dealing with the registration of paid lobbyists. However ... it may be an effective additional method through which to deal with lobbying.

It recommended that government encourage the formation of a suitably powerful association equipped with a discipline committee able to enforce 'a strict code of ethics.'

Finally the Committee suggested that the programme be administered by the Assistant Deputy Registrar General, an official of the Department of Consumer and Corporate Affairs also responsible for administering the Conflict of Interest Guidelines who would have considerable powers of investigation.

The Business Card Bill: the Two Tier Solution

With the handing down of the Committee Report, the issue of lobby regulation once again disappeared from public discussion and there was renewed speculation that 'intense lobbying' would put an end to the registration proposal. Certainly a number of organisations presented strong criticisms of the Committee report to the Minister of Consumer and Corporate Affairs, Hon. Harvie Andre, and reiterated arguments that had been made to the Committee. The Canadian Chamber of Commerce, for example, was entirely opposed and urged its numerous and far-flung membership to participate in a letter writing campaign. The Institute of Associate Executives took a more conciliatory position, accepting the creation of a registry, but urging that it be kept 'simple'. It opposed divulging financial information and listing the names of organisation members and it pointed out that it would be counter-productive to record every meeting concerned with administrative detail that association representatives participated in, but the Institute did suggest that organisations should submit 'a general description of their members, an indication of the types of issues of interest to their association, and the government departments with whom the association is currently in, or likely to, contact.'

In June, 1987, Mr. Andre tabled Bill C-82, the *Lobbyists' Registration Act*, stating that it addressed the public's need to know who is talking to government, but avoided the pitfalls of attempting to regulate lobbyists. Registration, but not regulation was its goal, seeking in simplicity a system that neither discouraged the general public nor created a process that would become constipated by its own insatiable appetite for information. For both the government and the Committee, the key to simplicity was to define a lobbyist as anyone who receives payment to represent a third party in discussions with public office holders. As we have seen, this absolves both volunteers and businessmen representing their own interests from the compass of registration. It accordingly goes some way to guarantee access to government to other members of the public.

By dividing lobbyists into two tiers the legislation went further than the committee, however, in simplifying the information required of some lobbyists. Tier I lobbyists were described as 'professional lobbyists' who represented 'clients' before government. Tier II lobbyists on the other hand, were employees either of interest groups or corporations who spend a 'significant part' of their employment representing their employer to government. Within ten days of undertaking to represent an interest on any one of a series of widely defined activities, Tier I lobbyists would have to register with the Deputy Registrar General, their own names, those of their client and the subject matter of proposed meetings or communications with officials. Tier II lobbyists would provide even less information: simply their names, the name and address of the corporation or organisation employing them. Neither is required to submit financial information.

The bill was much weaker than the Committee had proposed. Mapping services – which include some of the most influential firms – were not covered, nor was registration extended to firms engaged in indirect lobbying. Those lobbyists required to register were asked to provide much less information than the Committee had expected. The representatives of corporations and formal interest groups were not required to report their lobbying activities; interest groups were not required to file even minimal information concerning their objectives and supporters. Although Tier I lobbyists were required to register the undertakings they had entered into, it would be quite easy to avoid spelling out the real subject matter of meetings. On the other hand, a faithful application of the section would generate a blizzard of information that would overwhelm both the Registrar and those attempting to analyze lobbyists' reports. The proposed administrative arrangements were also flawed. The powers of the Registrar were insufficient. He or she would not be empowered to review the information provided by lobbyists or to verify it. Furthermore, as an employee of a government agency the Registrar would be subject to government influence.

The Bill was given a second reading on 14th March, 1988 in a brief debate that noted its shortcomings in comparison to the proposals of the Committee, but did not dwell on them. It was referred to a Legislative Committee which met twice and heard a handful of invited witnesses. During the hearings those Opposition members who had participated in the work of the Committee on Elections, Privileges and Procedure focused on the inadequacies of the two tier system, the unsatisfactory administrative arrangements and the less than compelling sanctions. They sought to expand the reporting requirements of the Bill and attempted to introduce a bar to the charging of contingency fees. They were unsuccessful. The chair – himself an Opposition member – found their amendments inadmissible and the bill was reported back for third reading with only technical amendments put forward by the government.

Dissatisfied with the scant attention paid to their concerns at the Committee stage, members of the Opposition gave the Bill its most searching review during the Third Reading. The deficiencies we have already noted were expanded upon and some startling examples of lobbying activity were put on record. Opposition members felt cheated. Because the report of the Standing Committee had been a compromise position, they had hoped that, 'the Government would introduce a Bill which nearly mirror-imaged the unanimous report of the parliamentary committee.' Instead a very much weaker proposal had been put forward and pushed through Committee. Rather than the legislation to register lobbying activity that had been promised by Prime Minister Mulroney in 1985, the Government had put forward a bill that required lobbyists to do little more than register their names and addresses. Bitterly they labelled it the 'business card bill.' Inevitably their protests were ineffectual and the bill was eventually approved by the Commons on a vote of 87 to 14 and was sent to the Senate where it was duly passed. An administrative unit of four persons is (1989) being established in the Department of Consumer and Corporate Affairs.

Analysis and assesment

The *Lobbyists Registration Bill* is uninspired. It deserves its soubriquet, 'The Business Card Bill'. The most significant thing about the act is that it exists. Lobbying has become an increasingly significant part of policy-making and the bill is a necessary step toward ensuring that it be conducted in an open manner that encourages a high standard of ethical behaviour on the part of both lobbyists and officials. The act has some worthwhile features. First, it affirms that lobbying is a legitimate and necessary part of modern public policymaking. Second, it covers not only lobbying at the legislative level, but also at the bureaucratic level where – in the Canadian political system – a very great part of lobbying activity takes place. Third, it takes pains to avoid creating administrative barriers to participation in policy debate by individuals and/or groups with limited resources. Fourth, it attempts to set up simple and straightforward reporting procedures.

In attempting to create a simple system of registration, however, it is seriously flawed. It excludes – as we have seen – certain kinds of lobbyists and some important lobbying activities. It requires insufficient information; the proposed administrative regime is inadequate, and the proposed sanctions are inappropriate.

The most serious of these weaknesses is the two tier system. It assumes that the objectives of corporations and formal interest groups can easily be discovered. This is mistaken. Many corporations and major interest groups are multifaceted organisations with diverse interests. If the goal of open government is to be achieved they should be required to identify for the benefit of other affected interests, the undertakings they are engaged in. Furthermore it is unsound to assume that the purposes and backgrounds of interest groups are transparent and can easily be investigated by the public. Under the proposed system an unscrupulous interest could quite easily establish an organisational front that would be immune to the disclosure rules applied to others. Similarly the reporting requirements are inadequate. Lobbyists should report lobbying campaigns rather than 'meetings'. The object of the campaign should be specified, as should the categories of officials to be approached. This initial campaign prospectus should be followed up with quarterly reports that identify actual interactions with the government and indicate any major changes in the undertaking. Such a procedure could be administered quite simply and would have the advantage of providing essential information in a digestible package to the public. It could be required of Tier II as well as Tier I lobbyists. This approach could also be used to address the need for information about the cost of lobbying campaigns. Lobby campaigns (in both Tiers) are frequently budgeted for as such. Consequently lobbyists should be able to generate global costs of campaigns quite easily and without divulging hourly charges. Other improvements can and have been suggested. Sunshine legislation would force government to divulge the names of lobbyists who have made representations concerning specific legislation; professional development amongst lobbyists could be encouraged; contingency fees should be prohibited, and so on.

Clearly, however, the Government has rejected such steps. At this stage we can only speculate on the reasons why. Obviously many will believe that lobbyists were successful in persuading the Minister, even the Prime Minister, that though registration could not be abandoned, its teeth could be drawn. Certainly many influential politicians and officials have taken up the lobbying business – during the course of the debate over registration, for example, the deputy minister of the Department of Consumer and Corporate Affairs became vice-chairman of Public Affairs International – and a number will have had opportunities to express their opposition to Mr. Andre and Mr. Mulroney. Their more immediate demands may have had greater influence than a poorly expressed public dissatisfaction with the policy process.

In some respects it is more intriguing to ask why the Prime Minister failed to carry through with a measure that he had himself proposed. Did he underestimate the influence of the lobbyists? Did he simply neglect the issue in favour of more urgent pressures, such as the free trade debate, the approaching election, and so on? Again, we will probably have to wait for the archives to be opened and the memoirs to be written before the puzzle is explained.

Despite the lacklustre outcome of the registration debate we need not be entirely disappointed. As Bill Neville commented on the Committee report,

> If I thought we'd get a law (like) the ... report ..., I wouldn't spend any time on this issue. But I've been around this place long enough to know that incrementalism will lead to opening it up again and adding another layer on the system.

The *Lobbyists' Registration Act* is so inadequate that revision may come even earlier than Mr. Neville would expect.

NOTE: I want to acknowledge the assistance I have received from politicians – especially Albert Cooper, John Rodriguez and Don Boudria; officals, lobbyists and fellow academics as I prepared this paper. In particular, I should like to thank those who commented on an earlier draft: Hugh Thorburn, Bill Stanbury, Michael Hind-Smith, Ken Imhoff, Clive Thomas and several officials who shall be unnamed. I also acknowledge the financial support of the Research and Development Committee of Dalhousie University.

PART II: Ways and Means of Influence

5 DIY: The Government Relations Functions of Large Companies

WYN GRANT

This chapter is concerned with government relations divisions, usually relatively small units highly placed in the organisational structures of very large firms with responsibility for coordinating a firm's relations with government. Whether the unit is part of a larger public affairs division, and the precise title used, will vary from firm to firm. It should be noted, however, that some firms also have a 'trade affairs' or 'regulatory affairs' function. 'Trade affairs' divisions deal with such questions as new regulations on the handling and transporting of goods and new documentation, as well as more exotic matters, such as exports of high technology goods to state trading countries, and they are necessarily in frequent contact with Customs and Excise as well as the Department of Trade and Industry and the Foreign Office. Regulatory affairs directors, frequently found in the chemical and pharmaceutical industries, will often be required to have a scientific background, and may be located within the company's research and development operation. A job description for one such post in a pharmaceutical company stated:

> The person appointed will lead an experienced team which has worldwide responsibility for ensuring that submissions to regulatory authorities are scientifically correct and meet the highest ethical and technical standards. They will also be responsible for the effective and efficient management of negotiations with these authorities.

Given the growth of environmental regulation, one can expect such posts to proliferate. However, specialised posts of this kind will not be the focus of this chapter, but rather the government affairs 'generalist' who has responsibility for attempting to coordinate a company's relations with government, including the European Community. Units headed by such government relations managers are largely confined to the top hundred companies in terms of turnover, and are particularly found in very large multinationals. They are particularly prevalent in industries such as oil and chemicals (operating on an international scale), electronics (with government as a major customer), or tobacco (vulnerable to political criticism). They are less common in industries with a less politicised operating environment such as food processing and retailing.

Three general points need to be made at this stage. Firstly, a large company will have extensive, day-to-day contacts with government and a government relations division cannot hope to (nor should it) undertake all these contacts itself. It is more appropriate that, for example, the manager of a plant should meet the local MP for an on site visit; that a technical specialist should have direct discussions with a member of the civil service on the implementation of a new European Community regulation; or that the chairman of the board should meet the permanent secretary of the Department of Trade and Industry to discuss the company's future plans, and the general economic environment. The task of the government relations division is to ensure that the company is aware of political developments which may affect its operations; to see that the company is not pursuing contradictory policies in its relations with government; and to ensure that those employees who are in contact with government are fully briefed about both policies and processes so that they can effectively represent the company's interests.

Secondly, a large company will undoubtedly make use of a number of mechanisms to influence government apart from direct face-to-face contacts. It will be a member of a large number of trade associations ranging from the CBI to small product associations, and will use these bodies to raise a number of issues that concern it and other companies. A large company will also probably make use of outside consultants, either to handle relations with Parliament, or to undertake specific projects.

Thirdly, the term 'lobbying' would be a somewhat misleading one to describe the bulk of the work of government relations divisions. Most such divisions are involved in a great deal of 'in house' work: engaging in issues analysis, and feeding the results to corporate planning committees, or even the main board; writing newsletters which keep senior management informed of relevant issues; and briefing and 'training' company representatives who are, for example, scheduled to appear before a Parliamentary committee. Moreover, even that aspect of a company's work concerned with interacting with government is usually rather more subtle than the term 'lobbying' implies. A company that has a sophisticated approach to government relations will attempt to develop a climate of well informed mutual understanding between it and civil servants and politicians so that, if an issue that affects the company arises, it is not necessary to build relationships from scratch. One government relations manager summarised the character of his task very well when he commented to me,

> Our objective is to ensure that politicians have a good understanding of what we're doing, and that our managers have a good understanding of what politicians think.

Comparisons with the United States

Many government relations divisions in British firms were set up in the mid 1970s, in part as a response to the uncertain economic and political environment of that period. Some of the first government relations divisions in Britain were set up by American multinationals (e.g. Ford, IBM) applying a general corporate public affairs policy to Britain; they were then imitated by British companies. However, even the American experience with government relations divisions is relatively recent. 'Back in 1968, for instance, only

100 corporations had offices in Washington; by 1978 that figure had jumped to 500. One business directory listed 1,300 corporations in 1986.' (Smith, 1988, p.31). It is also the case that the function of the 'Washington office' has changed over time. 'Before the 1970s, Washington offices were primarily for marketing and other commercial functions. The firms who maintained permanent Washington offices did so mainly because of their extensive commercial relations with the government.' (Yoffie and Bergenstein, 1985, p.125). Over time, political functions have become more important, and new Washington offices have often been set up with purely political objectives in mind. (McGrath, 1979, pp.66-69)

In comparing British and American experience, it should be noted that Britain is a metropolitan country with most corporate headquarters located in London; though now far more common than before corporate headquarters located in Washington are still relatively rare. As noted in Charles Miller's first chapter (2) in the past, when it was possible to talk of a functioning 'establishment' in Britain, 'government relations' was often handled on an informal level by company CEOs talking to ministers in their club or some other informal setting. The decline of such opportunities for informal social contact was one background factor encouraging the formation of government relations divisions in Britain.

What is clear is that government relations activities are carried out on a much larger scale in the US in terms of both the number of firms involved in such activities, and the way in which they are organised. Various estimates are available of the number of 'Washington offices'. Yoffie and Bergenstein (1985, p.125) note that 247 firms had their own staffs located in the capital, but also footnote another study giving the number as 545. (Yoffie and Bergenstein, 1985, p.137). Of 401 respondents to a sample of one thousand large and medium-sized firms, 42.7% had a company office in Washington. (Murray, 1982, p.145). A study focusing on *Fortune 500* companies found that almost 70% of those responding had a Washington office. (Wilson, 1987, p.22). Comparable British data is less systematic than that gathered in the United States, but suggests that less than 10% of the top five hundred British firms have a government relations division.

The government relations offices of British companies are also much smaller than those of their American counterparts. Wilson (1987, p.10) reports that the mean size of Washington offices was thirteen, and the median seven. In my own research, I have only come across one company in Britain which has a government relations division larger than those figures, and that was an American company with its European government relations operation based in Britain. ICI Americas Inc. has five government relations executives in its Washington office; ICI in Britain has one executive covering government relations (two if one counts the Brussels operation).

One important difference between government relations functions in the two countries is the extent to which they are involved in coordinating a company's trade association activities. One of the clearest findings of research on government relations divisions in Britain was that government relations divisions were very rarely able to coordinate the associative activities of their firms. (Grant, 1981). A principal reason appeared to be related to the internal structure and politics of firms. British companies are often highly decentralised internally, with considerable autonomy being given to product divisions; the finance function is often the main mechanism of central control. Product divisions or subsidiaries are often engaged in a continuing struggle with the corporate centre for resources and, above all, to preserve their identity. One means of underlining the distinctiveness of the product division is for it to be involved in its own trade association. Hence it is likely to resist any attempt by a unit located in the corporate centre (the government relations division) to intervene in its associative activities.

Research in the US reveals a very different picture. For example, one government relations executive told me that in the chemical industry, the 'integration of government relations and trade association activities is general to all firms'; this is certainly not the case for UK chemicals firms. The staff of the Washington office of ICI Americas Inc. are involved in twenty-four committees of five trade associations, as well as ten 'business advocacy' organisations. Admittedly, it would appear that, as one association respondent commented in interview, the chemical industry in the US has 'a very large contingent of government relations officers, more than any other industry' and that they are a 'close knit group, closely connected.' However, in the case of the steel industry, most of the big firms have a Washington office, and the head of that office will be on the American Iron and Steel Institute's government relations committee. British trade associations do not have government relations committees drawn from government relations staff. There is clearly much greater integration of a company's government relations and business association activities in the US than in Britain.

Are government relations divisions still necessary?

As was noted earlier, many government relations divisions in Britain were set up in the relatively turbulent conditions of the mid 1970s. Britain now has a more settled political environment, with a government that should, in principle, be well disposed to business. Do firms still need government relations divisions? After all, they have always been viewed with some suspicion within companies by managers in more traditional specialisms who are sceptical about the contribution that such units make to company profitability. Particularly in more traditional industries such as mechanical engineering and construction, government relations divisions have had a struggle to get accepted within firms, often relying on the support of particular members of the board. In both Britain and the United States, I have encountered examples of firms that have closed or curtailed their government relations divisions as a cost cutting measure.

There are a number of compelling reasons why large firms do still need a specialist 'in-house' government relations division. Despite the change in the political landscape since the 1970s, misunderstanding remains a feature of government-industry relations in Britain, whilst some Government policies have been seen as damaging to particular firms or to industry in general. Even policies which are potentially favourable for business, such as privatisation, may have implications for particular firms which need to be carefully monitored, e.g., the implications of electricity privatisation for large scale industrial consumers of electricity. Firms that have not developed contacts with the political system have found it more difficult to mobilise support when they have needed it, as Rowntree found when it fought its takeover bid from Nestlé. A contrast was drawn between Rowntree's experience and that of Pilkington which had been able to rally parliamentary opinion to its side when it faced a subsequently withdrawn bid from BTR. It was noted that Rowntree had been

> slower to mobilise support at Westminster. MPs have been privately critical of the company's efforts at lobbying. For instance, it has only just appointed an adviser on its Whitehall and Westminster activities. (*Financial Times*, 9th May, 1988).

Though Miller argues in Chapter 2 that this is to misunderstand the Pilkington story, the popular conclusion was that noisy lobbying worked. Competition policy offers a classic example of an area where government decisions have a considerable impact on the commercial future of an individual company: in some cases, whether it survives as an independent entity; in others, whether it is able to proceed with an important takeover bid on conditions that make the acquisition worthwhile. Of course, a lobbying exercise which is perceived as too blatant and intensive may be counter productive. When it launched its bid for British Caledonian, British Airways announced that it would 'run a very high-profile campaign for as long as we have to. Whatever resources are necessary will be allocated to the campaign.' (*Financial Times*, 3rd August, 1987). Although the deal was approved, 'BA's threat to embarrass the Government through a publicity campaign in the run-up to the autumn party conference if the bid was referred backfired badly.' (*The Independent*, 20th November, 1987). British Airways may also have under-estimated the importance of the European dimension. British Airways eventually had to make significant concessions to the European Commission on the terms of its takeover of British Caledonian, having apparently initially not appreciated the significance of the Commission's intervention.

Taxation policy is another area where government decisions may adversely affect a particular company whilst others benefit. A classic example is the so-called 'Mossmorran clause' (referring to the Scottish chemical plant of that name) inserted in the *1982 Finance Act* which had the effect of establishing a new regime for calculating Petroleum Revenue Tax which applied to all British ethylene producers except ICI. In the debate on the clause in standing committee, one member described events in the following terms:

> What is really being discussed is a Government undertaking given to Shell and Esso as part of an overall package to make sure that the Mossmoran project went ahead ... But then BP got to work on the Government and suddenly the amendments started coming in so that Government were able to satisfy BP's requirements ... That, of course, left ICI out in the cold because it was the fourth giant in ethylene production and, not unreasonably, it became concerned. (Finance Bill Standing Committee A, 24th June, 1982, columns 979-980).

Accordingly,

> ICI had a series of meetings with the Government at the very highest level. Meetings took place between the Chairman of ICI and the then Chancellor of the Exchequer, the Chief Secretary of the Treasury and other ministers and senior officials of the Revenue. (*Common Market Law Reports*, 26th June, 1985, p.592).

In fact, one former Treasury minister argues that both BP and ICI lost out because, although each firm had the backing of a minister, they failed in their lobbying campaign because they 'did not see eye to eye about the appropriate remedial action.' (Bruce-Gardyne, 1986, p.44). Rather unusually, this particular dispute was resolved through a court action brought by ICI against the Government.

A more general motivation for maintaining a government relations division is to be found in the Thatcher Government's emphasis on the development of direct contacts with companies. This can be seen as an outgrowth of a longer term tendency to encourage direct contacts with companies, and to bypass trade associations which were often perceived by civil servants as poorly structured, inadequately resourced, and insufficiently representative of the sectors they served. Growing concentration in the British economy also provided a rationale for the development of direct contact with firms. Although there has been a long history of direct contact between British government and firms such as ICI, it was only in the mid 1970s that a deliberate emphasis was placed on encouraging direct company-government contacts. A senior civil servant explained that, in contrast with the 1960s, 'where sectoral implications were carefully worked out with the help of the trade associations, in the 1970s there has been a greater realisation that government must also have contact with individual companies'. (Mueller, 1985, p.105).

This trend towards direct contact with companies was reinforced by the Government's decision in 1988 to abolish sponsorship divisions for particular sectors of industry which had served as the traditional point of contact between government and trade associations. The Secretary of State for Trade and Industry, Lord Young, made it clear that he intended to foster direct contacts with ministers, bypassing the traditional route of contact through trade associations. He described associations as 'the lowest common denominator, producing mutual dependency between sectors and sponsoring civil servants.' (*Financial Times*, 16th January, 1988).

The Thatcher Government has attempted to reduce the extent to which business decisions are influenced by government regulations. Writing in a personal capacity, the deputy head of the Enterprise and Deregulation Unit has noted that 'Despite the Government's strong enterprise philosophy, minimising the cost of regulation on business is no straightforward task.' In part, this is because government is pursuing policy objectives in areas such as environmental and consumer protection which may necessarily involve regulating business. Moreover, 'There is more public clamour for increasing controls than for reducing them. The assumption runs deep that problems are to be solved by regulating.' Apart from the emergence of new areas of regulatory activity, the earlier discussions show that more traditional areas of government intervention such as taxation and competition policy may lead to differential impacts on particular companies which cannot be handled through trade associations. Government relations divisions are needed as much as they were in the 1970s, although for somewhat different reasons.

Government relations at the European Community level

The European Community is having an increasing impact on the operating environment of businesses, an impact that will become more significant in the run up to the creation of a single internal market in 1992. Many of the issues can, of course, be dealt with by approaches to the British Government either on an individual company or trade association basis; certainly, this would be the most usual channel of approach when a matter is before the Council of Ministers. There are also European level industry associations, although, as most of them are associations of associations, faced with the problem of reconciling conflicts of interest between their various national members, their effectiveness is often more limited than that of trade associations operating at the national level. As one Brussels public affairs representative noted in interview, the process of securing agreement between the national associations 'can sap the energy of the [European] organisation.' It is significant that some leading German firms, in a country where coordinated action through an association continues to be seen as the preferred and legitimate method of exerting political influence, have appointed European coordinators to handle relations with the EC.

One deterrent to having a permanent public affairs representative in Brussels is the cost of running an office there, although some companies (such as ICI) have European headquarters in Brussels anyway. Another risk is that a representative in Brussels may 'go native' and become identified with the Community rather than his company. One public affairs officer recalled in interview the experience of another company who had had a representative who,

... got very close to everything that happened in Brussels, nothing could breathe without him, but he got further away from his company. They said, 'never again, we'll have an intelligent commuter.'

At best, the resident representative may lose a sense of proportion about the significance of matters being dealt with in Brussels. As one Brussels public affairs representative commented in interview, 'You've got to be business related, you've got to attach money values to issues. You can end up monitoring beautifully and passing paper, can become obsessed with minutiae.' Against that, it has to be said that one of the purposes of taking an interest in EC developments is to forewarn a company about a relatively obscure directive that might have a considerable impact on its activities.

The main focus of a public affairs representative's work in Brussels is the Commission. As well as contacts with the various directorates-general, this may involve cultivating relations with a Commissioner's cabinet, not just on matters which are the concern of that Commissioner, but also on other matters on which the Commissioner may be asked to express an opinion. Working with the Commission is aided by the fact that it is a very open and permeable bureaucracy, although some directorates-general are more open to industry influence than others. As one public affairs representative commented in interview, 'In Whitehall, a civil servant is really quite happy to talk, but he's looking over his shoulder at his minister, he's responsible to the minister, and he's looking over his shoulder at the party the minister belongs to.' The EC Commission didn't have that grass roots link and didn't mind people knowing when something started to be worked on 'because if it lets people know, then it gets some sort of input.'

Although one respondent noted that 'if you have a significant issue, you work it everywhere', public affairs representatives in Brussels devote much less attention to the Parliament and the Economic and Social Committee than they do to the Commission. Responsibility for monitoring Parliamentary committees may be handed over to a consultant. One significant difference from the government relations function in London is that the public affairs representative may often sit on committees of the European level federation, and may have a general responsibility for the company's relations with Brussels-based trade associations. Public affairs representatives have become closely involved with attempts to reform and rationalise European level associations initiated by their companies. In part, this involvement is a reflection of their presence in Brussels, although companies still send out experts to take part in technical committees (which constitute the majority of committees in most European organisations). The greater involvement of Brussels representatives in coordinating business association activity on behalf of their company may suggest that this aspect of government relations work has reached a greater level of maturity, although it may also reflect a feeling that there are more opportunities to influence the structure and activities of European associations at this stage of their development. Certainly, companies such as ICI have been more successful in efforts to reform

European level associations than in their attempts to reshape British associations so that they are more cost and effort effective.

It should also be noted that government relations divisions may be concerned with monitoring the activities of international organisations, particularly those that have policies concerned with activities of multinational companies such as the OECD and the UN. Companies with extensive interests in South Africa have had an interest both in monitoring developments there, and changing public attitudes towards South Africa, although this task has become less significant as companies have disposed of their investments.

Scanning the political environment

Most government relations divisions are involved in some kind of scanning of the political environment in order to identify issues which may affect their company in the future. This may be done in a more or less sophisticated fashion, ranging from keeping track of developments through reading particular magazines, to a formal procedure for the identification and prioritisation of issues. A company which emphasised the importance of issue management gave each of its government relations professionals an issue to manage, an organisation to monitor, and a programme (such as contact with MPs) to run. Each spring the head of government relations met with the corporate planners to decide what the strategic plan public policy issues were and which issues should be given priority. *Ad hoc* committees were formed when a public policy issue 'warmed up'. Thus, when the process of tele-communications liberalisation and privatisation was started, the company formed a strategy group to manage its public position in the issue. This was chaired by the government relations manager, and also involved marketing experts, product experts, and a press relations expert. It met weekly to define the company's position and external action plan. One product from these meetings was position papers which could be used both to brief a director going to meet a minister or MP, and also field managers who might be asked what the company's position was.

Although a government relations manager might well find himself or herself doing the rounds of the party conferences each year, rather more attention is paid by government relations units to the activities of interest groups concerned with particular issues. These are perceived as having an important influence on the development of the political agenda, leading to the emergence of issues on which the company may need a position. Indeed, the growing importance of groups concerned with environmental and social questions was given in interviews as one reason for the growth of government relations divisions. One respondent referred to the,

> ... social changes that lead to the increasing sophistication and success of single issue interest groups. When we think of strategies, we have to take that into account. In relations with government departments, if you had government on your side, that was all that mattered seven or ten years ago, now it's simply not

enough, it's necessary to understand these groups, how you might deal with them – 'deal' in inverted commas – by confrontation or compromise.

Although only one company went so far as to have a person working full time on the activities of environmental interest groups, most government relations managers would probably agree with the respondent who commented that knowledge of interest groups was a basic piece of intellectual equipment required in the job.

The extent to which the advice of the government relations division is taken into account when a company is making commercial decisions will vary from one firm to another, but as one respondent commented, it was difficult to 'try to bring the nebulous factor of social and political change into a process alongside other things which are more quantifiable and hard edged.' Another respondent described his job as

> ... always in danger. I can get a commitment from a director who says, 'I believe in what's being done and I think it's important.' But there's a whole series of profit centres in [this company], it's not just a question of convincing the Managing Director. He will say, 'I will back you in what you are doing, you have to convince the divisional heads, they will convince the plant directors.' It won't be a question of issuing an edict to them.

Even so, there is some evidence that some companies are taking the incorporation of political considerations into their corporate planning process more seriously. As one respondent commented, 'Ten years ago the political situation was a footnote to the business analysis, it is now a more fundamental part.'

Government relations managers like to talk of being proactive, but in reality they admit that for much of the time they are forced to be reactive. They are obliged to cope with the political consequences of commercial decisions taken by the board, or to respond to a government or EC decision that affects the company's operations. However, it is a management rather than a firefighting function, and this means that some anticipation of issues, and some attempt to cope with an increasingly complex political environment, can ensure that a company is prepared to cope with problems before they become too threatening. As one experienced government relations manager in a major company commented,

> It's very much seen on both [the government and company] side as 'forewarned is forearmed'. It would be a mistake if our masters were to get involved: on [the company] side main board directors, on government side ministers. The whole emphasis is to try and work things out at official level. It's an admission of failure to go to the minister.

Conclusions: the future of the government relations function

The government relations function is here to stay, although it is unlikely to develop on the scale to be found in Washington where a more fluid political system with considerable dispersal of power requires a number of points of access to be covered. In trade associations, something of a profession appears to be emerging in the sense that a person may start working for an association on graduating from university, and then move to other associations with skills that are seen as transferable as he or she moves up the career ladder. There is no comparable development among government relations managers. There are far fewer of them, and companies also often seem uncertain about the skills and qualities that they require. In some companies, a stint in the government relations unit for a couple of years is seen as valuable experience for a 'high flyer' being groomed for a senior management position. Other firms prefer to appoint individuals who are already senior managers and who thus have a thorough knowledge of the company. Yet others prefer to bring in retired civil servants or diplomats on the argument that it is easier for them to learn about the company than for those with industrial experience to learn about politics.

Whether or not the government relations function does become more professionalised, there are a number of factors which are likely to encourage its future development in Britain. Increasingly, the British political system is one in which decisions are made at both the national and European level. A failure to appreciate the significance of policy initiatives taking place at the Community level could prove damaging for a company if it has, for example, to make expensive alterations to its production processes as a consequence of a new environmental regulation. Conglomerates with firms in a number of different sectors of the economy may consider that their particular combination of interests is not well served by membership of a variety of business associations.

There are, however, two more general changes in the nature of politics which suggest that the government relations division is likely to become more significant in the future. Politics in western societies may be said to be shifting from a 'politics of production' to a 'politics of collective consumption'; one sign of this change is the emergence of Green parties in a number of countries. At the risk of some over simplification, the politics of the 1970s were characterised by employer-union conflicts, government prices and incomes policies, and a general distributional struggle over the roles of management and labour in the production process. In the 1980s, these conflicts have receded into the background, and environmental issues, ranging from the quality of the air we breathe through to the food we eat, have assumed a new importance. Note, for example, the way in which consumers have become concerned about food additives, a development that has implications for both the food processing industry and the chemical industry.

The other general change is the strengthening of a tendency for Britain to be a company state, a term used in Willis and Grant (1987) to characterise a state in which direct contacts between companies and government are seen as preferable to intermediation through business associations on the model of countries such as West Germany. (A third model is one which gives parties, or party factions, a key role in government-business relations, as in Italy, or also to an extent in Japan). Such a pattern of government-industry relations is rooted in a persistent tradition of individualism among British business persons which may be traced back to the industrial revolution. However, it has been reinforced and renewed by the Thatcher Government's preference for dealing direct with business; any future government would face the problem that the administrative apparatus which has existed for dealing with trade associations since the Second World War has been dismantled. In such an environment, the government relations division assumes a new importance. Indeed, government relations divisions may be able to make an important practical contribution to breaking down the mistrust of politicians which persists in the business world, and the lack of understanding of the problems and needs of business which is too often displayed by British politicians.

6   Making use of Westminster

IAN GREER

All serious political consultants in Britain make use of Parliament. Why? After all, some critics write off Parliament as irrelevant in policy making in this country. Some firms believe that consultants spend too much time focusing on MPs and not enough on Ministers and civil servants. Is time spent at Westminster, then, merely window dressing by consultants – impressing clients but not achieving any tangible effect upon policy? The answer is no. Parliament is relevant to policy making in Britain – and that is why consultants make use of it. It is one – not necessarily the most important one and by no means the only one – of the bodies involved in the policy cycle that anyone wanting to influence policy needs to cultivate.

The position has been put well in perspective by Professor Philip Norton (1984). He has identified three types of legislature,

> *policy-making legislatures*, which can not only modify or reject policy brought forward by government but can also formulate and substitute policy of their own.

> *policy-influencing legislatures*, which can modify or reject policy brought forward by government, but cannot formulate and substitute policy of their own; and

> *legislatures with little or no policy effect*, which can neither modify nor reject government policy nor formulate and substitute policy of their own – their task being to give formal assent to whatever is placed before them.

The US Congress is the only major legislature which is a policy-making body. Parliament in this country is, as it has been for most of its history, a policy influencing legislature. Britons traditionally look to government to govern; the role of Parliament is to respond – on behalf of the wider political community – and in responding to provide the limits within which Government may govern.

As a policy-influencing body, Parliament is thus a relevant body for political consultants. Policy may be 'made' elsewhere (i.e. in Whitehall and increasingly in Brussels) and consultants have regular contact with Ministers and officials; but once that policy is made it will then need Parliament's assent if it is to be given statutory force. Parliament has the power to throw the policy out or to amend it. It is significant that Parliament has proved more willing to use that power at the same time as there has been a growth in the number of consultancies. Again, the work of Norton has been important here, in showing a greater independence among backbenchers since 1970 (Norton 1978, 1980, 1985), roughly coterminous with the creation and growth of the commercial lobbying industry. The greater the independence on the part of MPs – and peers – then the greater their importance to consultants and their clients.

Anyone who doubts the relevance of Parliament need only be reminded of the *Shops Bill*, defeated on second reading in 1986 when 72 Conservative MPs voted with the Opposition. A host of other measures have been variously amended – or even not seen the light of day – because of parliamentary pressure, real or anticipated.

Prerequisites

Having established then that Parliament is a relevant body, in order to make effective use of it, there are two basic prerequisites. One is knowledge – knowledge of both parliamentarians and procedure. The other is using that knowledge to achieve the desired outcome. That is why consultants are especially valuable to clients: they have both the basic knowledge necessary and they know how to put it to effective use. Even if clients know who to contact (and few do – see the evidence cited by Rush, *et al*. 1988), they would rarely know how and when to make contact.

Knowledge of parliamentarians and of procedure needs to be extensive. There are 650 MPs and more than one thousand peers. They have varied interests, knowledge and ability. Consultants need to have a good working knowledge of every parliamentarian. Whenever a particular issue arises, MPs and peers can then be divided into four categories: those who are vital to contact (because of the positions they hold or because of their expertise), those who have some interest in the area and hence useful to contact, those who have no particular interest and hence should usually not be contacted, and those who are either hostile or whose support would constitute the kiss of death and hence should be definitely avoided. Who occupies these particular categories will vary from issue to issue. Hence, the contacts made will change rather like a chemical reaction.

Knowledge of procedure is vital. As I pointed out in *Right to be Heard* (1985, p.25), 'There is no point in mounting a campaign to defeat a Government measure if it only needs a minor amendment'. For the uninitiated, parliamentary procedures – and structures – are intimidating. Many (probably most) clients would have no idea of the difference between a Select Committee and a Standing Committee say, or whether it was permissible or not to approach a parliamentary clerk on a particular issue. Many would have little idea of the existence, let alone the role, of party backbench committees. Timing too is all important. Too many outside groups approach MPs to ask them to table amendments or oppose a particular clause in a Bill when the relevant clause itself has already passed through all its parliamentary stages.

Knowledge of when to act – and how to act – is thus the second prerequisite. What is the best way to get one's views across? In some cases, by a personal meeting. In others, by correspondence (and there are a host of 'do's' and 'don'ts' when it comes to writing to MPs). Both devices are a means to an end: that is, to get one or more Members (or peers) to take a particular form of action – table a parliamentary question, arrange a meeting with a minister, table an Early Day Motion (EDM), table an amendment to a Bill or speak in a debate, either on the floor of the House or in Committee. Knowledge of when to act reflects a good knowledge of procedure as well as good sources of information. Again, consultants save clients' time by monitoring parliamentary papers and other official documents, as well as being around Westminster regularly to know what is happening and, perhaps more importantly, what is expected to happen.

Types of campaign

In acting on behalf of clients, there are essentially two types of campaign that consultants engage in, each necessitating a different form of action within the Palace of Westminster.

One form of campaign is that of consciousness raising, getting a much higher – and more favourable – profile for the client in the political world. Such a campaign can and often does extend over a considerable period of time, sometimes running into years rather than months. It will entail having regular contact with targeted MPs and peers, arranging meetings for them with one's client, ensuring a regular flow of relevant (but not excessive) material and, if appropriate, arranging fact-finding visits to the client's factory or business site. Over a period of time a valuable network of potential supporters can be established with sympathetic MPs and peers being briefed and encouraged to take an interest in the client's long and short term objectives.

The second type of campaign is the reactive, or 'fire-fighting', campaign, acting on behalf of a client in response to a particular issue which has blown up very quickly or unexpectedly. A provision of a particular Bill or a specific proposal contained in a Green or White Paper, may affect the interests of a professional association, for instance (as happened in March 1988 with the publication of the Green Paper, *Review of Restrictive Trades Practices Policy*), or a particular industry or concern such as charities. Consultants are hired to respond quickly on their behalf, alerting sympathetic MPs and peers, arranging meetings if time permits, and ensuring that the appropriate action is taken (amendments, motions or questions, depending on the form of the problem) in order that the Government knows that it will have a battle on its hands to get the provision through. In some cases, it is sufficient to ensure Government knows there is a problem: it will often be willing to consult on the issue, even modify its own proposals, if it realises that as drafted what it intends will have unintended consequences.

The 'who' of parliamentary lobbying

In lobbying Parliament, who should – and, in the case of consultants, does – one concentrate on? As will be clear from what I have said already, it will depend on the specific goal sought by the client. However, as a broad generalisation, MPs and peers fall into two categories: those who are relevant by virtue of their own personal interests and constituency representation; and those who are relevant by virtue of the (temporary) positions that they hold. Let us now look at some of those who fall into these categories.

Most MPs upon arriving at Westminster find it is to their advantage – for both political and practical reasons – to be reasonably selective in the areas of policy upon which they concentrate. There are few who fall in the 'jack of all trades' category (and those that do need to be treated with some caution); most like to be known as someone with something useful to contribute in a few key areas of policy. Often this interest in particular subjects at Westminster is just a continuation for the Member of interests pursued before becoming an MP and in many cases derives from a previous career (lawyers in the House, for example, are particularly prevalent, whilst scientists are few and far between). In other cases, MPs will actually spend some time looking around for policy issues to pursue, and having selected one or two will then duly set about researching them in some depth in the hope of carving out a name for themselves among their colleagues as something of an expert.

Having done so, these members become the targets for consultants working in that field. If they are able to demonstrate their knowledge and interest – by making an intelligent and incisive speech on the floor of the House, for example – then the Minister will sit up and take note of what they have to say (indeed, it is not uncommon for some backbenchers to know more about a certain subject than the responsible minister). For the Member's part, he will appreciate the briefing provided by consultants and the opportunity to discuss the issue in some depth with the client.

Whatever disparate interests they choose to pursue in policy terms at Westminster, all MPs are united in their concern about what is taking place within the boundaries of their own constituencies. Indeed, there is evidence that MPs are taking an increasingly active role in constituency casework, partly out of choice and partly out of a need to respond to the ever- increasing demands of their electorate (see Cain *et al.* 1987). Even those Members in safe seats now devote a significant proportion of their time to such casework. In pursuing a particular campaign, therefore, consultants need to be aware of all those members for whom there is a constituency implication, be it in terms of job losses (or potential gains), environmental protection or the affect of the unified business rate.

These then constitute the members who are relevant for consultants either by virtue of their personal knowledge or interest or because of their constituency representation. Given that their interests or their constituencies are unlikely to change (unless they lose their seats of course) they comprise what might be termed 'constant friends'.

This is not to say that those who fall in the second category don't always prove to be constant friends, but simply that the positions that they hold aren't constant. As long as they remain in such posts, however, consultants need to be aware of them and of the extent of their influence.

Among this latter group are Ministers' parliamentary private secretaries (PPSs). They are far more prevalent now than ever before, no longer being the sole preserve of cabinet ministers. Most Ministers of State, and even a few parliamentary under-secretaries of state, will now have their own PPS. In addition to being more of them, the extent of their job has also increased over the years. Their principal role is and always has been to provide the minister with feedback on the strength of feeling among backbenchers either to specific proposals or to policy direction in general. In turn, they also convey messages on the minister's line of thinking to their colleagues. Increasingly, however, as more and more outside organisations seek the ear of the minister, the PPS is serving as a valuable channel of communication between the Minister and such organisations.

Like ministers themselves, the calibre of PPSs will vary enormously as will the extent of their influence. Some enjoy very close links with their minister (note, for example, close relationship in the 1960s between Dick Crossman and Tam Dalyell as recorded in *The Crossman Diaries*), others have a far more cursory relationship. But whatever the relationship, they should not be ignored as they serve as an important conduit between the Minister and the outside world.

Another group of Members who should not be ignored by anyone seeking to raise an issue at Westminster is the Opposition front bench team. The spokesmen shadowing a particular Department are guaranteed the opportunity to speak at the beginning and end of debates in the chamber and those 'leading' for the Opposition in committee on a Bill have plenty of scope for probing into the finer detail of a piece of legislation and in exchange for co-operation can often wrest important concessions from the Government. They may also of course at some point become Ministers themselves.

Others who are relevant by virtue of the positions they hold include those who sit on, or serve as officers of, parliamentary committees. There are several different types of committee, each very different in its status and range of activity.

The real focus of attention for anyone wishing to influence the passage of a bill should be the Standing Committee appointed to examine its provisions. It is here that the legislation is subject to its most detailed examination. Anything from 16 to 50 members, reflecting party strength on the Floor of the House, go through the bill literally clause by clause. Often members are simply encouraged to turn up and to vote when required but not to participate in the proceedings. It can have its uses however. It only takes two or three Government Members on a smaller committee to join with Opposition Members to amend the provisions of a bill; as happened frequently in the 1970s and has been witnessed more recently on a number of major bills, including those reforming financial services in 1986 and copyright law in 1988.

Contrary to the impression given by their name Standing Committees labour under the handicap of being appointed on an *ad hoc* basis. They are not committees on which MPs serve continuously; hence to influence a bill at Committee Stage, one has to wait until the membership of the committee is announced – usually just a matter of days before the committee starts to sit.

Unlike Standing Committees, the departmentally-related Select Committees are permanent bodies. Established in 1979, there are currently 13 such committees. Despite their comparatively short existence they have become a recognised and accepted part of the parliamentary landscape and enjoy a high degree of political visibility, notably so in the case of the Treasury and Civil Service, Foreign Affairs, Defence and recently the Social Services Committees (and, under the chairmanship of Christopher Price in the 1979-83 Parliament, the Education Committee). There are eleven members on each committee and the competition for places is fierce. They undertake a number of major enquiries each session (see Drewry, 1985; Englefield, 1984) and provide a useful opportunity to get views heard and on the public record. Although the committees are now permanent, the membership is not and hence it is advisable to establish links with more than just one or two members of the committee.

Both the Conservative and Labour parliamentary parties have a number of committees which meet regularly to discuss issues of concern to them. The Conservative committees tend to meet weekly and to cover a wide range of topics (currently there are 23 such committees, plus six regional committees); Labour committees, which tend to be less well supported, have been reorganised to parallel the subjects covered by the select committees. Unlike Conservatives committees, peers also serve on them.

The party committees, though less well known than the Select Committees, have a much longer history and politically are often more significant. The Conservative committees in particular, which date predominantly from the 1920s, are closer to the party's policy-making processes than are the Labour committees. Committee officers are elected annually and some establish quite considerable reputations – and influence – in Westminster. The long-serving Conservative MPs Sir William Clark and Michael Grylls, for example, are best known for being chairmen respectively of the Finance Committee and the Trade and Industry Committee. Party committees have far more flexibility in their programmes than have Select Committees and so inviting a party committee to make a fact-finding visit to a particular factory or proposed development makes more sense than making a similar invitation to a select committee when it is already investigating an unrelated topic. Consultants can play an especially valuable role in making contact with party committees on behalf of clients and will often make all the administrative arrangements for visits and fact-finding trips. Contact with Conservative committees is invariably through the chairman and secretary – the two most important officers.

The final group of committees that can be valuable for the purposes of companies and other bodies – and hence valuable to consultants – are committees in the House of Lords. They are few and far between; there are no party committees and virtually all bills have their committee stage taken on the Floor of the House. But what their Lordships' House lacks in quantity it makes up for in quality. This is especially so in the case of the two sessional or permanent Select Committees – on Eurpean Communities legislation and Science and Technology. The EC Committee works through seven sub-committees and almost one hundred peers are actively involved. (This compares with 16 MPs on the equivalent Commons' Committee.) The committee fulfils a valuable function of scrutinising draft EC legislation, and has acquired a formidable reputation not only in Whitehall but also in Brussels for the quality and authority of its reports (see Grantham and Hodgson, 1985). Topics covered by reports from the committee in 1985/86 included indirect taxation and the internal market, disclosure of significant shareholdings, consumer protection policy, disposal of waste oils. Similarly, the Science and Technology Committee, bringing together Fellows of the Royal Society with leading industrialists (something no Commons' committee does), has proved both informed and persistent. Its 1987 Report on Civil Research and Development was especially influential in eliciting a re-structuring of, and greater commitment to, the government's infrastructure for dealing with the R & D needs of the nation. Such Lords committees – as well as *ad hoc* committees established to investigate particular topics – are especially valuable to affected outside interests by virtue of the fact they invite, and receive, extensive evidence, both oral and written.

Having then identified the individuals one needs to make contact with, either because of their personal interests or the positions they hold (the two categories are far from mutually exclusive), it is then possible to set about constructing a campaign to influence them. This brings us to the how of parliamentary lobbying. What is the best way of achieving contact and making effective use of Westminster?

The 'how' of Parliamentary lobbying

The point at which one makes contact with targeted parliamentarians comes at a relatively late stage in a campaign to influence legislation or increase a client's profile in the political world. As I noted in *Right to be Heard* (1985: pp. 26-28), there are essentially six stages in a typical campaign:

(i) a thorough study of information about the client and an identification of the client's problem in relation to government and the policy-making process;

(ii) an analysis of those parts of the process most central to the problem (which minister has responsibility and the like) and of all existing legislation, regulations and judicial rulings;

(iii) devising a strategy to achieve a solution to the problem – for example, a stage-by-stage programme to build up support within Whitehall and Westminster to achieve a particular legislative change;

(iv) and here parliamentarians come more into the picture – this involves the implementation of the strategy, usually entailing representations to ministers, civil servants and parliamentarians (as well as others beyond the policy cycle, including journalists) targeted at stage two, and employing methods devised at stage three;

(v) constant monitoring of opinion within Whitehall and Westminster, in other words to achieve some feedback (which can then determine what further action may be necessary);

(vi) constitutes the final outcome – hopefully the one desired by the client.

The method of contact with parliamentarians will vary according to the nature of the client's problems and the time available to make contact. If one has to act within a matter of hours, there is not going to be time to arrange elaborate seminars and issue invitations to make fact-finding visits to a client's plant in a county far distant from London! It will also vary according to the political consultancy employed. Some consultants – myself included – are prepared to deal directly with MPs and peers. Ian Greer Associates is a well established firm with a good reputation among parliamentarians of all parties. When we write to them, they know we can be trusted and that the points we make are well founded and well researched.

If time permits – and the client's problem suggests it is appropriate – meetings between clients and targeted MPs and peers are arranged, either at the client's offices or in the Palace of Westminster. The most effective meetings are invariably those where the senior management of the company meet with parliamentarians on an individual basis; that ensures that the message is an authoritative one and that the parliamentarians feel they are being treated on a serious and personal basis. (It also means that the message can be geared to the particular interests of the Member.) Such meetings may be supplemented by seminars or presentations to groups of Members, either a group drawn together by the consultant on the basis of the MPs' particular specialisms or an existing group such as a party committee or an all-party group. These meetings, especially if they involve visual displays (videos, tour of a plant etc), tend to take place at the client's premises.

Meetings may also be arranged at Westminster, either because it is most convenient to the Members involved, is necessary for reasons of time or is required by the procedure involved. If one is seeking to influence the provisions of a bill, for example, contact with members of the standing committee considering it will – while the committee is considering it – necessarily take place in the Palace of Westminster, and more often than not in the Committee corridor.

Meetings at Westminster may also take the form of hiring a room – usually one of the four small dining rooms – for a reception. These can be useful, but they are rarely valuable *on their own* and their usefulness is being diluted by over-use. MPs are becoming increasingly immune to being swayed by a pleasant lunch and a ready supply of drink. Indeed, some Members come along to receptions (invited by fellow members) just to make up numbers and have no great interest in the body on whose behalf the reception is organised. One-to-one meetings in a client's office, or a serious seminar for a carefully selected group of Members, are far more productive in achieving the consultant's principal goal: getting the client's message to those who need to hear it.

Arranging meetings at Westminster are clearly appropriate as they involve MPs – and active peers – at their 'place of work'. But for MPs, of course, Westminster is not their only place of parliamentary work. In some cases, it is appropriate to arrange to meet Members within their constituencies. This is obviously so in the case of client's whose premises – and workers – are in the Members' constituencies. It may also be appropriate – whether by meetings or correspondence – in the case of groups whose Members are spread over a number of constituencies. Members alerted to problems that are likely to affect constituency interests – loss of jobs, factory closure, siting of a nuclear waste dump, takeover of a local firm by an overseas predator etc – are often among the most powerful and persistent advocates on behalf of the affected interests. The task of the consultant is to make sure that they are alerted to the problem and, once alerted, well briefed in order to take parliamentary action.

For political consultants, the 'how' of lobbying thus entails three particular and inter-related tasks: pinpointing those who need to be contacted, providing the arguments that will be persuasive, and making the necessary arrangements to ensure that those arguments are put over effectively. Lobbying is thus a multi-faceted business, and parliamentary lobbying constitutes but one stage of a complex process.

With what effect?

Having sketched out what consultants do in relation to Westminster, there remains the central question: what effect do they have? There can be no doubt that they do have some effect, acknowledged by parliamentarians as well as clients, and some illustrative examples will shortly be offered.

The overall effect, though, as Grantham and Seymour-Ure have shown (1989) is difficult to quantify. This is especially so given the number of campaigns undertaken to raise a client's profile – the 'consciousness-raising' campaigns. By what objective scale can such campaigns be judged? Indeed, they may be impossible to assess given what might be termed the 'hidden success' element of such campaigns. How does one measure Government inaction caused by anticipation of the reaction? By that, I mean that raising a client's image at Westminster, ensuring a positive image – and ensuring the Government knows that the client now has friends in Westminster – can result in the government not taking action that otherwise it might have done had the interests affected been 'friendless' within the political domain. To use the terminology of social science, such 'non decision-making' on the part of Government is not usually observable and certainly is not quantifiable, but I am convinced it is now far more prevalent in the corridors of power. Ministers and civil servants are today far more sensitive than ever before to parliamentary opinion and political consultants have proved valuable in ensuring that they are aware of the strength of opinion on key issues.

Another problem with quantifying the effectiveness of consultants is the fact that often now consultants will be hired by interests on both sides of a particular issue. The *Shops Bill* is a good example; so too is the 1988 battle for the take-over of Rowntree Mackintosh by Nestles. (Rowntree Mackintosh hired a consultancy, so too did Nestles and the other Swiss company battling for control, Suchards – the battle centring on Parliament and the need to persuade the Secretary of State for Trade and Industry to refer – or not refer – the bid to the Monopolies and Mergers Commission.) As a result of such activity, it is near-impossible to quantify clearly the effect of consultants qua consultants (as opposed, of course, to the effect of particular consultants). What such cases reveal, though, is the value of consultants in ensuring that the message of competing interests are clearly heard. It is not often the case that some industrial or financial Goliath hires a consultant in a bid to win political support over the claims of some tiny David. Rather it is two (or more) Goliaths presenting competing claims (large retailers versus the Church, in the case of the *Shops Bill*, for example) and often not knowing the political system sufficiently well to know how to get their message across. Hence the value of consultants.

Though not quantifiable in precise terms, there are numerous instances of consultants achieving the goals of their clients (see especially Grantham and Seymour-Ure, 1989), certainly sufficient to justify the expense of hiring consultants. In some cases, for relatively modest fees, consultants have helped achieve changes in legislation or policy that have saved the client millions of pounds. From the client's point of view, hiring a political consultant is thus a worthwhile investment; indeed, not to do so is increasingly a false economy.

The value of consultants in achieving desired goals is best illustrated by way of example. I offer two, which help put some flesh on the skeleton of consultants' activity sketched above.

Case Studies:

Plessey

The giant electronic and defence firm, Plessey, approached Ian Greer

Associates in January 1986 after the Office of Fair Trading had referred a hostile merger proposal by GEC to the Monopolies and Mergers Commission (MMC).

A campaign – which was to be both broad and deep – was constructed, the aim being to alert those at all levels in the political domain to the damaging implications of the merger, not just for Plessey itself but for the array of small businesses which relied so heavily upon it.

A number of meetings and briefings were arranged with members of the Cabinet (who would be involved in the final decision affecting the company) as well as with the relevant shadow cabinet spokesmen. The intention, however, was not just to try and influence the Cabinet directly, but also indirectly by influencing those in the political environment occupied by Members, carefully selected on the basis of the criteria outlined earlier, as well as with the appropriate backbench committees. As a result of these briefing sessions, aided by an exhibition and the production of a concise booklet highlighting Plessey's case, an Early Day Motion supporting the company was tabled and signed by 170 Members. Members were also encouraged to table parliamentary questions as a further device to keep the issue at the forefront of the Government's mind while the MMC considered the proposal.

By August of that year, when the MMC reported to the Secretary of State for Trade and Industry, there were few people at Westminster who were not at least aware – if not well versed – on Plessey's reasons for opposing the merger plan. The Secretary of State duly accepted that the proposal was not in the public interest and that the merger should not be allowed to proceed.

British Airways

In July 1984, just weeks before Parliament rose for the summer recess, a Government-commissioned report by the Civil Aviation Authority recommended that Britain's state-owned airline, British Airways, be reduced in size and that in the interests of competition, a number of its inter-continental routes be transferred to its major rival, British Caledonia.

The BA management were horrified by the proposals, not least because of the effect they would have on the company's capacity to compete effectively at an international level. The first thing Ian Greer Associates did was to research the strength of feeling at Westminster to the recommendations. This revealed that despite their magnitude they had attracted considerable cross-party support. BA therefore had a battle on its hands and with the House about to rise, limited opportunities in which to get their case across.

Having familiarised ourselves with the major issues involved, we immediately set about pinpointing key parliamentarians and arranging meetings. With time of the essence, we had to be selective, concentrating on those who not only had some existing knowledge and interest in airline policy but who could be relied upon, if not to support BA's case, to acknowledge the arguments being put forward for opposing the CAA recommendations. A series of well-honed briefing papers were prepared for such meetings and prior to a major debate in the Commons on the CAA report, a personal briefing was given by the BA chairman, Lord King, to 18 MPs.

A number of the Members identified and approached by Ian Greer Associates decided to table an Early Day Motion urging their colleagues to reject the CAA report. Pressure was kept up during the summer months and during the autumn conference season, nearly 40 briefing sessions were held with Members from all parties. In October, much to BA's relief, the Government announced that it had rejected the CAA's main recommendations, going instead for a limited exchange of routes between the two airlines.

Both examples sustain the general thrust of this chapter. While it is true that many of the problems of clients are best resolved in discussions with civil servants before a government commits itself in public on a policy, there are many issues where we need to recognise that Ministers are politicians as well as administrators and they are sensitive to the views of their fellow politicians in Westminster.

7 Issue Advocacy in Parliament: the Case of the National Consumer Council

DR. MARTIN SMITH

Introduction

The interests of 'the consumer' have moved centre stage in British politics in the 1980s. Of course this does not signify that consumer organisations now win all their battles in Whitehall and Westminster; there are some successes and some failures. It *does* signify that consumer principles inform a wide range of public policy debates and that consumer issues have acquired a greater resonance amongst politicians of all persuasions. There has been a consequential effect upon the terms of a number of key political debates. It signifies, too, that the influence exerted by consumer organisations within the UK legislative process is, though not great, greater now than it has traditionally been.

A full account of the many reasons for this overall shift in the pattern of influence would take us well beyond the scope of this chapter. However, issue advocacy in Whitehall and Westminster is obviously not undertaken in a vacuum: it is related to complex patterns of social and political change. Two of these changes are particularly important in setting the scene, and the context in which the National Consumer Council – and other UK consumer organisations – engage in Parliamentary activity.

First, as regards the general balance of political *power*, consumer organisations are still relatively weak compared to most producer or supplier interests (the CBI, the NFU, large corporations, financial institutions, the professions and, in a different category, the trade unions). Relative powerlessness here principally means inferior resources – human and financial – and weaknesses in campaigning skills and experience. Consumer organisations are usually the underdogs in any contest with, say, British Airways or the pharmaceutical industry or the accountancy profession. This imbalance in lobbying power is no longer always decisive, but is nevertheless an inescapable and constraining fact of life for the National Consumer Council in many of the forums – including Parliament – in which the big decisions are taken.

Secondly, however, there is a countervailing factor. The agendas of British domestic politics have become significantly more consumer-oriented in the 1980s. Cause and effect are difficult to disentangle, although the impact of 'Thatcherism', with its distinctive, if selective, anti-Establishment bias, has undoubtedly been critical. Whatever the reasons, the general proposition – a change in the character of domestic political agendas – holds true on both the Right and the Left of British politics. Each of the parties are making some sort of bid to become *the* consumers' party.

Much of this can be attributed to good old-fashioned party opportunism. It would be surprising if that were not the case. But there is a more substantial aspect to it. A number of key public policy debates – on the delivery of local authority services and the future of public health care provision, to take two examples – are now being conducted in terms which demonstrate that consumer organisations are beginning to impose their own analyses and perspectives on the politicians. 'Consumerism' – the process of political activism through which the consumers and users of goods and services attempt, via their representatives, to obtain a better deal for themselves – is gradually moving in from the margins of British politics.

Consumerism used only to be concerned with High Street issues like faulty goods and misleading prices. Increasingly, the principles developed by consumer organisations within the framework of this relatively narrow, traditional interpretation are being used to analyse the use or consumption of publicly provided services like transport, health, education and social security. Thus passengers, patients, parents/pupils and claimants are being encouraged to see themselves as 'consumers'.

In 1988, politicians of both the Right and the Left confirmed this identification. Kenneth Baker presented the Government's *Education Reform Act* as an attempt to make 'the consumer' sovereign in the market-place for schooling; while Neil Kinnock endorsed the wide-ranging first phase report of his party's policy review team on Consumers and the Community. This broad and relatively new construction of the scope of consumerism informs all of the work of the National Consumer Council, including its Parliamentary activities.

The character and organisational peculiarities of the National Consumer Council

The National Consumer Council (NCC) is a curious organisation. It was established in May 1975 to represent the interests of consumers generally to central and local government, to industry and to other bodies as appropriate. It is a non-statutory body funded entirely by the taxpayer. It is a private limited company supported by the Department of Trade and Industry. Its chairman, vice-chairman and Council are appointed by a Secretary of State yet its policy-making procedures are independent of Government. It has a particular remit to represent the interests of poor and disadvantaged consumers and does not undertake any product testing. (It is the Consumers' Association, not the NCC, which publishes *Which?* magazine). This strange combination of characteristics makes the NCC perhaps unique in UK representative politics.

The character of the organisation is of central importance to any account of the scope of its Parliamentary activities. The NCC has no regulatory function; its only power is that of persuasion. It conducts research, it forms policy and it makes recommendations. In short, it *lobbies* – wherever and whenever it is appropriate to do so and resources permit.

NCC's strengths and weaknesses

The peculiar character of the NCC brings with it both advantages and disadvantages for lobbying purposes. In its thirteen-plus years, some appointments by Government to membership of its Council have undoubtedly had a political flavour – in both directions. Each successive chairman however – Michael Young (Lord Young of Dartington), Michael Shanks, Michael Montague and Sally Oppenheim-Barnes – has actively striven for party political neutrality. The occasional controversial appointment has made no lasting impact on the Council's perceived party neutrality, a perception which has been consistently reinforced by the careful tone of its major policy statements.

Perceived political neutrality is essential to the effectiveness of the Council's lobbying. So also is its complete independence from commercial interests. These two qualities characterise the NCC as a genuine public interest organisation, a status which opens more doors than it closes.

The special nature of the Council's links with its supporting Department, the Department of Trade and Industry (DTI), is important. Relations with DTI's Consumer Affairs Division are generally cordial. There are benefits to the NCC here in terms of access to information and policy-making procedures. It should be noted, however, that much of the Council's business with Whitehall is necessarily with departments other than the DTI. Indeed, the last three large pieces of work commissioned from the Council by central government have each dealt with non-DTI issues – banking services, European air transport and the Common Agricultural Policy. The only major departments of state with which the NCC had no significant contact on policy matters between 1984 and 1987 were the Ministry of Defence and the Foreign Office.

Departmental support (or 'sponsorship') is not an unalloyed advantage. The DTI provides the NCC's 'bread and rations' through a grant-in-aid mechanism, and the Council is formally responsible to a DTI junior minister for the conduct of its business. This relationship of financial dependence has not compromised the NCC's policy-making independence or lobbying freedom. There have of course been occasions when NCC has been in disagreement with the Government at both ministerial and official level. However, such disagreements have never resulted in actual political interference. Experienced consumer affairs visitors from overseas have frequently expressed amazement that a body which is entirely funded by central government should on occasion be so robustly critical of it, apparently with impunity. A reason – not the only one – for this absence of political interference is that the quality of the Council's published reports is widely acknowledged to be exceptionally high. This, perhaps, is the Council's greatest strength. Without it the Council's Parliamentary lobbying would be much less effective.

Lobbying by the National Consumer Council; organisation and resources

The enormous breadth of the NCC's remit means that the scope for lobbying by the Council is almost limitless. The NCC's working definition of the proper scope of consumer affairs includes goods and services, in both the public and private sectors. The Council must clearly respond to proposals and priorities which are not its own, in addition to pushing ahead with its own agenda for change. In practice, much of the NCC's lobbying is determined in response to present and future legislative programmes, though events in Whitehall and Westminster may themselves be a consequence, in whole or (more frequently) in part, of initiatives taken at an earlier stage by the NCC and its allies.

The Council allocates considerable resources to the task of attempting to persuade officials engaged in pre-legislative and other consultative work. In 1986 it responded to some fifty consultative documents at the request of no less than seven different government departments. This activity is mainly performed by the Council's senior research and development officers under the direction of their managers.

Parliamentary work is complementary, though in the nature of legislative gestation, rarely simultaneous. Parliamentary effort explores most available avenues: Government Bills; Private Members' Bills; select committee enquiries; adjournment debates and Parliamentary Questions. It is frequently assisted by media campaigns organised by the NCC's press office.

All Parliamentary activity is organised and executed 'in-house'. The Parliamentary Office, which between 1986 and 1988 comprised a Parliamentary Officer, an Assistant Parliamentary Officer and a Legal Officer, is grouped with press, publications, library and general public relations functions in the Public Affairs Group. The Parliamentary Office is responsible for developing political strategy and tactics, subject to the approval of the Director. Other NCC personnel supply policy advice for briefing purposes.

Resource constraints determine the extent of the Council's lobbying at any one time. The Council has a current policy prospectus which embraces issues in housing, education, health, consumer (goods and services) law, the Common Agricultural Policy, consumer credit and debt, insolvency, the advice services, the regulation of utilities, air transport, financial services, the pedestrian environment, freedom of information and social security – not an exhaustive list. Though not all these issues are politically 'live' at any given moment, the scope for appropriate Parliamentary action is frequently greater than the resources required to proceed on several fronts simultaneously. The Council therefore has to make choices in targeting its lobbying effort. It also depends heavily on its existing contacts and reputation at particularly busy times, as in the 1985/86 session outlined below.

Criteria for Parliamentary action

In deciding whether or not to embark upon a particular piece of lobbying, or similarly, whether or not to discontinue a project already begun, the NCC applies a number of criteria.

These are the seven most important:

(i) the relative importance criterion: is the issue intrinsically important on a consumer scale of 1 to 10?

(ii) the success probability criterion: what are the chances of success, given the Government's known position, the prevailing balance of the parties and other relevant factors?

(iii) the complexity criterion: how complex are the substantive points at issue, and does the Council have the intellectual capacity at staff level to cope with the consequences of engagement?

(iv) the obligation criterion: is the Council obliged to intervene by a previous commitment or by the nature of a particular request?

(v) the insider/outsider criterion: is the NCC already on the 'inside track' on a particular issue by virtue of its status and connections, or could it achieve that position?

(vi) the other players criterion: would the Council's point of view go by default if it chose not to pursue a given argument or set of arguments in Parliament, or would it be taken up by other lobbying interests?

(vii) the topicality criterion: is it the kind of issue that could be cranked up by an effective publicity campaign, or is it going to be difficult to generate interest in its implications?

What Bills the Council chooses to lobby on in any one session will depend heavily on the advice given by staff in answer to these questions. Usually, there is a difficult balance to strike. In the 1985/86 session for example, work on the *Gas* and *Airports Bills* was halted following Commons completion, in spite of the importance of the issues, partly because it seemed clear that the Government would make no further concessions and partly, in the case of the *Gas Bill*, because work was being carried on by the then National Gas Consumers' Council. In the same session the *Shops Bill* was a priority for the NCC because it did raise intrinsically important issues for consumers, the Council was on an inside track, public interest was high, and the Council was obligated by previous commitments. Similarly, it persisted in lobbying on the *Financial Services Bill*, also in the 1985/86 session, because the prospects for success appeared to remain high throughout the Bill's Parliamentary passage.

Occasionally, legislation is introduced which is so fundamental to the Council's work, and so central to the responsibilities of its supporting department, that a high – even an exclusive – priority is given to it. *The Consumer Protection Bill* in the 1986/87 session was an example. This Bill – an omnibus measure dealing with product liability, consumer safety and misleading price indications – because it ranged so widely across the traditional consumer agenda, was the predominant feature of the Council's Parliamentary work for the session.

On product liability, Council policy required the NCC to contest aspects of the Government's approach which, in reality, had long previously been hardened up in the arena of the European Commission. Consumer interests had been defeated during this all-important earlier stage of the lobbying process, and the prospects for reversing this position in Westminster were always likely to be poor. The arguments were nevertheless pressed throughout the Bill's passage through the Lords. The Government was indeed defeated by an NCC-inspired amendment on the scope of the 'development risks defence' – a temporary victory soon after reversed. Subsequent examination by the Commons was curtailed by the announcement of a general election.

The process of making decisions of the 'drop further work'/'don't drop further work' variety is most complex where longer-term strategic campaigning is concerned. Some battles can be worth fighting and losing in the short term for the sake of agenda-setting or perception-altering gains on the more distant horizon. Even in this context, however, it is useful to keep most of the criteria listed above in mind as a kind of efficiency yardstick. Since Parliamentary lobbying is a completely open-ended activity capable of swallowing up huge amounts or resources, some mechanism for questioning the utility of active lobbying is essential.

The 1985/86 session

To illustrate the range of choices and opportunities that present themselves, there follows a detailed examination of the NCC's legislative interests in the 1985/86 session. Although in some respects this was an unusually heavy year (for Parliamentarians as well as lobbyists!), it was not exceptional in the diversity of the challenges which are a feature of NCC life in the second half of the 1980s.

Throughout the session, the NCC was overstretched on the Parliamentary front. Its Council committed itself to lobbying on the following Government Bills: the *Airports Bill*; the *Building Societies Bill*; the *Education Bill*; the *Gas Bill*; the *Shops Bill*; the *Financial Services Bill*; the *Social Security Bill*; and the *Housing and Planning Bill*. It was also invited by a Conservative back-bench member of Parliament to draft and advise on the substance of a complex Private Member's Bill on consumer safety.

It was only possible to sustain work on all these fronts at once because the organisation was flexible enough to re-allocate resources away from other important activities. Five senior members of staff were involved in writing

Parliamentary briefs during January and February 1986. Even so, trying to keep nine balls in the air was an impossible task, forcing a number of tactical withdrawals. Work on two Bills was dropped completely (see below). Considerable problems remained, some of them determined by the Parliamentary timetable. This was most graphically illustrated one Thursday morning in May when, at opposite ends of the Commons Committee corridor, two amendments drafted by the NCC on different Bills were called almost simultaneously.

1. *The Airports Bill (now Act)*

This provided for the privatisation of the British Airports Authority (BAA). The NCC takes no general view on public/private ownership questions. This is partly because this is ideological territory and as such is the proper province of the political parties, and partly because *who* owns an industry is less crucial as a consumer issue than *how* that industry delivers its goods and/or services. The Council is however interested in the wider issue of the regulation of monopoly utilities – in this case the provision of aeronautical services to airlines and of non-aeronautical services (car parks, duty-free shops and refreshment facilities) to the travelling public – and in competition policy.

In the early stages of proceedings on the Bill, it seemed that the prospects for influencing its outcome might be good. The Council had recently completed for the Government a major study of European air transport (*Air Transport and the Consumer*, HMSO, 1986) which had been favourably received. Contacts at official level in the Department of Transport were excellent.

The Council's main concern was that the declared thrust of the Government's air transport policy, supported by the NCC, which was broadly pro-liberalisation, appeared to sit rather oddly with some of the more restrictive and monopolistic provisions of the Bill. There seemed to be no guarantee that a privatised BAA would not use its powers to protect existing monopolies or oligopolies on either the aeronautical or non-aeronautical side of its business. The structure of regulation proposed in the Bill, giving, among other things, an intriguing new role to the Monopolies and Mergers Commission (the duty to conduct retrospective quinquennial reviews), was in the Council's view unsatisfactory.

NCC staff drafted a series of amendments on competition, regulation, access to information and consumer representation at airports. All were tabled. The arguments on competition and regulation were well aired in the Commons, and contributed to one Government defeat (later reversed) in Committee. However the signals coming from officials were uniformly discouraging. There was nothing substantial to point to by way of ministerial commitment by the time the Bill had completed its passage through the Commons. In view of other pressures, further Parliamentary work by the NCC on the *Airports Bill* was therefore dropped.

2. *The Building Societies Bill (now Act)*

The NCC's most important influence on the *Building Societies Bill* was entirely pre-Parliamentary. By legislating, among other things, to empower the societies to offer their customers a wider range of services, including cheque books and credit cards, the Government was responding directly to one of the recommendations of the Council's report *Banking Services and the Consumer* (Methuen, 1983), a major study which had itself been commissioned three years earlier by the then Minister of Consumer Affairs, Mrs Sally Oppenheim MP.

NCC lobbying on the main liberalising provisions of the Bill was supportive and largely confined to Commons Second Reading. It was judged, correctly, that the forces opposed to these provisions were too weak to do significant damage. What remained to be done was a simple piece of opportunism in which the initiative was taken by a back-bench Conservative MP. The Bill as drafted did not provide for a Building Societies Ombudsman. Cross-party support was obtained for amendments which inserted provision for a statutory Ombudsman scheme (the first of its kind in the UK).

The supporting arguments were drawn principally from the NCC's 1983 banking report. The detailed drafting of what is a complex scheme was done by government officials after ministers had indicated their support for the principle.

3. *The Education Bill (now Act)*

The NCC's main contribution to proceedings on this Bill was to bring together a coalition of parent/pupil interests comprising the Advisory Centre for Education, the Confederation for the Advancement of State Education, the National Association of Governors and Managers and the Welsh Consumer Council. The NCC acted as a clearing house for the exchange of views and supplied what were, in effect, Parliamentary consultancy services.

A number of amendments were drafted and promoted – on the composition of governing bodies, procedures for electing governors, arrangements for training governors, and on the presentation and content of governing bodies' annual reports. There were no direct successes in Parliamentary terms; subsequently, however, the substance of many of these arguments – particularly on training for school governors – has been accepted by the Department of Education and Science (DES).

One proposal advanced by the Council and its allies during proceedings on the *Education Bill* has yielded fewer fruits. This was the proposition that provision for the election of pupil governors should be given statutory effect. Since enactment, the DES has issued guidance in a circular on the desirability of senior pupils being involved in the work of school governing bodies.

There was one particular difficulty in working on this Bill. This was the squeezing out effect of the public interest focus on other, larger issues addressed by the Bill – specifically corporal punishment and freedom of speech in universities. This made it harder for the Council and its allies to generate media interest in its own concerns and thereby increase lobbying elbow-room in Parliament.

4. *The Gas Bill (now Act)*

The *Gas Bill* provided for the privatisation of the British Gas Corporation and, amongst other things, for the replacement of the old National Gas Consumers Council (NGCC) by a new Gas Consumers Council (GCC). The NCC worked alongside the NGCC and agreed an appropriate division of labour.

The Council achieved a remarkable success early in the session by persuading the Commons Select Committee on Energy to endorse much of the NCC's critical approach to the Bill (Commons Select Committee on Energy, 1986). However, it proved more difficult to translate this achievement into legislative effect. The main lines of the Bill had been agreed between the Department of Energy and the British Gas Corporation (BGC) well in advance of publication. The Government's firmness of purpose was reflected in the exceptionally tight drafting of the Bill and its near complete refusal to accept amendments. The only significant changes that were made to the Bill (and its accompanying Authorisation) in Parliament were on matters which NCC and NGCC had raised. The two most important concerned the duties of the new Director-General of the Office of Gas Supply (OFGAS) and the extension of the powers of the new Gas Consumers Council to cover complaints about appliance sales, service and installation.

These were satisfying achievements. Nevertheless, the Council's failure to persuade the Government to strengthen the Director-General's powers to deal with the abuse, or suspected abuse, of the BGC's effective monopoly in a key consumer market, was disappointing. It had become clear by the time the Bill had completed its Commons' passage that the Government would not yield any more ground. Further work on the Bill was therefore dropped.

5. *The Shops Bill*

The *Shops Bill* provided for the de-restricting of shop opening hours. It closely followed the recommendations of the 1984 Auld Committee (*Report of the Committee of Inquiry into Proposals to Amend the Shops Act*, Cmnd 9376), which in turn substantially reflected the abolitionist arguments put forward by consumer organisations. The one important difference between Auld and the Bill was that Auld recommended the retention of wages council protection for shopworkers, whilst the Bill only conferred protection on the under-18s.

The NCC attempted to assist the Bill's progress through Parliament whilst not expressing any view on the issue of shopworker protection. (Employment questions formally lie outside the scope of the Council's brief). Consumers' Association, the National Federation of Consumer Groups, NCC and others repeatedly drew attention to the ludicrous anomalies created by the *Shops Act 1962,* and to the evidence of majority public opinion which was, and has remained, consistently pro-liberalisation.

In spite of this effort – and to almost universal astonishment – the Bill was defeated on its Second Reading in the Commons in April 1986. The margin of the Government's defeat, 14 votes, was exactly equal to the number of votes cast against it by the Ulster Unionists. Sixty-eight Conservative MPs entered the Noe lobby; another thirty-eight abstained or stayed away.

In retrospect, it is clear that the Bill's supporters had lost the initiative in public relations terms some weeks before the final vote. The Keep Sunday Special group fought a skilful (and generously funded) campaign. Nevertheless, the Bill would still have received a successful Second Reading and would still, most probably, have been enacted in some form, had the Government not made two or three serious tactical errors, culminating in a quite disastrous piece of front bench mishandling on the day of the key Commons debate.

In retrospect too, it is clear that consumer organisations did not lobby hard *enough* to prevent what was undoubtedly a very major Parliamentary defeat – for them as much as for the Government. The NCC must take its share of the responsibility for this failure.

6. *The Financial Services Bill (now Act)*

The purpose of this Bill was to establish a new regulatory framework to govern the conduct of the City and to protect the interests of investors. This was new territory for the NCC and staff were surprised by the amount of discussion that took place in Westminster around the issues on which the Council had provided briefs. This was due in part to the fact that opinion within the financial community was sharply divided on a number of matters; it was useful to the protagonists in these arguments to be able to call on NCC's aid from time to time.

The Council set itself a number of objectives. It tried to get a complete ban on cold-calling written into the Bill, and failed. Proposals for greater disclosure of commissions and charges were advanced with partial success. NCC won half a victory at the very last ditch with arguments for proportional lay representation on the governing bodies of self-regulatory organisations, and could also claim some credit for getting proposals to license individual salesmen dropped (the argument being that such proposals could not be effective).

However, the evaluation of 'success' and 'failure' in lobbying on this Bill was – and remains – difficult because of the amount of important operational detail left to delegated legislation (regulations and codes of practice). The many representations that have been made since enactment on a variety of key issues have been led by Consumers' Association.

7. *The Social Security Bill (now Act)*

During the passage of this Bill, NCC focused on proposals for a Social Fund to replace the existing single payments system. In particular, the Council attempted to persuade Parliament to insert into the Bill provision for an independent system of complaints redress for clients. With others, NCC argued that the proposed new arrangements would place too much discretionary power in the hands of DHSS officers, and that specific criteria should be drawn up to help claimants know their entitlements.

The NCC Parliamentary Office drafted amendments designed to create an independent appeals procedure for users of the Social Fund. A variation of one of these amendments was successfully tabled and pressed in the Lords but was subsequently reversed by the Government in the Commons. The Council also argued that the Social Security Advisory Committee should be given a specific duty to monitor the workings of the new Social Fund; an amendment tabled to this effect was lost.

A collection of defeats and unsatisfactory 'compromises' was all that NCC had to show for its work on this Bill, in spite of the fact that the substance of Council's arguments was articulated on all sides in Parliament. Like other critics, the NCC ran hard up against the immovable obstacle of the principle of a cash-limited Social Fund.

8. *The Consumer Safety (Amendment) Bill (subsequently Act)*

This was drafted by counsel for NCC as a Private Member's Bill at the request of Conal Gregory MP, a backbench Conservative. It was in a sense, therefore, the result of a piece of reverse lobbying. Gregory had drawn twentieth place in the annual Ballot. He had long been concerned about safety matters, particularly unsafe childrens' toys, and was determined to take a Parliamentary initiative designed to tighten up the law. He approached NCC and asked for Council support. The Council provided back-up policy advice and expert drafting assistance, in addition to public relations and media services, throughout the Bill's passage through Parliament.

The purpose of the Bill (now consolidated in the *Consumer Protection Act 1987*) was to amend the *Consumer Safety Act 1978* by providing the relevant enforcement officers with greater powers to stop and seize imported goods suspected of being dangerous. It gave effect to some of the recommendations of the Government's White Paper *The Safety of Goods* (Department of Trade and Industry, 1984, Cmnd 9302). It was a small step in the right direction, though more far-reaching changes were subsequently presented to Parliament by the Government in the 1986/87 session.

The Council was delighted to have been able to assist in the enactment of the Bill. The resulting legislation was, however, far from perfect from a consumer point of view, as indeed it remains following consolidation. In lobbying terms the hand that the Council had to play in negotiating with the Department of Trade and Industry, on Mr Gregory's behalf, was not a strong one because of the fragility of the Parliamentary procedure involved. The Government could have killed the Bill at any time. NCC therefore felt obliged to recommend to the sponsoring MP a number of compromises which were as difficult for it to support as they were for Mr Gregory to accept. Lobbying must always balance the desirable with the attainable.

9. *The Housing and Planning Bill (now Act)*

This provided, amongst other things, for the commercial re-development of local authority housing estates. NCC staff drafted a number of amendments on arrangements for consulting tenants living on estates being considered for re-development. These were tabled by Conservative members during Commons Standing Committee proceedings. They were not accepted by the minister as drafted, but the tone of the Government's response was encouraging. Subsequently, the Government did agree to specify in circular form the factors that were to be taken into account by the Secretary of State when approving development plans; one of these was to be the question of whether or not tenants had been consulted. Other amendments on tenant participation in housing management schemes made no headway.

Other Parliamentary work in the 1985/86 session

The heavy burden of work imposed by the need to respond to the Government's legislative programme and work on the *Gregory Bill* left the NCC little time for ancillary Parliamentary activity. The one other substantial contribution during the year was made in the Lords.

The Council made a major input into the work of a House of Lords Select Committee's investigation into European consumer policy. The final report of this Committee, published late in the session, was a very helpful analysis of the way forward for EEC consumer policy.

Conclusions: 'success' and 'failure'

It is exceptionally difficult to make conclusive evaluations of 'success' and 'failure' in the lobbying business. This is especially true of the labyrinthine world of issue advocacy, which the NCC inhabits, a landscape which should be carefully distinguished from that of commercial lobbying where 'winners' and 'losers' are often more easily identified.

What the two activities have in common is that they both take place in a working environment in which, or so it sometimes appears, the world is divided more or less equally between those who claim too much and those who (more wisely) claim too little. The reality is that very few lobbying interests are ever able to achieve their goals unaided; that is why the NCC invests so much effort into putting together alliances.

No Parliamentary session is exactly like any other; and no Bill presents quite the same challenges, opportunities and risks as any other. Much of the NCC's lobbying is long-haul work and must be judged against correspondingly wide horizons. In the Parliamentary session I have used as a case study, there were some long-term successes, particularly in the financial services field, and some major failures, notably on shop hours. The overall conclusion, however, is that the Council has more than enough to show for its efforts to justify the high priority which it gives to Parliamentary and allied activity.

8 Policy and Influence: MAFF and the NFU

BARNEY HOLBECHE

The NFU was set up and maintained by farmers to do well by them. That was our *raison d'etre* and we go about it in a purposeful way. The title is *Policy and Influence: MAFF and the NFU*. I shall go a little wider than that. As I hope to describe the NFU's interests in Government go wider than MAFF. The agricultural industry is a very large industry and one which touches from time to time on a whole range of Government departments. In fact I was looking at a list and there are hardly any that we don't deal with on a regular basis: the Foreign Office is one. We deal with virtually all the rest. The other thing I would like to underline from the title policy and influence is *influence*. Influence I think is the right word because in no sense could the NFU claim that it is in a position of power. We cannot pull any levers anywhere. What we can do is persuade people who have got access to the levers to operate them in directions we think will be beneficial. We are very much in a position of influencing and encouraging and persuading.

About the NFU : It was established in 1908. It represents the interests of farmers in England and Wales and has sister bodies in Scotland and N Ireland with whom we work closely. (Even more so now that we are members of the Common Market and so many of the decisions that affect the industry are taken in Brussels as opposed to London in pre EEC days.) The farmers are owners and occupiers of the land. The NFU is not a trade union which is a common misconception ... There is a lot of confusion about this. I cannot think of another trade federation that has the word 'union' in its title. Opinion polls that have been conducted suggest that a good third to 40% of the public that responded to a questionnaire saying who do you think the NFU represent said it was agricultural workers rather than the farmers.

We have over 90,000 working farmer members in England and Wales and quite a lot of associate members like bankers and representatives of local firms who take out an associate membership in order to receive papers on what the NFU is up to, etc. We are funded entirely from subscription income; the subscrip tion nowadays usually goes up almost annually ... the subscription is now £45 basic and 55 pence per acre which is estimated will result in an average sub. of £105 per farmer with a yield to the NFU of something over £10 million. Now that average sub. of over £105, is of course, a pretty high figure for a voluntary organisation. You will appreciate that there is no way that we can insist that farmers belong to the NFU, but we reckon something like 75% of active commercial farmers do take up membership and naturally, because we are not in a position to insist, quite a large amount of our effort particularly at local branch level is spent on going around trying to make sure that people are paying their subscriptions on their full acreages. It's a pity that such a lot of effort has to go into that, but I think that it is probably true of any voluntary organisation that the act of attracting money from people is a desperately time consuming thing and there we are. We try to get round that sort of thing by variable direct debit and the like. Of course farmers respond very much to how much they feel the NFU performs ...

The structure of the NFU is important in giving an understanding of our lobbying activities. One very essential feature is that the NFU is a democracy from our local branches up to county level. We have 49 county branches in England and Wales through to our National Council and our national leaders. The Council of the NFU consists of about 100 farmers who are delegates from each of our county branches. The number of branches per county varies according to size of membership so Anglesey and the Isle of Wight get 1 and Devon gets 4. Most of them get 2 or 3. Most delegates are elected annually and they have to come back from meetings in London and report at the local meetings. They are held accountable to the farming community and if the farming community perceive that they have failed in representing the interests of Shropshire or Suffolk or wherever then the chances are they won't get elected next time round. Some council delegates only last a year, some last much longer. Until recently one 'father of the house', as it were, had been on the Council for 25 years. A lot has to do with the confidence which the farming community has in a delegate's ability to represent their interests. The NFU acts as a sort of agricultural parliament. As you would expect there are committees dealing with all sorts of agricultural commodities such as livestock, cereals, and so on and there are also the so-called services committees which deal in economic policy, legal matters (we support all sorts of test cases), a technical committee and the committee I'm most concerned with, the parliamentary committee which, as its name implies, scrutinizes legislation going through Parliament affecting agriculture. The office-holders of the NFU, president, deputy president and vice-president, are elected annually – there is an interesting rule in force which I haven't observed in any other organisation. The President, in his second year, has to have 80% support from the Council in order to continue in office. In other words all it needs is 21% of people to vote against him and he is out. This has the advantage that, for the leader of the NFU to continue in office over a number of years, clearly he must have the overwhelming support of the Council behind him.

In the case of Lord Plumb, for example, he was president for nine years and eventually resigned ... although there have been cases of casualties in the past through this pretty tough rule. Many organisations have presidents or leaders who are elected for one year – then they leave after the end of that period of office. They have just learned the job – are becoming most useful to the organisation and their period of office ends....

In the NFU we have something like 300 local branch secretaries whose bosses are the 49 county secretaries. We are now in the process of rationalising into ten regional administrative centres. The staff are all permanent paid officials of the NFU although the local branch people are also local insurance agents for the NFU Mutual Insurance Company. There's a headquarters secretariat in Knightsbridge with something like 150 staff including about 80 executive staff. These staff in London act in the manner of civil servants to our political masters. My immediate political masters, for example, are the chairman and vice-chairman of the parliamentary committee. I am in regular contact with them about issues as they come up and how we are going to handle them.

I have gone out of my way to stress the importance of democracy in the NFU because I think it is an important factor in the way the organisation works and I think that it helps to make the NFU as representational as the rather inefficient processes of democracy can allow. There are a number of other pressure groups whom we come across ... who are not, I would suggest, as directly representative of the interests they seek to serve as is the NFU. There are some bodies I can think of for example where their decisions are made by a handful of permanent officials or by a council/executive committee where members are invited rather than elected. The people who ultimately decide NFU policy – the NFU Council – are people who have been elected. (They may have been influenced on the way by the permanent officials, but, at the end of the day, it is the elected people who have the say over what the policy is, and how the money is collected, and how it is spent and so on.)

So the name of the game for the NFU is leadership. This doesn't mean to say we are constrained in adopting new ideas by the pace of the thinking of our slowest and most conservative farmers, but equally it does mean the NFU must not get significantly out of step with what the majority of farmers are thinking and doing at any one time. Because that way disaster lies! It is clearly essential, in order to maintain credibility, that the NFU is seen to be truly representative of its members and one of the ways in which we achieve this is by constant two-way communications between farmers on the ground and the NFU and its leaders. This means frequent attendance of our leaders at local meetings; firstly, to tell members what is going on in the NFU nationally to explain current policy difficulties or threats we face and what we are to do about them and, secondly, to hear from the farmers themselves what their views are on the problems, what priorities they attach to objectives.

This process has several benefits. It means that NFU leaders can develop NFU policy in the light of their judgment on the art of the possible and the current views of farmers. It also means that farmers are better clued up than they would otherwise be for lobbying their MPs in the constituencies. One of the advantages of the agricultural industry is that because the industry is so geographically dispersed (unlike, say, car factories where there are only perhaps half a dozen direct constituency interests) farmers have a direct input into a large number of MPs on a constituency basis. These troops on the ground are a very valuable political resource and, therefore, it is essential from a NFU point of view that they are supplied with up-to-date ammunition to fire at their targets.

Lobbying

The NFU is sometimes referred to as a very effective pressure group on behalf of its members and a model to others. If this is so it is not because there are any magic techniques known only to the NFU nor that there are any special arrangements behind closed doors. It is sometimes suggested that because the NFU works closely with the Ministry of Agriculture, the government department responsible for the NFU, in some sense the Ministry is the NFU's poodle and that it will obey the orders of the NFU whatever they may be. That really just isn't so. There are issues where we are in agreement, but equally there are plenty of issues where we fall out and we're not afraid to say so publicly. For example, in 1980 the Ministry took into their heads to abolish prior approval for capital grants whereby the farmer had to have a written piece of paper before the grants would be paid. This system had an advantage from an environmental point of view that you could influence the way a farmer was going to carry out a particular operation in the countryide. This was an important way of vetting and checking that the farmer was not going to do something silly and result in adverse publicity for the industry and so on. The Ministry maintained that they were going to make a huge saving... anyway we felt it was the wrong decision for the reasons I've indicated and in that case there was a grand alliance (involving, incidentally, at least the tacit support of the Department of the Environment) between the conservation lobby and the NFU to have them stopped. I regret to say we didn't quite manage it although ironically in 1986 the Ministry took on a new statutory duty to balance the interests of agriculture and conservation!

I think that although it is nice to have this reputation of being effective if you look at the evidence we lose far more cases than we win. I would like to suggest that this also applies to any other pressure group. What I think is a reasonable aim is to get some of what we want most of the time. Occasionally, we get all of what we want although, usually, it's on very limited issues where that happens and, equally, there are occasions when we don't get anything of what we want – which causes great distress amongst our members. But one of the techniques involved is to get the best deal going and then explain to the farmers that this is the best deal in the present circumstances. Each issue and circumstances around it are different so the approaches must be varied accordingly. Some lobbies do seem to have difficulty in judging well the art of the possible – to see what is on and what is not – and they tend to be rather plaintive about a compromise solution that may have been worked out that does not meet all their requirements. I believe we have to be realistic on this. After all the Government is supposed to be running the country not the NFU, or the consumers, Friends of the Earth, RSPCA or CBI. When we are all lobbying, it is obvious that all of those interests, which are often conflicting, cannot possiby get all of what they want all of the time. It's a very competitive atmosphere. When a good deal has been obtained, of course we try to seek credit with our members – but not at the expense of damaging relationships with Government and politicians. Tomorrow is another day and another issue.

About qualities and techniques. Luck and skill obviously have a role in lobbying, but most of all the qualities required are pretty mundane – maintenance of relations I would put pretty high up the list. That means once you have set up a liaison system with civil servants and the politicians it has got to be maintained and updated. It is important to be vigilant about changes that take place in the staffing of government departments; changes that take place with politicians,by-elections, Government reshuffles, for example. It's important to keep tabs on the House of Lords. Some elderly peer might not have been in the House for years, but you may discover he has a 40 year old son who is an active farmer and might be prepared, eventually, to do some work on agriculture.

Patience and persistence are also qualities which are very important. Some issues may take many years to achieve progress on. For example, the issue of the control of dogs may be rather trivial to some, but not to farmers when some 10,000 livestock are either killed or maimed by uncontrolled dogs every year. We have been trying for 70 years to get something done on that and it is just beginning to move a little now perhaps. It really does take a very long time on some issues, so it is really important to be patient.

It is also important to have an enthusiasm for the political decision-making process in general – not just in agriculture – because Westminster in particular is a very exotic hot house of current issues and dealings and movements. A big issue in some other department of Government may have an indirect influence on the way in which agriculture is dealt with....

We have to have a certain amount of stamina. Some of these activities in Parliament take place in the middle of the night. I think 5 o'clock in the morning is my latest. It doesn't happen that often, but, on major bills, for example the *Wildlife and Countryside Bill* ran on for many days well into the night and, even if you brief politicians to represent your point of view and there's nothing more you can do, it's always a good thing to be there – partly to feel the atmosphere, but also to show your solidarity with those people who have been kind enough to accept your brief to do something.

Finally, the other quality you require is a sense of humour when for example your favourite private member's bill, which you have spent a year gearing up for, goes down the Swanee because of some procedural mess up which might take place in the Bill which is at the head of the queue. This sort of thing happens not infrequently.

Techniques of Lobbying

Regular contact with politicians is obviously essential – that means backbench MPs, cabinet ministers and junior ministers. I do think the latter are important. A lot depends on their personality and particular ability and I do think they are well worth cultivating. The House of Lords is particularly important at the present time with this Government having a large majority in the Commons. With one or two notable exceptions the Lords is about the only place we can get the Government defeated, so it's well worth doing a bit of work there.

Another aspect of regular contact is that it is very much a long term process. Political lobbying is not a smash and grab. You shouldn't go down to Westminster and grab a politician by the lapels and demand that he does something. You've got to cultivate them and it takes time. Like gardening some of your plants will come up nicely and others not at all. The only way you can find out which ones are to be successful is to try it....

Another important factor is to have a united front in presenting a particular viewpoint. We do everything we can to resolve internal policy differences between farmers behind the closed doors of the NFU before we come out in public and take a particular line. My experience is if you allow your dirty washing to be seen in public the chances are it will become dirtier still and that's not particularly helpful to winning your cause. So, decide what you want first, whether you've got full support from your membership and then get on with it.

Getting in early is a very important golden rule. We have a sort of intelligence role on behalf of the farmers to keep our ears to the ground to find out what new initiatives are being proposed and what legislation may be coming on with the object of influencing it from the outset. It may be legislation that we like and that we simply want to make sure that it's in a form preferable to the farming community. It may be legislation to which we are hotly opposed, or it may be something in between. Whatever it is we will be wanting to take an interest from the earliest stage. There is no question that once a piece of legislation reaches Parliament you may be able to tinker around the edges, but the prospect of getting any significant changes at that stage are very remote indeed – particularly with a Government majority like the present one. Therefore it makes it that much more important to seek to try to get it right before it ever enters Parliament.

Briefing of politicians is obviously absolutely essential. You try to aim for the briefest of briefs. Politicians are busy people. You write them a 6-page paper and it will probably end up in the bin, unless of course they are specialists, in which case they will come back for more in any event. It is important that briefing should be accurate. There is no sense in giving a politician something which doesn't tell the whole truth or which distorts the case. The case must obviously be presented in the strongest possible way. It can also be presented in different forms according to the recipients. Therefore the sort of brief that would be given to a Conservative back bencher might be different from that given to a Labour back bencher depending on what points you want to bring out. It is perfectly possible to do that and maintain intellectual honesty and consistency of argument!

So, yes, detailed briefs can be used for the specialists; we also draft suggestions for parliamentary questions with the intention of either extracting information or pressing the Minister to take a particular course on a particular issue. Also, as you would expect, if there is a piece of legislation we want to have changed then we are in the business of drafting amendments to the legislation and then hawking the amendments around the politicians with a view to having them tabled and debated. It's a very hit and miss affair. It's very much a question of win some, lose some. We don't, generally speaking, go in for mass lobbying of politicians except when there is a strong demand from the membership to do so. My feeling is that getting hundreds of farmers to Westminster and trying to get them to meet their MPs is a very haphazard business. It rarely has much effect. You can often be much more effective in a quiet more selective sort of way than you can bringing up a vast army of people to London. Sometimes it's helpful from the point of view of the farmers who feel frustrated and they want to do something. But really it does not tend to be very effective.

Another technique is that we can play an entrepreneurial role. When a problem needs resolving the first thing to do is to decide who can make the decision to have the change made that we want and then we try to bring together the problem, the politicians who might be concerned with it, and the means of resolution. One example I can use concerns burst water mains. Until relatively recently, if you had a water main going across your farm and it burst, a tremendous amount of damage could be caused, but the water company was not responsible for compensating you for that damage unless negligence could be proved, and so a change in the law was required. We looked at the cases we had had in the past five years and we identified the constituencies where these cases had taken place, and we narrowed it down to one case where the MP concerned was a back bencher who was a lawyer (it was a legally complex issue) and who also, personality-wise, was someone who would not take no for an answer. So he was the ideal candidate. We then looked for a vehicle and a Water Bill was going through Parliament at the time concerned with something quite different – not this issue at all. We got him to raise it on the second reading. He was selected for Standing Committee – he ran our amendments there and eventually we'd persuaded the Government of the rightness of this cause and the Government itself came forward with a suitably drafted amendment later in the Bill's progress. So that was an interesting case of trying to bring all the bits of the jigsaw together to reach the objective that you want.

Another aspect of this entrepreneurial role is finding allies: allies are very important. Within reason I don't mind who the NFU goes into an alliance with if there's a reasonable prospect of obtaining success. It is often the case that if several organisations or bodies are saying similar things to a wide range of politicians there's more chance of making progress on that issue than if you're just saying it yourself. And, equally, those allies might be Government departments in certain instances.

Credibility

In presenting a case to the Ministry and to politicians your case must be accurate, reasonable and politically attractive. Generally speaking, the strength of the case will determine the progress that can be made with it. We have been successful on some weak cases, but there are many more examples where little progress has been made on good cases. The important thing is not to discredit the source by over-selling any particular argument. There is a need to produce good hard evidence to sustain claims.

We look for a professional relationship with politicians. We work together where we can. In terms of party politics, it is true that some Tories see us as natural friends, some Labour members see us as part of the natural enemy. Ironically we're probably neither. Agriculture goes on as politicians come and go – we must continue to deal with them all!

The sad tale of the eggs and salmonella scare in December 1988 provides some interesting material for the student of politics and lessons for others. Farmers have seen with horror how quickly a sector of their industry can be devastated by unsubstantiated allegations about its products, but can take some comfort from the striking demonstration of how effective their organised lobby can be. By failing to obey the first rule of politics (if you are in a hole, stop digging!) a colourful but inflexible Junior Minister has seen that the old adage that 'any publicity is good publicity' does not hold good. And taxpayers have seen with dismay the bill they must foot for serious Government mishandling of a problem which it allowed to become a crisis of its own making and which otherwise need not have resulted in grave damage to an industry, the loss of many jobs in it, and significant calls on the public purse. The normal close contact between Government and affected interests is mutually beneficial in usually preventing the development of such crises.

Note: This chapter was based on an oral presentation to the Public Administration Committee Conference in September, 1985. It was updated in December 1988. 'Published in its original form in *Public Policy and Administration*, vol.1, No.3, 1986.'

PART III: Criticisms and Conclusions

9 The Ethics of Lobbying: Why James VI [I] was Right

ALAN DOIG

James VI [I] may have been a lousy king but he knew enough about the qualities needed to be an MP to warn the handful of voters in 1620 not to elect to Parliament young, inexperienced men, 'that are not ripe and mature for so grave a council' or 'curious and wrangling lawyers who may seek reputation by stirring needless questions' (Porritt, 1903, p.381). The objections to lawyer-MPs, voiced often during the next 200 years, concerned, in addition to their frequent absences in the courts and their solicitation of Crown patronage, the blatant use of their parliamentary position to tout for work as spokesmen in the House for those seeking Commons' approval for the vast amount of private legislation. It was not until 1858, however, that the House tried to stamp out such paid advocacy by resolving that it was a breach of privilege 'to bring forward, promote or advocate any matter in the House on an agreement for payment'.

Yet in 1969 a Commons Select Committee was earnestly discussing the need to distinguish between 'advocacy of a cause in Parliament for a fee or retainer' and 'the advancement of an argument by a Member who, through a continuing association with an industry, service or concern from which he may obtain some remuneration, is able to draw upon specialist knowledge of the subject under debate' (*Select Committee on Members' Interests*, HC 57, 1969, para 110).

Parliament has traditionally sought to differentiate between behaviour that it will or will not tolerate, and the latter has invariably been governed by a belief that a Member's independence and freedom of action should not be compromised or controlled. The 1858 resolution reflects this tradition in that, bearing in mind that being an MP has never been seen as a full time, and before 1911 not even a salaried, occupation, Parliament has dealt with the question of outside financial interests or income by imposing restrictions where they impinge on or compromise an MP's parliamentary duties. The 1969 Select Committee, set up by the Labour Government in response to concern over the increase in lobbying and the activities of some lobbyists both inside and outside the House, wanted to distinguish between paid advocacy and interest-representation that involved payment from outside interests. It wanted to extend the 1858 resolution by banning advocacy and allowing interest-representation but insisting on, for the latter, a clear declaration of interest with the failure to do so to be treated as a contempt of the House (the second most serious offence against its standards). The Select Committee thus wanted to ban the 'mischief' of advocacy in all its forms but allow speaking on interest-related matters when to do so was 'in the public interest', so long as the interest was disclosed. It believed that the 'honour' of MPs was the best means of policing its recommendations and rejected the idea of a Register and a special committee to deal with interests.

In 1974, after some well-publicised abuses, the then Labour Government overturned the whole thrust of the 1969 conclusions by introducing both the Register and an attendant Select Committee and requiring a disclosure of financial interests, whether acceptable or not. Much of the current concern over lobbying stems directly from those decisions and from the failure of the Select Committee to clarify what its function is and its failure to come to grips with the basics – what is lobbying, what is unacceptable and acceptable behaviour by lobbyists and MPs, how should lobbying be policed, and by whom – and reflected the Select Committee's failure to understand the nature and problems of lobbying generally within the decision-making process of Westminster and Whitehall.

British Political Culture, Lobbying and The Public Interest

The 1985 Report of the Select Committee on Members' Interests intoned that 'the principal (sic) of "lobbying" is not in question. It is the right of any citizen to lobby his Member of Parliament and if he considers that his case can be better advanced with professional assistance he has every right to avail himself of that assistance' (*Select Committee on Members' Interests*, 1985, HC 408, para 3). It is also the practice, if not the principle, of policy and decision-making in Britain that lobbies and lobbyists have an integral role to play, a role that has been institutionalised by successive governments' faith in the quasi-corporatist approach of representation, consultation and cooperation and by the incorporation of lobbies and interests into the myriad of advisory and executive bodies that surround the central machinery of government. All lobbies and interests, however categorised, aim to influence policy and legislation, whether at formulation, decision or implementation stages, in their favour. Such influence may range from the professional lobbyist seeking to protect the Bristol Channel Ship Repair Yard from nationalisation plans, to the charity Age Concern seeking 'to raise the threshold of interest in aging in an area where there are many competing interests for people's time.'

There is nothing wrong with such contacts or relationships which have a crucial role in the development of policy agendas, the implementation of decisions, the mobilisation, articulation and involvement of specific interests in a way that political parties cannot provide, and the provision of a countervailing balance to centralised government power (Davies, 1985, p.xv). On the other hand it is equally important for 'governments and politicians to preserve an area of autonomy, to protect the point at which politics comes to rest from the infinite demands to which it is subject ...' (Robertson, 1982, p.194). In other words, there should in principle be a point where governments have the privacy and freedom to make decisions where, for example, wider public or national interest, or those without an organised voice, can have due consideration over and above the demands of specific or special interests.

In practice the role of lobbying and the presence of 'permanent' lobbies, the existence of specific and specialised clients or constituencies of Whitehall departments, has meant that accommodation, cooperation and agreement with those lobbies and interests invariably predominates, with means rather than objectives the point of discussion. Such lobbies and interests have long learned to exploit shared cultural, social and educational backgrounds as well as to play by the Whitehall mores of trust, responsible behaviour, secrecy, compromise and gradualism which has resulted in the development of communities of interests and consensual decision-making. Thus 'part of the reason for the Department of Transport's bias towards the road lobby is that the lobbyists and the civil servants come from similar backgrounds ... and almost without exception they share the seemingly trivial details of social conditioning ... that are so important in prejudicing attitudes to transport policy' (Hamer, 1987, p.112). Furthermore closeness is often encouraged to facilitate decisionmaking. The Select Committee on Defence approvingly noted that the Ministry of Defence 'has assured us that the Procurement Executive's door is always open to the Defence Manufacturers' Association ... We welcome the wider dissemination of information and recommend that these briefings be as comprehensive as possible and that the Ministry should be as open as possible at all levels with the relevant parts of the defence industry and act in partnership with them.' (*Defence Committee*, 1981-82, HC 22, para.77)

Departments can, as a consequence, be 'captured' by their major client or interest or, conversely, departments can come to see certain interests as their 'property' and essentially become lobbyists on their behalf, in areas as diverse as transport, food, agriculture as well as defence. As Self and Storing said of the Ministry of Agriculture's almost symbiotic relationship with the National Farmers Union:

> Politicians and civil servants are likely to regard their tasks as completed when accommodation between the parties has been reached. They tend to lose sight of their broader obligation which is not only to accommodate the interests of conflicting parties but to search out and to promote the broader public interest. (Self and Storing, 1971 ed, p.220)

As a result:

> One cost involved in the increasingly close relationship between groups and governments is that the policy process has if anything excluded the general public from any effective influence ... policy-makers have retreated into a definition of 'public interest' that may be rather narrow in that it tends towards assuming that public interest equals the balance of organised pressure in a given policy area.
>
> (Richardson and Jordan, 1979, p.174)

Independence, Impartiality and Influence

On matters of wider public concern the influence of permanent lobbies can have important implications both for Ministers and the public on matters from nuclear energy to what we eat. When the Department of Energy decided that the US-designed Pressurised Water Reactor (PWR) was the future for nuclear power stations, it was the line forcibly taken with Governments. Tony Benn has claimed that when he tried to suggest gas cooled reactors;

> The Permanent Secretary marched into my office, with all his officials, including the deputy secretaries, the chief scientist and he said: 'We want the pressure water reactor' and I said: Well I take a contrary view, I want you to draw a paper on the advanced gas cooled reactors and he declined to do so. I had to go to my political advisers to do it and the Permanent Secretary then briefed the CPRS and other departments in the Cabinet against me.
>
> (*Treasury and Civil Service Committee*, 1985-6, HC 92, Vol II, p.145)

Once the Department and its clients in the energy industry had made up their minds 'research and practical development in the many alternative ways of producing or conserving energy has had, on the whole, little or no support from the Thatcher or previous British governments'. (Baker, 1988, p.91) Furthermore when opponents to PWR had their say before the 1981-85 Layfield inquiry into the proposed 'Sizewell B' nuclear power station, 'what did the Layfield Report achieve other than to delay public and Parliamentary debate until it was too late to substitute any alternative for the PWR? ... it may have fostered the dangerous illusion that energy policy in general and nuclear energy policy in particular are beyond the capacity of ordinary people and must be left to engineers, economists and QCs'. (Baker, 1988, p.96)

The British Nutrition Foundation (BNF) was set up by major food manufacturers to promote 'good food habits'. It was sponsored primarily by processed food firms and many of its committees have members on various DHSS and MAFF committees. It was represented on the National Advisory Committee on Nutrition Education (NACNE) which, in 1981-3, prepared a report arguing that Western food was a major cause of non-infectious disease. Many of the fat– and sugar-laden foods whose intake would need reducing were products of BNF's sponsors. BNF were not happy with publication. Their Director-General who resigned in 1984 spoke about the 'unhealthy cosy' relations with Whitehall with both sides keen to silence the report:

> The tactic was to delay it and delay it again, so that everybody would get fed up and at no point would it see the light of day. If that failed then it was to be published as low key as possible with as little reporting as possible and no official support. The most important point was to persuade the Department of Health

that on no account should it be published as a Department of Health report ...
It should be as hard to get at as possible by making a small print run ... and to
present the report as a discussion paper by a bunch of scientists who were not
even eminent. (Cannon, 1987, p.356).

The NACNE report was eventually published in Autumn 1983 by the Health
Education Council (this troublesome body was later abolished as an independent quango) but ignored by Ministers and civil servants alike. The
DHSS's Chief Medical Officer, who on retirement moved to chairmanship
of a BNF committee, accused the report of exceeding its remit and of being
unsuitable, on scientific grounds and balance, to DHSS, BNF and MAFF
representatives on NACNE.

It is practically impossible to break the interaction of Government
Departments with major related economic interests. There is nothing
unconstitutional or illegal about such relationships but they increasingly
favour certain groups who seek to cement their closeness by employing MPs,
former MPs (usually ex-Cabinet Ministers) and former senior civil servants.
Parliament has been critical of the destination of these civil servants, and the
one-way traffic (few outsiders move in), with the Treasury and Civil Service
Committee arguing:

> At a time of increasing closeness and interdependence between government
> and the private sector, that the traditional independence and impartiality of the
> Civil Service is in danger of becoming eroded or compromised ...'
> *(Treasury and Civil Service Committee*, 1984, HC 302, para 1.6).

The Government and the Civil Service strenuously deny any such consequence, arguing that such moves are, as one former senior civil servant put it,
in the public interest and that any restraints would damage

> ... a Service wholly and altruistically devoted to understanding the condition
> and to serving the interests of the citizens of this democracy
> *(Treasury and Civil Service Committee*, 1984, Appendix 15).

What evidence there exists – and both Governments and the Civil Service
refuse to reveal who goes where under what, if any, conditions – suggests
that, if they are not trading on their expertise or experience as consultants to
the highest bidder, the civil servants involved usually sign up with organisations with Government dealings. While the traditional worry of favours for
jobs rarely happens, the recruitment of former civil servants helps interests
form a 'Whitehall' dimension to their activities because they are conversant
with the processes and personalities:

> By employing former civil servants certain groups are able to weigh the group
> contest in their favour. It is the groups that are the best-organised, best-
> financed and most 'respectable' that can afford and attract civil servants. This

is an added element of advantage to the 'insider' groups which already dominate the British policy-making process. (Jordan and Richardson, 1979).

Such An Utterly Trivial Matter: MPs and their Interests

In March 1988 the normally well-behaved Commons Defence Committee, having tasted government blood over the Westland affair, decided that the House could no longer rely on the Government's word that 'all is well' with the process that approves the movement of 'a high number of former MOD employees ... to a defence related post without any hindrance' (Defence Committee HC 392, 1987-8, para 48.9). It wanted to be sure that the movements were both in the public interest and that the benefits of interchange 'do not accrue to industry at the expense of the public service and the taxpayer' (*Defence Committee*, HC 622, 1987-8, para 13). Their annoyance at the lack of cooperation from the Government, and its refusal to provide any information other than broadbased facts and figures, is to be welcomed. As yet, however, the Select Committee on Members' Interests has not studied how far interests are penetrating the parliamentary part of the policy and decision-making processes and how far the broader public or national interest is being eroded in what should be a crucial 'area of autonomy'.

The purpose of an MP was clearly and unequivocally laid down in 1947 when, in response to the question of trade union sponsorship, the House resolved that the duty of an MP was, 'to his constituents and to the country as a whole, rather than to any particular section thereof'. Parliament has had a history of periodically fighting off any interest, from the Crown to the East India Company, that has sought to threaten the independence and freedom of an MP and to place him in a position of advocacy, dependency and control, particularly when money has been the medium.

In resolutions carefully enshrined in *Erskine May*, the bible of parliamentary practice and procedure, an MP cannot promote or oppose any bill, resolution or matter, submitted or intended to be submitted to the House or any committee in return for a bribe, fee, compensation or reward. It is also forbidden to offer a fee or reward to a Member for drafting, advising upon or revising any bill, resolution, matter or thing intended to be submitted to the House or its committees. An MP also cannot enter into a contractual agreement stipulating he should act in any way as the representative of that body or organisation in regard to any matters to be transacted in Parliament. Furthermore, since MPs did not receive salaries until 1911 and most have always had personal business or other financial interests, a requirement developed that they were forbidden to vote on any matter in which they had a financial interest and expected, on grounds of frankness and prudence, to declare such an interest before speaking.

Anyone looking at the various resolutions as a whole would assume that MPs were forbidden from acting on behalf of outside interests for money while being nudged to declare their own interests when speaking. Yet the whole tenor of the 1974 Resolution – the general requirement to disclose any financial interest and to complete an entry in the Register – is that, so long as there is disclosure, MPs are not restricted in their relationships with outside interests. This contradiction stems from the panic engendered by the Poulson affair – the Government wanted to act, rather than establish another committee – and from the tradition of not seeing previous resolutions as laying down general guidelines for future practice. Indeed many of these resolutions were *ad hoc* reactions to a particular set of circumstances; for example, one was, 'less the consequence of high moral principle than an orchestrated plan by some hungry MPs to reach the trough of Crown patronage' (Doig, 1984, p.53). Others were directed at specific categories rather than the generality of MPs and were, in any case, impossible to police in an institution dominated by the 'gentleman ethic' and a complacent belief that a Member is able, and expected to be able, to 'distinguish between his personal interests and parliamentary duties'. It is hardly surprising, therefore, that MPs have dismissed concern over financial interests as, in the words of Conservative MP Anthony Grant, 'an utterly trivial matter'.

The Rise of the Lobbyist

Into this atmosphere of apparent unconcern, the growth of lobbying has made steady progress. As noted in Chapter I it first emerged as a cause for concern in 1947 when the Lynskey Tribunal investigated the role of a middleman, Sydney Stanley, who traded on his political connections to solicit funds from businessmen eager to circumvent post-war restrictions. With evidence that acceptable lobbying was shading into influence-peddling Prime Minister Clement Attlee announced a Select Committee to look at such activities. Its report noted that large firms and trade associations had the staff and contacts to lobby, quite legitimately, the government and the civil service. It did not, however, see any future for the 'intermediary', the private middleman:

> If an individual desires to set up as a professional intermediary, he must be able to attract a clientele, and in order to do so he must be able to offer some services of value to his prospective clients. The only services he can render are a knowledge of the workings of the system, with or without the addition of personal acquaintance with individual officers. It is difficult to see how a private intermediary can acquire this knowledge. (*Committee on Intermediaries*, 1950 Cmd 7904, p.67).

What it did not foresee, however, was the possibility of those from within the 'system' setting themselves up as intermediaries and selling their knowledge, access and contacts. Although political PR was in its infancy at the time the Select Committee was reporting there were an increasing number of clients seeking access to the decision-making processes who turned for professional help to those individuals with advertising, public relations and, more importantly, political backgrounds, such as political journalism, government PR work and party activism. During the 1950s these individuals laid the foundation of political lobbying as a commercial activity. They knew how to exploit their political contacts and their PR expertise, and they pioneered many of the techniques used today; the provision of detailed briefings, the use of 'fact-finding' missions, the creation of climates of favourable opinion and the hiring of MPs as consultants. While their impact on Parliament was marginal at first the abilities of PR in orchestrating clients' interests was clearly demonstrated in the mid 1950s battle for the introduction of commercial television where 'the outside interests seemed to have exerted more effective influence than Conservative voters, constituency organisations, or even members of the Parliamentary Party' (Wilson, 1961, p.208).

PR was clearly an area where the increasingly active role of PR men seemed 'another testimony to the age-old weakness of democracies run by amateur politicians in the face of well-informed and determined professionals ...' (Turner and Pearson, 1966, p.159). Furthermore, 'the new post-war Tory MPs were "young men on the make", eager to obtain financial rewards and the hallmarks of status. They were bitterly hostile to socialism, which they interpreted as limiting individual opportunities for personal advancement.' (Wilson, 1961, p.95).

They came together in what MP Francis Noel-Baker described in 1961 as the 'grey zone', the jobs that paid fees and retainers but required no special qualifications or fixed hours of work and where the roles of advisor and consultant 'need not become generally known'. The growth of so-called 'public relations', and of the power of pressure groups, he warned, 'means that Members of Parliament have themselves become more attractive allies for business interests than they have been in the past. The door, in fact is wide open for a new form of political corruption ...' (Noel-Baker, 1961, p.91).

Turning a Blind Eye

Despite the lesson of the 1941 Boothby case, when the late Conservative MP was severely reprimanded by a Select Committee for failing to disclose an interest and for lobbying in expectation of a financial reward, MPs happily signed up for jaunts to Spain, Ghana and the Central African Federation, often organised by fellow MPs employed by PR firms, and threw 'the mantle of Westminster respectability' over their private business affairs. As the late Tory MP Anthony Courtney said: 'I had acquired for the benefit of the firms with which I was connected improved personal contact with the Board of Trade and other Ministers' and, for their activities abroad, 'an aura of official Government blessing through the fact I was now a Member of Parliament' (Courtney, 1968, p.63). It took the shock of the 1968 Greek Junta affair – when the military government's PR firm claimed to have a British MP working behind the scenes to influence other MPs – to persuade a

Labour Government to set up the 1969 Select Committee on Members' Interests and the Poulson scandal to force the next to introduce its 1974 requirements on disclosure and the establishment of the Register. Yet the Government reaction in 1969 was, 'what do we get out of this ... don't we merely damage the Government at this stage?', while in 1974 Labour MP Brian Walden reflected the views of many of his colleagues in arguing:

> If my experience of life is any guide, there is nothing so disappointing to the prurient as a revelation. Once they actually know what is going on, their interest in it will subside rapidly. The suspicious will go to lusher pastures where someone is trying to conceal something ... (*Hansard*, Vol.874, c.456).

He was right, of course. Once the public furore had died down, the new Select Committee later reported arrangements for entries in the Register to an emptier and less interested House which decided to leave the definition of a 'relevant' financial interest, and the amount of detail to be entered up to Members' discretion. Worse, the Select Committee did not propose any action against Members who refused to make any return for the Register, including 'nil' entries, and delayed publication of the Register until 1980, thus nullifying any practical effect of the 1974 Resolutions and ensuring the issue of Members' interests did not have a high profile.

Indeed, the Labour Government even tried to avoid investigating the circumstances behind the 1974 Resolutions, particularly those of the MPs who had had dealings with Poulson. James Callaghan argued that, 'it seems to me that in view of the obscurity of the position it may be as well to focus on the practice for the future rather than to re-run the past, about which so much has been said.' (*Hansard*, Vol.917, cols.1449-50). Prodded by *The Observer* the House did look at the activities of MPs involved with Poulson but gave that task not to the new Select Committee on Members' Interests but to an *ad hoc* committee, whose conclusions it refused to accept, simply deciding to 'take note' of them and avoiding drawing any general principles from them. The sacrifice of Tory MP John Cordle, whom the Select Committee decided had not only failed to declare an interest but was also found to be advocating the interests of his employer in a parliamentary speech, was arguably less the result of an insistence on standards than a party tactic designed to protect Reginald Maudling from censure as the House closed ranks in case anyone should assume that it was acting like a 'sanctimonious lynchmob'.

Wolves In The Fold?

Faced by this collective indifference, or unwillingness, to deal with the issue of lobbying, lobbying has been an entrenched part of parliamentary life. This falls into three specific areas: MP-lobbyists, the interaction of MPs' business interests and government policy, the role of the professional lobbyist. The number of MPs holding consultancy, advisory or similar appointments is now substantial. The 1985 Register showed some 150 MPs holding 280 consultancies; the 1988 Register showed some 180 MPs holding nearly 300 consultancies. Interestingly there are a number of MPs holding multiple consultancies and a small number who hold consultancies but appear to have no other business or commercial interests. There are also a small number, around 5%, who have directorships or consultancies in PR firms. Clearly outside interests see MPs as worth recruiting and employing. On the other hand, problems can arise because there are no clear rules on advocacy versus interest-representation and because the poverty of the information currently available does not allow anyone to judge whether an MP is working as a lobbyist or because that is where his or her own interests, experience or expertise lie. Furthermore the Register does not carry financial and other contractual details of MPs' relations with outside interests to ascertain what they are expected to do and the level of financial commitment involved. It is equally difficult to judge whether the pursuit of the interest is complementary to or conflicts with the party or wider public interest.

In 1980 Tory MP Anthony Steen was talking to the Association of Consultant Architects about the value of having an MP on their side. In an internal aide-memoire, the association were allegedly told that,

> ... MPs have little opportunity on their own to concentrate on any one group's interests or problems unless they have a special reason for doing so ... If, however, a special interest group is prepared to sponsor an MP, or group of MPs, to pay them fees for their care and attention, this has proved to be an effective method.

The benefits are, apparently, that the MP, or MPs, could,

> ... at the ear of government, explain problems with particular care to Ministers, take the extra trouble required to put down questions, to prepare speeches on special interests that would otherwise go by default. (Roth, 1981, pp.i-ii).

The chairman of the Motor-Cycle Association told Tory MP Keith Speed, whose Westminster Communications public relations company had saved its members some seventy thousand pounds in backdated VAT on motor-cycle tests, 'this is a good example of how having a friendly man in the House of Commons can be enormous assistance to us' (*TV Eye*, 1984). Another MP, Sir Marcus Fox, a co-owner of Westminster Communications, was hired by the leading figure in the Association of Private Open Cast Operators to push the NCB to relax restrictions on open cast coal mining. Fox, with the help of a few colleagues, started 'inquiring and pushing' so that there was 'no doubt that the Coal Board now understand that there is a strong feeling in Parliament that this is an area that's got to be encouraged' (*World in Action*, 1984).

Fox's belief that there was a relationship between the activities of an outside interest and general Government policy also raises the second area of MP-lobbying; the intertwining of business interests with ideological attitudes. Former Labour MP Maureen Colquhoun wrote of her experiences on an Oil Taxation Bill Committee that the men from the oil companies 'write notes to the Tory members of the Committee. They were effectively advisors to the Tory opposition on the Bill. They slotted additional information to the Tory members of the Committee, who already had prepared briefs, during the process of examining the Bill.' (Colquhoun, 1980, p.128).

With the advent of a radical Conservative government committed to ending state ownership and intervention, and opening up the opportunity for commercial expansion, both MPs and special interests have been noticeable in their attention to the decision-making processes, something the Labour Opposition have intermittently queried (to no real effect). Of the July 1988 debate on the *Finance Bill* Labour MP Nick Brown complained that 'it was companies, and not constituencies that were being represented at this stage of the *Finance Bill*' with property not people motivating the changes being proposed by MPs on behalf, he alleged, of 'an extraordinarily long list of vested interests, interests that could not possibly be those of the majority of any of these Members' constituents'. In 1987 Labour MP Ron Lewis argued that Tory MPs with interests in the alcohol industry should not be on the Standing Committee of the *Licencing (Amendment) Bill* which would 'increase the profits of the drinks trade'. In April 1988 Labour MP Bob Cryer, a longtime critic of MP-lobbyists, wanted to know whether Tim Smith, a Tory MP and a consultant to accountants Price Waterhouse, was putting down questions on Whitehall spending on management and computing consultancy contracts that could be related to Price Waterhouse's development of a business plan. He also drew attention to an internal memo from merchant bank Morgan Grenfell's parliamentary consultant, Tory MP Andrew MacKay, when he claimed that the bank had urged more use of the 'considerable talents' of the MP who was apparently responsible for reviving the bank's 'political acceptability' following its involvement in the Guinness affair.

The strongest complaints have been aimed at the lobbying for the Channel Tunnel legislation and contract where nearly 40 MPs and peers have had links with the varous consortia. A BBC *Newsnight* film alleged one MP, Tory David Atkinson, had failed to register an interest while another, Tory MP Den Dover, allegedly cast a crucial vote on the choice of construction schemes as a member of the Transport Select Committee – and was an £8,500 registered consultant to one of the competitors. Earlier, the whole issue of what type of link there should be across the Channel had been the basis of intense lobbying campaigns by professional lobbyists:

> The Channel Tunnel Group, which included four major UK construction firms and two clearing banks, with a former Ambassador to Washington as its chairman, employed according to the *Sunday Times*, 'Streets, a leading financial public relations company, and GJW Government Relations for lobbying. Some 30 meetings have been held in Parliament by the Channel Tunnel Group to gets its message across to MPs.' A second rival – Channel Expressway, the road/rail link – 'planned its lobbying with military precision to make up for lost

time'. Its chairman headhunted an experienced lobbyist from a PR firm who, 'using her nine years' lobby experience, built up a list of 300 MPs and active peers with an interest in the channel link, either as transport, trade or foreign affairs specialists'. Groups of ten MPs were dined and had the project explained to them. Said the *Sunday Times*: 'the move worked brilliantly'.

(Doig, 1986, p.518)

In Whose Interest?

There has been an equal concern over the number of MPs with related interests who were involved in the recent Committee Stage of the *Cable and Broadcasting Bill*, an exercise in parliamentary decision-making noteworthy for 'the assiduous presence of lobbyists, hovering just outside the door of the committee hearings armed with detailed briefing sheets for its members' (*The Observer*, 1st July, 1984). Radical or wideranging initiatives by the Government, which are not part of an ongoing policy agenda with the permanent lobbies, have been a godsend for professional lobbyists because the rapidity in processing, and often ill-thought-out detail of, the legislation allows them to offer their clients a parliamentary rather than Whitehall input. They also have the organisation and expertise necessary for interests to respond rapidly to one-off or unexpected developments and mobilise the necessary parliamentary support.

Thus both the two main rivals for the Channel Tunnel contract used professional lobbyists as well as MP-consultants. The Law Society used a professional lobbyist to oppose a bill to end solicitors' monopoly on conveyancing. In the contest between Guinness and Argyll for Distillers both sides – and the Bank of Scotland who were drawn into the fray at one point – called on the services of professional lobbyists (Kochan and Pym, 1987), two of whom were also involved in the Westland affair.

The success of the professional lobbyist has depended on skilfully deployed persuasion and briefing techniques, the identification of sympathetic MPs, the cultivation of influential MPs and Ministers and payments to MPs ('MPs can't be expected to give us the detail as a labour of love, can they?' said one lobbyist). They reinforce their professional expertise by obtaining access to the House itself where discreet meetings and conversations, use of the Polis information database on MPs' backgrounds and parliamentary interests, use of Commons' rooms for entertainment and early acquisition of official documents gives them both a spurious legitimacy as well as a privileged means of pursuing their clients' interests.

Lobbyists obtain this access primarily as research assistants to MPs. Peter Luff formerly a director of Good Relations Corporate Affairs, a firm of professional lobbyists, was research assistant to Anthony Grant (he of the 'utterly trivial matter') who was a consultant to Good Relations. Luff frankly described the relationship as 'essentially bogus' but necessary to obtain a pass to the House because it was 'the only way I can gain access to certain information', access to information which, he said, 'my clients, I believe, have a right to have' (*Select Committee on Members' Interests*, HC 408, 1985, p.42,44). Luff is not alone in this unusual relationship: in 1983 Douglas Smith was managing director of Political Research and Communications International (PRCI) whose chairman was Peter Fry, MP. Smith was Fry's research assistant, a usefully placed post when PRCI won a contract to lobby on behalf of a new airbus consortium and since he could access Polis to find out which MPs were concerned with noise regulation and who could have their fears allayed by a letter promoting the aircraft's quiet engines. The 'bogus' relationship, however, goes further. Private rooms and dining facilities are much prized by lobbyists to host meetings for clients and MPs (on one occasion an MP even attended a presentation on the value of double-glazing). One device for arranging such functions is the 'all-party' group a proto-official parliamentary committee often resourced, and serviced by a lobby, such as Age Concern for the All Party Group for Pensioners. In 1985 PRCI went so far as to propose funding an official visit to Sweden by the Commons Environment Committee to study aspects of nuclear waste disposal, a subject that interested a PRCI client, but for which there were no official funds available. John Biffen, Leader of the House, drew the line at that; private funding for official Commons business would be 'inappropriate'.

Inside the Fold

In 1986 Home Secretary Douglas Hurd warned of Parliament's need to free itself 'to some extent' from the 'strangling serpents', the pressure groups and the interest groups. At the same time these groups, as a 1985 lobbying seminar suggested, are part of 'an increasingly competitive and cut-throat environment which recognises little in the way of compromise'. All is fair, the seminar blurb argued, in 'the need and opportunity to influence decisions, or policy, which could vitally affect the profit, or the loss, to a business or even an entire industry'. Lobbyist Peter Luff was quite clear that his clients, 'part of the British commercial and industrial scene', required 'access to decisions taken in this place which have a material effect on their interests.'

Certainly lobby firms are not backward in trumpeting their influence and privileged access. In 1982 Bob Cryer quoted from the publicity blurb of Lloyd-Hughes Associates which claimed 'regular relationships with the British Government, Cabinet and other Ministers and their Civil Service advisers at all appropriate levels' and a success deriving 'from confidence that we can match promises with performance'. It even professed that 'Ministers or senior officials have asked us to help in creating a particular climate of public opinion to enable them the more easily to assist one of our clients whose case they have accepted'. Cryer went on to quote the claim of Charles Barker, Watney and Powell that they provided the 'secretariat of several all-party committees' and that of David McDonough and Associates

Ltd about their 'working lunch concept' which the firm saw as an effective weapon in the corporate communications strategy and for which they could 'recommend' a suitable place including, 'in appropriate circumstances', the House of Commons.

Such is the importance of access for the professional lobbyist that some will go to extraordinary lengths to obtain it. In May 1988 Paul Singer of the Escalus Public Affairs Consultancy wrote to Tory MP Robin Maxwell-Hyslop:

> I have recently established a lobbying business and require a Pass for the House of Commons.
>
> Because of the lack of Parliamentary recognition afforded to the industry, such a pass needs to be obtained via an MP. I wonder, therefore, if it would be possible for me to secure one through your good office, assuming that you have not filled your allocation.
>
> With the position of lobbyists being a rather grey area, I suggest that a Pass be issued under the guise of a research appointment. In order to make this above-board, but also to give something in return for sponsoring a Pass, I am prepared to undertake any work for you.
>
> As for security, I have no doubt that I would clear any vetting procedure. If you require a reference, my cousin, Professor Brian Griffiths, Head of the Prime Minister's Policy Unit, can provide this.
>
> I hope that we will be able to meet for a further review of the matter and I look forward to hearing from you. (*Select Committee on House of Commons (Services)*, HC 580, 1987-88, appendix 7)

Maxwell-Hyslop was furious, writing to the Serjeant at Arms that he interpreted the letter as 'offering me a corrupt inducement to enable the sender to obtain a pass to which he is not entitled'. He wanted the letter drawn to the attention of whoever or whatever committee issues passes – and it ended up in the appendices of a report of the House of Commons (Services) Committee, an unusual destination but not surprising given that Parliament has generally been reluctant to indulge in stringent policing of the activities of professional lobbyists and MP-lobbyists.

Sleeping Policemen

Even the 1969 Select Committee on Members' Interests thought that the 'public scrutiny' of the whole range of a Members' financial interests was apparently the 'proper activity for journalists, compilers of reference books and academics; it is not essential to the way the House conducts its business' (*Select Committee on Members' Interests*, HC 57, 1969, para 75). Other Committees have been equally ineffectual. The Select Committee on

Privileges, proposed by the 1969 Committee as the possible means of policing its code of conduct, will only consider allegations about MPs and lobbying within the context of the general reputation, character and good name of
the House. It has tended to avoid the question of the truth or justification of
allegations, preferring to focus on the propriety or otherwise of making them
and their effect on the House's public image. The Select Committee on
Members' Interests set up in 1974 spent its early years tinkering with the
categories and criteria for the Register while begging the House not to 'diminish your Committee's standing' in publishing the Register without deciding what to do about those MPs refusing to make a return. Finally, in the face
of the House's failure to take any action (or interest) to enforce one of its
own Resolutions or, with the Labour Government's connivance, to allow a
debate on the behaviour of the leading 'refusenik', the Committee published
an incomplete Register because of 'demand' for it. It quickly failed its second test when Labour MP Brian Sedgemore wanted it to rule on whether the
Prime Minister's 'batting for Britain' over a contract in Oman where her son
was a consultant with the successful contractor was an interest that should
have been declared. Apart from Mr Sedgemore's own ingenious demonstration of a financial link via Denis Thatcher, the allegations also concerned the
issue of whether, as in other areas of the public sector, non-pecuniary
interests should be declared or included in the rules. The Committee
thought better of answering that and, by sticking to existing rules, was able
to say that there was no breach by the Prime Minister and therefore no need
to 'investigate the validity of these allegations'.

Its first full investigation of lobbying was a pusillanimous affair beginning
with its over-polite welcome to lobbyist Sir Trevor Lloyd-Hughes – 'today is
an unusual, almost unique occasion in the history of Parliament', – continuing by skating over quotes from the firm's publicity material – Lloyd Hughes
called it a commercial document for 'trying to sell my services' – and ending
by refusing to allow the Deliverer of the Vote, whose office issues official
documents, to give named examples of those journalists and research assistants who were abusing the office for their own 'sidelines' and 'professional
purposes'.

Given that the Committee wanted to consider the position of 'those who
seek, for reward, to influence the decisions of the House by direct communication with Members' it effectively avoided the issue of MP-lobbyists by
choosing not to require them to register who pays them how much to do
what. The reason for this extraordinary decision was apparently the need to
balance public disclosure and the right of privacy, including the 'privacy of
the client'. Its second objective, to ensure that an MP knows the source and
'true nature' of any approach and the 'standing' of the person making it, was
equally half-hearted. Professional lobbyists were not to be registered
because of problems of definition and enforcement but lobby journalists,
secretaries, research assistants and all-party and parliamentary groups were
to register. This information was not available to the public, there was no
requirement of any verbal declaration (the information was only available in

the Library) and there was to be no control over access to the resources and facilities of the House. Furthermore it would appear that registration has been less than successful; the various categories of those required to register have not rushed to do so and the information, given the turnover of staff, is often quickly out-of-date. Of more concern is the fact that, of the 330 current entries, 50 indicate 'a connection with parliamentary consultancy or research services or public relations' with a further 50 working for charities, professional bodies or non-profit making organisations 'presumably in some kind of representative or lobbying capacity or in providing assistance to members supporting the aims of those organisations or bodies.'

Since, in the words of chairman Geoffrey Johnson Smith in March 1988, the Select Committee on Members Interests is now viewing 'the apparent increase in lobbying' with concern – again – it may do well to take guidance from the humble House of Commons (Services) Committee which, in culling the above information on the activities of staff in relation to the issuing of passes, has recommended that 'automatic access' to the House should not normally be granted to those whose primary interest is the propagation of interests, commercial or otherwise. Responding to complaints of some MPs that some lobbyists are running their businesses from the House, the Services Committee, traditionally concerned with American interns hogging the photocopiers and with trying to find rooms for MPs, has come out strongly against such practices; 'it is quite intolerable that the services of the House ... should be available for commercial purposes. This practice is an abuse of public money, and should be stopped' (*Select Committee on House of Commons (Services)*, 1987-88, para.52).

It is also intolerable that the democratic processes should also be used for commercial purposes and, bearing in mind the Services Committee's warning that such practices are the 'tip of a larger iceberg ... whose progress should be halted', something must be done to provide Parliament with that 'area of autonomy' in which MPs can pursue the interests of their constituents and the country as a whole.

Ignoring the cant about contributing to the democratic process, lobbyists and lobbies are in business for themselves and their clients. They should not be allowed to ride on the back of the lack of research and other support for MPs by making good those inadequacies, nor should MPs be allowed to trade on their parliamentary knowledge to pick up congenial work with or for lobbyists. Part of the solution rests with providing the information lobbies want outside the precincts of Westminster; part lies with the proper resourcing MPs need to carry out their parliamentary duties. More important is the will needed for Parliament to return to fundamentals and decide what behaviour is or is not acceptable for an MP. That depends on an effective Select Committee on Members' Interests and a comprehensive register as well as the clarification and codification of past precedent for current practice. It is interesting to note that the Americans and Canadians have handed this issue over to independent ethic offices; they have also, like the Australians, decided to require lobbyists to register. If nothing is done, said

Peter Smith, past president of the Institute of Public Relations, there is a risk of a major scandal. It is one thing for the civil service to reach accommodation with lobbies to formulate policies; it is another for professional lobbyists and lobbyist-MPs to decide on and legislate for those policies. An utterly trivial matter is now a major cause for concern.

10 Lobbying: The Need for Regulation

CHARLES MILLER

> ... And the hired guns must surely be the political lobbyists ...
>
> Sometimes, client manipulation can occur. Take two rival clients, say a government consortium and a pressure group. Neither is likely to understand that the lobbying community is a tight-knit circle that protects its own interests.
>
> The rival lobbying firms will often exchange intelligence to prolong a situtation – and therefore their fees.
>
> Lobbyists arouse suspicion in Westminster because they seem motivated by cash, not conviction, and can change sides capriciously ... In practice, many of them will acquire members' research passes to gain privileged access and acquire free copies of Hansard and government reports (often worth hundreds of pounds) from the Vote Office.
>
> (Anita Chaudhuri, *The Times* 22nd June, 1988)

The author of this piece follows immediately to say, 'They provide a valuable service to their clients ...'

Lobbyists have to cope with a lot of this. Most consultancies have files bulging with cuttings alleging sharp dealing, abuse of the system and other chicaneries all pointing to the suggestion that it is impossible to seek to influence public policy without cutting ethical corners. The old images of lobbying, redolent with descriptions of the arm-twisting tactics used by operators in the New York legislature will not, it seems, be buried for some time.

Professional practitioners cannot understand why so much attention should be focused on allegations that are almost certainly exaggerated. Their concerns have moved past questions of right and wrong to the more nebulous issue of sound professional practice – defining it; adhering to it; and devising a regulatory system to protect consumers from those who cannot comply with it.

Two years ago, the author of this chapter was talking to two gentlemen, who might be described as Old School, at a City banquet. One was a senior Cabinet Minister; the other is now head of one of our most respected financial markets. The conversation turned to lobbying. Both parties believed it was utterly wrong: we elect our legislators; it is undesirable that we should interfere with their quinquennial mandate, they concurred. They voiced a concern that many feel. Lobbying is seen by a great number of people as a process by which the wheel of democracy is buckled. Lobbying enables individuals as groups to secure an advantage in public policy or legislative terms over others. A Congressional lobbyist quoted an elegant statement of the position from a Capitol Hill hearing:

Beset by swarms of lobbyists seeking to protect this or that small segment of the economy or to advance this or that narrow interest, legislators find it difficult to discover the real majority will and to legislate in the public interest. As government control of economic life and its use as an instrument of popular welfare have increased the activities of these powerful groups have multiplied. As the law-making money-raising and appropriating agency in the Federal government, the acts of Congress affect the vital interest of these organised groups, many of which maintain legislative agents on or near Capitol Hill. These agents seek to transform the aims and programmes of their groups into public process by having them embodied in general legislation, by changing the tax laws to suit their own purposes, by using their influence to reduce or eliminate the appropriations for agencies they dislike, and to increase the appropriations of agencies they favour, and by pressing for ratification or rejection of treaties, presidential nominations and constitutional amendments. A pressure group economy gives rise to government by whirlpools of special interest groups in which the national welfare groups create delays and distortions, the public welfare suffers in the warfare of private groups, and Congress becomes an arena for the rationalisation of group and class interests. (*First Report* from the Select Committee on Member's Interests, 1984-85, HC 408, p.13)

Looked at in that way, the case against lobbying, and in particular, those who earn their living by doing nothing but, seems reasonable. Yet cursory cross-examination dissolves the argument. Even if we overlook Government's desire to open vast numbers of policy issues to public consultation each year, it is clear to most people that the complexity of the modern day work of Whitehall and Parliament is such that effective policies cannot be formulated in a vacuum. Without information, the process atrophies. If organisations do not inform the system, it almost certainly fails to represent the wishes and needs of the electorate accurately.

Taking this argument a stage further, the right to petition the source of power has been a constitutional principle since Magna Carta. Then it was the King; now power lies in a variety of institutions, but the validity of the citizen's right to make a case to Government is undiminished by time. On the contrary, as Government has moved into every aspect of individual and corporate life, that right – as Ian Greer put it, the 'Right to be Heard' – has become more precious and of greater necessity.

Government is a tribunal. It proposes decisions and then adapts them on the basis of the quality and weight of evidence presented on either side, or it receives external proposals and reacts once it sees who is effected and how strong are the arguments for adoption, rejection or modification. At every stage, the policy process is participative, or at least as participative as both sides wish to make it. Lobbying – the making of a case to those whom we elect or pay to run the country according to our wishes – is not only desirable but essential.

If the concern is raised at the way it is done, rather than at its validity in a democratic system, the solution seems to be in Government taking a tougher, more objective attitude to pressure or the influence of money over ideas. As Robin Oakley, *The Times*' political editor, commented (12th July, 1988), 'It is up to Government to ensure equity between individual pleaders.'

Later, in the same article, referring to an Institute of Directors' conference on lobbying, he states,

> What business wants from the lobbyist, one contributor put it at the IoD conference, is to have the decision making system as far as legally possible wired for sound. But the process of contact for companies which matter should be permanent and two-way. Civil Servants like to give Ministers good advice. For that they need to know ahead of time what industry itself is planning.

He expressed a constitutionally impeccable view. Denial of the right and need to lobby must bring with it increased isolation of Government from the wishes of those who appoint it.

Our two eminent gentlemen above – both of whom it should be noted have done more than their fair share of lobbying in their time – may therefore have been confusing principles and methods. There is nothing wrong with lobbying; it is the way it is done that causes concern. Increasingly those concerns are directed at those who do nothing but lobby and, what is more, do so not in their own cause, but as the paid representative of others.

When we consider the points of principle raised against the use of professional intermediaries in dealings with Government, it is easy to see that most are rooted in a lack of respect for the role of the lobbyist, not a fundamental feeling that such work damages democracy. Lack of professionalism, which feeds those roots, is itself an ethical issue, not simply because it may carry with it abuses of the system (whether innocent or intentional) but because it inevitably leads to an absence of good faith between client and adviser. Unable to comprehend the system or secure concrete solutions for their clients, the bad consultant is often forced to pass – or concoct – misleading information to organisations or create a placebo (one common expression is 'structured hospitality') to disguise his inadequacies. It is sad that so many agencies and clients genuinely and innocently believe that such conduct is worthwhile.

Professional lobbyists have clear obligations, not only to their clients and Government, but to themselves:

(i) The duty to be properly qualified for the work at which they are representing professional expertise.

Since professional lobbyists have never consistently discussed the point on a collective basis, there is no agreed understanding of 'properly qualified'. There is no practising certificate, no professional examination, no form of vetting by Government akin to the process of becoming a Parliamentary Agent. Clients have no way of knowing whether a consultant in this field has the ability to solve their problems other than through past record (which may not be an adequate guide: would the amendment have gone through anyway; were they pushing against an open door on a policy issue; did the client do most of the work?); recommendation (which may be based on empathy more than a genuine agreement of worth – most MPs and Ministers, for example, have their favourites, but their testimonial as often as not will be swayed by the style with which they were handled); or, more reliably, contextual experience. A drugs company with a Pharmaceutical Price Regulation Scheme problem could have no better guide to its chances of success than to employ a former Health Minister or head of NHS procurement. They implicitly discharge their duty to be qualified, to be 'Fit and Proper' in City regulatory terms. Others have a greater burden of proof to carry.

(ii) The duty not to misrepresent credentials or services. An experienced observer scanning the literature of many lobbying firms would be struck by the claims made. Other professions are far stricter in preventing exaggerated or misleading statements being represented by their members. If we are to believe such claims, most consultancies are impeccably connected, have access to much inside information, and can boast a wide range both of impressively qualified staff and successful case histories. All is well with the world. Concerns about ethics and professionalism are a thing of the past.

If only. There is a plethora of cases where the lack of a code of conduct to cover the profession has enabled firms to get away with murder. Consider the consultancy that retyped Hansard extracts before sending them to clients in order to claim the information was derived from its inside sources. Consider statements made by some firms to a leading international journal seeking to assess their qualified staff. Both the numbers and the length of Government service of their staff are known to have been markedly exaggerated. Consider carefully the wording of the claim made by one firm that, with its client facing an MMC reference, they (and I must of necessity paraphrase) 'watched the changing political climate and advised that there would be no political intervention and that it would be counter-productive to lobby. The consultancy's advice helped to ensure that there was no reference'. Consider the firm that advised its client to meet a large number of MPs, Ministers and EC Commission officials and pay for backbench opinion surveys in a case investigating the redrafting of some UK Regulations. Yet barely any contact was made with the Whitehall officials responsible for the redrafting. The client was advised that they were not important. Few, if any of the client's objectives were achieved. The great lacuna in the ethics of professional lobbying lies not just in the lack of a Law Society or Institute of Chartered Accountants but, more basically, in the absence of a body of recorded precedent or accepted consultancy practice. Most firms, therefore, honestly feel they are doing the right thing most of the time, and there is no rubric against which others can question such beliefs. There is no question, however, that the better firms know other consultancies (or perhaps, to be more accurate, some consultants in those firms) regularly and consciously recommend action they know to be unnecessary for the sake of prolonging a case – and a fee – that has long since run its course. There are certainly also instances of companies who have paid agencies to solve problems which basic professional research would have revealed never existed.

So much of this stems from the lack of expertise of many of those employing lobbyists. Most finance directors are accountants; most in-house counsel are trained lawyers. They know the tricks of the trade and can keep a tight check on their auditors or solicitors. Few executives responsible for dealing with Government have first-hand knowledge of the system with which they must work. There are few manuals or courses to guide them. The duty placed on lobbyists to educate and honestly advise their clients must be greater where it is so easy for people to be misled by proposals that flatter to deceive.

There are three further guidelines which cannot, despite the above, be questioned.

(iii) The duty to tell the truth; which appears self-evident except that it is tied to the less obvious requirement of professionals to ensure that their clients represent the whole truth to Government. The nature of the policy formulation process is such that, despite the inadequacies many (including the author) attribute to it, factual misconceptions are eventually exposed – if not by officials then by those outside groups with an interest in so doing. A Conservative backbench lawyer adds his observation to the wry statement of Bruce George MP (c.f. Chapter 2) on the need for honesty:

> The lobby against Greek cement imports in 1986 was convincing at first sight but did not tell us it was itself operating a cartel. Further representations were treated sceptically as a result.

Most lobbyists are not subject experts. It is their duty to ensure that at the least their client warrants, in writing if necessary, that its case is accurate and, preferably, independently to vet such cases and to see whether they stand up to examination. It is not enough simply to advise a client on techniques of advocating its version of the truth. They have a duty to the system to ensure that it is not misled.

(iv) The duty to disclose their interest. While interests of commercial confidentiality make it difficult in some instances to be open about clients or motives in dealing with Government (most usually in seeking to obtain information) it should be the norm that lobbyists identify their interests when contacting parliamentarians or officials.

(v) Lastly, the duty not to abuse the institutions of Government or the House. It is this aspect that shares top billing with a sense of intrinsic naughtiness in the catalogue of high sins compiled by so many critics of professional lobbying. There have been a number of successive flavours of the month, mainly arising from the willingness of tame MPs to be exploited; e.g. the securing of parliamentary research facilities and the booking of Commons Dining Rooms to impress clients. It is not surprising that Robin Oakley refers, as much in angst as cynicism, to the world of the lobbyist thus (*The Times*, 12th July, 1988),

In any decent restaurant within a limousine's purr of Westminster today you are flanked by Jermyn Streetshirted smoothies with well practised pouring arms, introducing clients to a Peer they once met on the 6.08 back from a conference in Leeds.

Yet the result of this wave of criticism, much of which is justified, has apparently been only to send the miscreants rushing to check their collars. There is still no shortage of operators who are long on salesmanship and shorter on professionalism just waiting to treat clients like emperors and sell them new clothes. Oakley concludes, referring to the author of this chapter:

> What is required too, and what he has so far failed to persuade his fledgling profession to set up is an effectively regulated register offering a 'kite mark' for lobbyist firms which are willing to submit for examination their literature, staff and qualifications, to subscribe to an agreed code of conduct and to operate some form of consumer complaints procedure. (ibid.)

He is correct. If the profession of lobbying is to be regarded as just that it has only two options: to regulate or be regulated. That it has not submitted to the strictures long ago accepted by others with whom it would like to stand proudly is a reflection of the lack of agreement that exists on competent regulatory bodies and the form and substance of control.

No-one is even sure whether a regulatory body exists at present. If it is accepted that the business of dealing with Government-related issues is a public relations discipline, the Institute of Public Relations, which represents individual PR practitioners, and the Public Relations Consultants Association, covering agencies, fit the bill. Both have codes of conduct which appear appropriate. The PRCA's code of conduct, for example, imposes a duty of fair dealing and of listing of clients and payments to legislators. It also prohibits the payment of inducements to legislators contrary to the public interest, engaging in 'any practice which tends to corrupt the integrity of channels of public communication or legislation', and proposing to clients 'any action which would constitute an improper influence on organs of government or legislation'. Members are lastly warned against circulating false information or misleading targets on the identity of their clients.

Despite the unimpeachable wording and the undoubted good intentions of both PR organisations, many of those calling themselves professional lobbying firms display feelings ranging from reluctance to disgust when it is suggested that they should practice under the auspices of either. Such emotions stem from five sources. The reputation of PR is such that a large proportion of lobbying firms believe it would damage their image to be associated with it. They also feel that the PR industry has wrongly represented lobbying to be one of its disciplines; that the use of PR techniques by unqualified consultants has contributed to the apparent opprobrium in which professional lobbyists are held and that effective lobbying relies only marginally on such devices; and that these would-be regulators have little or no inside experience of Government and would be unable to detect much of the unprofessional advice and negligent actions that better-versed observers such as Robin Oakley are able to highlight. IPR itself admits that the more professional firms are not associated with it:

> Some agencies are openly and solely in the lobbying business, though few of these would be represented in the IPR membership. (IPR submission to the Members' Interests Select Committee, 13th May, 1988 p.12).

The PR codes, additionally, do not seem to cover the vetting of staff. Although there are IPR-approved examinations and even a sponsored MBA, an understanding of Government and of the principles of working with it is not part of either curriculum. Clients would not therefore be given the guarantee in using a lobbyist that he or she had satisfied a minimum objective standard of professional knowledge: the same guarantee that can be seen hanging behind the accountant or surveyor's desk.

In recent years, the Commons Select Committee on Members' Interests has conducted two inquiries into lobbying. It is appropriate to view the responses of IPR and PRCA. In 1984-5, PRCA favoured a regulatory register of lobbyists administered by Parliament (*First Report* for the Select Committee on Members' Interests, 1984-85, HC 408, paras 86-88) so did IPR (ibid. p.35, para 17). By the time the committee came to examine the issue a third time (the first being an *ad hoc* review in 1974), PRCA was still advocating a register, but now it is to be administered by itself (submission to the Select Committee, 1st July, 1988, p.4). IPR was by 1988 also casting doubt on an 'official' registration system (submission to the Select Committee, 13th May, 1988, p.3). While the difficulty of defining lobbyists (should the term cover just paid advisers or extend to in-house staff? Should pressure groups be included?) was cited as the reason for this about-turn, the suspicion was mooted that other forces were at work. In the three years following the 1984/5 Select Committee's Report, both Government and the media increasingly recognised that lobbyists and PR consultants were different animals. By the time the Committee looked at lobbying again its view (clearly observable to any reader of the oral evidence) that lobbying and PR were synonymous had changed. It was felt that PRCA and the IPR were retrenching and, by proposing registers administered by them, seeking to re-assert control over the subject.

The growing attention paid to regulation of lobbyists in the mid to late 1980s focused two strands of concern about the profession. Its ethics obsessed the media; the quality of the way it did work was of greater interest to practitioners.

The lobbied were in two minds: keen to see consultants supervised, forced to play the game; keen to discourage professional intermediaries; and desirous of improving standards such that only the best could practice for gain. Many MPs were not concerned either way. If they and their colleagues wished to accept retainers, book rooms or do other favours for lobbyists, so be it. It is their club; they may act as they like within it. The growth in lobbying from all sources had anaesthetised enough of them into a dull acceptance that lobbyists were an inevitable sufferance, like advertising or traffic jams.

By no means all legislators and practitioners favour regulation by Government. Efforts by consultants to formulate their own tough codes have not materialised. An attempt in 1985 by the leading firms outside the PR industry to discuss professional standards was effectively sunk by the Public Relations industry's organ, PR Week. They have not met since. The majority of their individual representations to the 1988-90 Select Committee enquiry are believed, however, to favour a Parliamentary administered register. While the profession is split between the PR and non-PR camps, with the two being apparently irreconcilable, it may be the only way forward.

As Paul Pross' Chapter 4 documents, the Canadian Parliament is considering legislation to regulate lobbyists as we write. Both Australia (1983) and the United States (1946) operate registers. The registers will at least be controlled by the centres of power in both countries but the central problem is untouched by foreign legislatures. The aim of the Australian and American legislation is merely to control by identification. Anyone lobbying for pay must register, with a Government Department in the former case and with Congress in the latter. Yet the register will only tell analysts or legislators who is doing what on behalf of whom. They are introverted, run for the benefit of Government. They do not tell clients whether those on them are properly qualified to do their job, nor do they impose any detailed code of ethics or practising principles on those who register.

To date, as in other regimes, Parliament (Whitehall seems disinterested and the Select Committee did not invite a view on regulation from the Cabinet Office) has given little thought to the users of lobbyists. There seems no reason why Government should have the protection it feels it needs and yet business and industry should be met with the smugness of caveat emptor. After all, if Government demands that driving instructors and employment agencies should be registered, not to mention Parliamentary Agents, why should the public not be protected effectively from unscrupulous lobbyists.

The consensus view among professionals is that abuses of the system are negligible, if much publicised. But while there are major industrial managers who still believe that, as one put it, it is 'custom and practice' to organise champagne receptions to maintain the voting support of friendly MPs during a late sitting on a Bill, it is easy for those who know no better to appeal to their views. On the other hand, there have been property developers who have sought to use lobbyists to bounce the Department of the Environment into using legislation to restrict competition to them in local authority deals. A poorly qualified consultancy would probably not have the knowledge to advise its client of Government's probable reaction to such tactics.

The clearest yet most pragmatic solution probably does lie in the establishment of a register, but a voluntary one. After all, those who do not apply for inclusion say much about themselves. The Members' Interests Committee will gain all the comfort it, and the rest of the Government needs, if it requires applicants:

1. To declare that at least 25% of their income is derived from advising third parties on the processes of Parliament and Government with the principal purpose of influencing public policy or legislation.
(This criteria seeks to follow the Supreme Court's definition of a lobbyist in *United States v Harriss* (1954).

2. To declare the full educational and career experience of all executive staff. In the absence of any better evidence, this must be the most objective guide to the quality of a firm. Public declaration of staff qualifications would also encourage all firms to improve their recruitment procedures.

3. To declare all clients where they retain the firm for the purposes defined in 1 above.

4. To deposit with the Committee all promotional literature. This requirement would act as a safeguard against misrepresentation or exaggeration.

Outside organisations and parliamentarians have traditionally distrusted the idea of registration of lobbyists. They have cited (and some of the evidence so far given to the 1988-9 lobbying enquiry restates this concern) that registers create elites, monopolies and privileged classes. It entirely depends on how the system is structured. The right registration process is one that sets qualitative criteria, unlike the Washington register which simply requires limited disclosure. Ask lobbyists to deposit the right information with the right authorities and standards and ethics will quickly improve. Ask them just to leave their names at the door and a self-glorifying clique could easily be created.

It is not regulation of lobbying that is needed, but of lobbyists. If they will not help themselves then, sooner or later, Government will have to impose hard medicine on a practice that wishes to be called a profession.

11 Effective Lobbying: the Hidden Hand

GRANT JORDAN

Two Channels of Influence?

It is tempting to hold that there are two main channels of influence and that lobbying organisations are conveniently divided between those that operate on the Government/civil service world of Whitehall and those that operate on the MPs in Westminster. In fact while there is a difference in emphasis in some consultancies there seems to be a general agreement that Whitehall is the effective channel. The effective lobbyist is therefore the unseen professional. In *Lobbying Government* (1987) Charles Miller spells out that the view that 'Parliament is all-important' is a myth. He argues that the current vogue for 'Parliamentary Consultants' is misguided. In his Bow Group pamphlet (1984) with Roger Hayes he noted:

> It is far easier to develop an understanding of Parliament and familiarity with Members than with any other part of the public policy system. With the very limited experience of working either with or in the Civil Service that exists in most consulting firms, it is natural that they should place their emphasis on the most visible and accessible element of Government. Yet few of the issues that concern interest groups are really decided in Parliament, and for a consultant to direct his clients down the parliamentary road because he knows no better or is unable to exhibit more effective experience is to turn what is often an administrative or technical matter into a political one.

They continued,

> Other professional people who omit to take the most cost-effective action for their clients can be sued for professional negligence.

They note however that clients rarely object to being given the Westminster treatment – whatever its effectiveness,

> Introductions to well-known Members, lunches in the House in private dining rooms or the Harcourt Room and the undeniable splendour of the Palace of Westminster are inevitably more impressive than the dull effectiveness of Whitehall.

In similar vein Norman Tebbit (1985) quoted with approval the President of the Institute of Public Relations who claimed, '... the primary task in government relations consultancies is to avoid the need for lobbying campaigns.' Tebbit warned that high profile campaigns would in the long term harm, 'your political and Government relations.' Companies can educate the market to expect to work at a parliamentary and political level – when this is not necessary.

In the first session to hear evidence of the Select Committee on Members' Interests' inquiry into lobbying in 1988/9, Robert Adley MP argued,

> Would [the witness] agree and share my concern that there are however lobbyists who have an inbuilt financial incentive to purport to their clients the proposition that Members of Parliament are extraordinarily influential in everything under the sun and that they, the lobbying organisations, will be better able to extract larger fees from their clients the more their lobbying organisations can tell their clients that we as Members of Parliament are extraordinarily influential. Is that a fair summing up of the position about the mythical influence we have over some of these important decisions?

In his evidence to the first session of the Committee, Stanley Orme MP added,

> ... I really do believe some of these fancy organisations kid ... that they can influence Members when in actual fact they probably do nothing of the sort. (HC 518 i)

David Burnside of British Airways reported that there were consultancies who created barriers rather than communication between their clients and Parliament.

> They often mislead on the relationship between Parliament and the Government and would spend much of their client's money in influencing Members of Parliament when perhaps they should be spending a great deal more time with civil servants at the right level in the departments concerned. It is because of the mystique of the place ... that so much time is spent with Members of Parliament rather than dealing with a technical boring subject by directing themselves perhaps towards government departments.

Douglas Smith of Political Communications has argued,

> I don't want to minimise Parliament. I've got my friends there. But we are, as you know, living in an elective dictatorship. MPs can be useful to back up Whitehall contacts; if civil servants can see you can get MPs to raise merry hell they're more likely to take you seriously. But the best lobbying is done by getting access to the right civil servant.

The same *Guardian* piece that quoted Smith quoted Andrew Gifford of GJW as having contact with civil servants virtually every day. He claimed,

> There will be people in our office who know the various permanent secretaries quite well, either from the civil service or from working with senior politicians. We'll be on good, friendly terms.

David Rose (*The Guardian*, 8th January, 1988) quoted him claiming that prevention is better than cure,

> Last minute lobbying in reaction to measures which have already been publicly announced is always extremely difficult, and clients are more likely to benefit from a steady intelligence service forewarning them of Government activities in their field, when action can be taken early.

Although identified as a major lobbyist within Parliament, Ian Greer in his evidence to the Select Committee also argued that one of the changes in the last few years was the awareness by clients, that it was too late to call in consultants at the eleventh hour – 'some are now starting to realise the value of actually making representations well in advance. Therefore, there is an opportunity to ensure that the Civil Service side in advance of legislation is then tackled properly.' (HC 518-vi, p.104)

The evidence from the Contract Cleaning Maintenance Association, in 1989, to the Select Committee on Members' Interests made the point that while as an organisation it did not usually lobby Members of Parliament, it did speak 'at some length quite often' with Central Government Departments and, from time to time Ministers.' Their Secretary General explained, 'We feel that we can manage our own affairs reasonably well without the intervention of Members of Parliament. (Mr. Hall himself was an ex civil servant, formerly responsible for MOD privatisation policy and a former political adviser to the Director-General of Warship Construction at Bath.) (HC 44-v).

However, Whitehall contacts are flowers that are difficult to cultivate. If there is a suspicion that lobbyists are trading on the relationship then the shutters can go down. Therefore an honest claim of access can be damaging if it is picked up by the Whitehall side – and an exaggerated claim will lead to a lobbyist being 'frozen out'. This Civil Service reticence perhaps pushes lobbyists into writing and advertising in a way which gives undue Parliamentary prominence. They cannot put Whitehall in the front of the shop window – because some have no access – and those with access have the sense not to flaunt it. Thus though most lobbyists would claim that the long term cultivation of Whitehall is the most effective means of lobbying, their own published list of clients and cases give far more weight to Parliament.

Jock Bruce-Gardyne's (1986,p.152) perspective as a Minister also lead him to the conclusion that the 'insider strategy' is preferable,

> ... the safest solution for the corporate lobbyist is to fix up his trade association, and then to watch his trade association fix the civil service. For once the deal is done, the honour of the civil service is engaged. If it fails to deliver its Ministers bound hand and foot, it hangs its head in shame. Whereas the lobby which (only) converts the politicians is inevitably confronted by the resistance of the civil service.

He set out the batting order as follows:

> First, win the argument behind the scenes in Whitehall if you can ... Second, if you cannot, then try to identify a Minister who ... is likely to be well-disposed ... Only if both of these approaches have been tried and failed does it become desirable to go public.

Finer (1958, p.21) claimed that:

> When a group wants something, it will try to go to the ministry first. This is not because the civil servant is the true ruler of the country. There are three very sensible reasons for doing so. In the first place, where the minister and his department have the power and the authority to give or withhold, it would be folly to kick at their door before bothering to find out whether it was not, in fact, wide open. Secondly it may be bad manners. The relationship between some lobbies and a ministry may be very close, each side having something to give the other ... Part of the unwritten code that governs the relationship of the Lobby and the civil service lays it down that neither side shall *wantonly* embarrass the other ... good manners coincide with self-interest in putting matters to the ministry before going any further. There is a third reason for doing this: it is the only way of finding out 'how the land lies'...

Evidence mentioned earlier submitted to the Select Committee on Members' Interests in 1988 by four academic members of the Study of Parliament Group confirmed that Parliament was not the prime target of interest groups. Of a sample of 350 organisations only 7.6% thought Parliament was the most influential point of access. This compared with 31.6% for Ministers and 28.5% for Departments or civil servants.(HC 518-iii, para.13)

The Government Report produced by Public Policy Consultants in 1987 found that well over half of a survey of MPs themselves reckoned that their influence was over-rated by lobbyists. One MP observed (1987, p.17):

> We are not powerful and we do not make policy – that's done in Whitehall. MPs can have an input, mainly on constituency matters, but many other uses of MPs, for example in contested take-over bids, are not as effective as lobbyists think.

Thus the phrase that is commonly used in this area – Parliamentary Consultant – appears to mislead. The consultants appear to be mainly Whitehall consultants – but perhaps the term Parliamentary Consultant sounds less threatening to our popular democratic theory. It might be that some consultancies do work mainly in Westminster and are best described as Parliamentary – others though perhaps use this phrase to attract clients who themselves have not perceived the difference between the Whitehall and Westminster worlds.

We are then reinventing the American conventional wisdom. Lewis Dexter (1969, p.71) recommended that American interests lobbied in Congress only, '... when the executive department is almost uniformly hostile ...' His examples were of outsider groups – the anti-Vietnam movement, chiropractors who were denied recognition by medical orthodoxy and the National Health Foundation whose anti pollution arguments were then seen as heresy by the relevant Federal agencies. Parliamentary strategies are thus by no means the most effective, but if such a strategy is undertaken then there are still differences of type and impact. Here again the 'law' appears to be that it is the less obtrusive campaign that might well be (normally) the better. Professor Finer claimed (1958, p.54)

> ... the stronger an organization's relations with MPs, the less public notice it arouses; and, conversely, that fuss, noise, mass lobbying and similar demonstrations are often an indication of the failure of an organization to achieve effective Parliamentary relations.

In an American source (Berry, 1984, p.116) the contrast is drawn between the mechanics of lobbying in the legislature versus lobbying the Administration. It suggested that in the former context there was a great premium on being around, on being visible. It was suggested that information was gathered, influence exerted, through casual encounters. One lobbyist was quoted, '*You have to be seen*. Even if the legislators don't know who you are, if they see you often enough, they'll start to think that you belong.'

In contrast it was acknowledged that the lobbyist dealing with civil servants might find that his targets would feel uncomfortable at too frequent meetings. While the civil servant might recognise that he needs the information and the consent of the group, he might not wish to compromise his neutrality... Such a distinction makes sense when transferred to the UK – though the British House of Commons is less important in legislating than is Congress. However this takes a one shot view of the activity. Over time the relations that are built up in being useful to the Opposition and to back benchers can be 'cashed' when Oppositions become Governments and backbenchers become Ministers.

Within the field of activity there is a need to set out different types of operation.(See particularly the chapter by Ian Greer). There is the provision of information on political and Parliamentary developments for the client. There is background climate control. There is the fire brigade campaign – planning and executing a campaign to redeem a situation that might appear lost. Increasingly Parliamentary lobbying appears not to be legislative in its goal but to use backbench pressure to influence Government in its discretion over takeovers and other matters. The lobbyist can be a general adviser over the political climate rather than employed to attain well defined objectives.

Two Lobbying Styles: Contacts versus content.

As well as two channels of influence, two different types of lobbying organisation can be identified – the 'contact man' versus the 'advocate'. One type is very much the 'facilitator' in getting clients together with Members of Parliament or civil servants. This is often defended as being the less damaging style in terms of our traditional political operations. The lobbyist is assisting clients to make their own representations.

This kind of approach is however criticized by some as being professionally bankrupt in that the lobbyist is simply acting as a high grade secretary with an address book and a telephone. The alternative view is that the lobbyist should be much more active in constructing – and even presenting – the case for the client. The analogy here is again with the lawyer who doesn't consider his remit is to get the client in the court at the right time – but will present the case because he knows the way in which a case should be put.

The 'contact man' or dating service approach was savaged in a piece in *The Economist* (5th March, 1988):

> Go to Locketts, a plush Westminster restaurant, on any weekday lunchtime, and you play 'spot the lobbyist'. It is easy: pick out a Member of Parliament who looks well-fed but bored. He will be sharing a table with an earnest-looking industrialist who smiles rather too readily, and a stripey-shirt-and-spotty-tie clad PR man who seems well intentioned but slightly vacant. The industrialist will be flattered by the MPs attentions: the MP will be pleased to prove that there is indeed such a thing as a free lunch; and the PR man will take the profit from what will often have been an expensive waste of time.

However there may be a market for such activity! The clients may be getting exactly what they want. Dexter (1969, p.146) has noted that clients are sometimes only seeking to enhance their own personal prestige:

> They want to feel they have a pipeline to some 'inside dope'; they want to meet famous people. In such cases, a Washington representative who tries to do a job which is best for the organization ... will prove irritating.

This American view was again echoed in *The Government Report* (1987, p.18). A back bencher told research staff from Public Policy Consultants:

> Much parliamentary lobbying is unnecessary. People like to meet MPs. They feel they are striding the corridors of power but they are not. Similarly, there is a suspicion that many companies allocate a budget to entertaining MPs, whether parliamentarians want or need to be entertained or not, and find it easier to spend the money than to reallocate it. The Commons dining rooms are full every day. They sell only an impression of power.

The advocate style is particularly associated with some of the smaller single subject consultancies (perhaps an ex civil servant specialising in his former area of work). They have the intimate knowledge of the policy area that allows them to arrange the argument not the menu. Again the distinction has been made in the US. Dexter (1969, p.131) distinguishes as follows:

> They (some lobbyists) can and do waste a good deal of time in focussing on influence relationships rather than the merits of the case – or in trying to cultivate influence of their own through contacts, rather than dealing with the issues.

How to lobby

Several lobbyists are on record in this book, and in other of their works, explaining the methods of the lobbying profession. The Head of the Legal Department of British Coal, Ronald Cowles (1988), has also given a perspective from within the public sector. American sources include Berry (1984), Dexter (1969) and Cates (1988). To a surprising degree there is a consistency in all these accounts. The British sources also seem to marry well with US accounts.

This chapter does not seek to explain the mechanics of lobbying in the sense of how, for example, to organise the circulation of an Early Day Motion to publicise an issue. One example of the practical issues involved is available through accounts of the Sunday shopping issue. The Keep Sunday Special Campaign divided its approach (on a budget of over £200,000) into five –

(a) preparing briefs for selected Members of the House of Lords, and distributing by mail.

(b) preparing briefs for selected Members of the Commons and distributing by mail.

(c) sending to every Member of Parliament copies of the Press Pack produced for the launch of the campaign.

(d) writing letters to each Member of Parliament between November 1985 and April 1986, enclosing Press articles and other research information.

(e) sending a fresh Red Rose to selected Members on Friday 14th February, in a perspex box, decorated with the words 'We love Sunday'.

(HC 44 – iii)

This chapter dwells on the development of relationships rather than the particular activities used to obtain that access.

1. Tides.

Ian Greer makes the point that different sorts of legislation will appeal to Governments of different complexions. It follows therefore that the political strategy will have to take into account whether the Government is basically, well or ill disposed. Charles Miller in his book also notes that it is a matter of ascertaining the Government's intentions and susceptibilities and then selling ideas that fit in – 'The best-selling work is persuasive rather than coercive'.

Greer argues that in general it is also easier to 'sell' an idea from the outside of the Administration later rather than earlier in its life. The Government has enough to do in its first years of office to implement party legislation – without looking for further ideas. We can pick up Dexter's (1969, p.63) observation for the US that, 'Most lobbyists, most of the time, act to reinforce, strengthen, aid and reassure congressmen and staff who tend to be on their side. They relatively *rarely* argue with known enemies.'

2. The earlier the input, the more effective it is.

There is an iron law from lobbyists that the time to influence legislation is the drafting or even the pre drafting stage. This may be a perfectly obvious point but as the recent publicity has been on Westminster lobbying, it is worth letting the lobbyists themselves underline the Whitehall emphasis. Even Greer, with his strong Parliamentary associations, says in his book that by the time a Bill reaches the House of Commons it has been months in preparation and most politicians and civil servants would feel that anyone with a serious interest should already have known about it and made their representations in good enough time for them to have been taken into consideration. This supports the notion of the 'extended legislative process' – that legislation is not simply something associated with the parliamentary stages but involves lengthy 'pre digestion' within Departments, between Departments in inter-Departmental discussion, and between the parent Department and their client interest groups.

Jenny Jeger now with GJW argued that, 'Approaches are made to MPs only if the pressure group has to have an item of contentious legislation passed, if legislation is going through the House where all the group's objectives have not been fully met by prior consultation or if the group wants to get information out of the government. The groups which mainly deal with MPs are the weaker, less elaborately organised "cause groups" and they are often inadequately equipped for the purpose.'(Mackintosh, 1978, p.68).

In Chapter 8 Barney Holbeche of the NFU said, 'Getting in early is a very important golden rule ... There is no question that once a piece of legislation reaches Parliament you may be able to tinker around the edges, but the prospect of getting any significant changes at that stage are very remote indeed ... Therefore it makes it that much more important to seek to get it right before it ever enters Parliament.'

Charles Miller in *Lobbying Government* observes that the formulation of policy is similar to the conception of life; it grows, takes form and by the time it emerges into public view – parliamentary consideration – it may be too late to do anything except try to lose some rough edges.'

Miller (1987, pp.97-8) also makes the point that:

While outwardly upholding the legislative position of Parliament and the role of Ministers, many officials become understandably biased against those who base their advocacy to government on MP-geared pressure on Ministers without consulting those to whom those Ministers would normally turn for advice. The answering of Parliamentary Questions and responses to legislative amendments could in many cases be obviated if outsiders consulted with officials in good time.

He observes that officials always stress that they can only advise the Minister, but says (1987, p.99), 'While this is technically correct, the great proportion of administrative judgements ... are by officials who have been well trained in the largely fictional convention of Ministerial Responsibility.' Later he returns to the advantages of a negotiation approach with officials rather than encouraging an adversarial mood by harassing them with PQs or late night Adjournment debates. He notes that, 'It should be remembered, however, that a battering ram is not needed if you can walk through the door. Pressure should in most instances be a subsidiary weapon in your plans.' He (1987, p.132) argues that, 'The amount of noise made by advocates is usually in inverse proportion to the strength of their case or their abilities.' Smith similarly notes that, 'Policy formulation is a cumulative process. Parliament stands at the end of it.'

For Smith (1986, Section 3.1), 'Most important is an acquaintance with key civil servants; departmental officials know better than anyone else which way things are moving.' He says that it is when political obstacles are particularly great that representation at official level should be combined with intermittent parliamentary and media initiatives.

Ronald Cowles claims that except in terms of broad policy, the Civil Service plays a far more important part in generating new legislation than Parliament or ministers. (1987, p.3) He noted that this did not imply that the direct approach to civil servants was the only means of attempting to attain objectives, but that, '... care should be taken if that pressure is applied in parallel that it does not prove counterproductive. There will be many instances where quiet persuasion of those responsible for drafting new legislation will be more effective than putting them on the defensive *vis-à-vis* their political masters.' He concludes, 'For if there is one essential ingredient in successful lobbying, it is get in early, before what is objectionable has become engraved on tablets of stone.'

Norman Tebbit (1985) has warned that, '... it is *necessary* to have a good cause. But that's not *sufficient*. It must also be made sufficiently early, be well presented, and be put to the right people.' He complained that many fire brigade operations were ill advised in that they were too late to be effective and only drew attention to the adverse changes affecting the company. 'What is sometimes also not realised is that the best way to avoid damage by fire may be to have decent fire precautions.' Not only is responsive Parliamentary 'fire fighting' type activity not as effective as pre emptive lobbying, it is more controversial. The less open the lobbying the less complaints there will be. Dexter (1969, p.61) has claimed that the Washington representative who reacts – or is forced by his client to react – to some congressional proposal without determining priorities is not even a semi prepared emergency fire-fighter, 'He resembles more nearly a mother who spends hours bandaging a child's minor cuts when both that child and her other children have major unanswered needs and illnesses.'

He claimed later (1969, p.80), 'Even on Capitol Hill, the main job of Washington representatives is not lobbying as such. Rather it is using Congress as a means of influencing the administrative branch ...'

The stress on the early input has been inevitably carried over into advice on dealing with the EC. An article in 1988 in the Department of Trade and Industry; *British Business* advised, 'It is important that lobbyists' views are presented to the Commission as early as possible (preferably before the publication of a proposal) to make sure that the text which emerges is acceptable.'

3. The 'piggy back' approach

Ian Greer's book points out that it is easier to adopt or 'extend' a Governmental bill relating to the topic in hand rather than to try to create interest in a virgin bill. A civil servant explained that Departments too use the opportunity of legislation for one purpose to 'kill another bird': the actual metaphor he preferred was that while the patient is under the anaesthetic anyway the surgeon might as well take out his tonsils. Holbeche gives an instance of the NFU waiting on a Government Water Bill to appear to use one of its interested MPs to insert a clause dealing with the problem of burst water mains and compensation for landowners. The original bill had nothing to do with this but the NFU counted on the fact that the Government was too concerned with the central thrust of the Bill to offend any member of the Standing Committee on a point of detail.

4. The scale of change.

Quite clearly the degree of success in any campaign will relate to the sort of change required. It might be that the change is quite marginal to the thrust of the bill – while of key importance to the affected interest. It might even be that the Government will see the undesirable consequences as soon as representations are made.

Two of Greer's examples in his 1985 book fit this general category. He describes the campaign against the 1981 Bill to liberalise the monopoly of the Post Office. As drafted the Bill would have inhibited the developing air courier industry. After pressure, Ministers accepted the need to suspend the postal monopoly for 'time sensitive' deliveries. The 1981 *Finance Bill* also had unintended consequences for the life insurance industry. Again the Government eventually put forward its own amendment.

These sorts of changes – and the likelihood of success – are different from those where there are objections to a major piece of legislation or where the Government is quite well informed as to the consequences. (e.g. the proposal to put VAT on newspapers and books). Smith (1986) gives the example of the objections of the fast food business to *Miscellaneous Provisions (Local Government) Bill* in 1982. As drafted this would have allowed local authorities to oblige 'take aways' to close by 11 p.m. The compromise agreed – closure by midnight – was, in the scale of the field, a significant victory for the industry's lobbyists. Smith is thus making the point that the realistic ambition is to nudge the Bill in the direction sought – not to force the Government to stand on its head. Jacqui Lait who was parliamentary adviser to the Chemical Industries Association has presented the work of the lobbyist as whittling away at unfavourable legislation. She claimed that major policy reversals were not her aim, 'just legislation that we can live with.' (quoted in Faulder, p.185).

5. Bargaining

Connected with the fact that most lobbying is about marginal change rather than confronting a secure government majority, it allows the development of a bargaining mentality among participants. Smith (1986, 3.1-10) later observes that lobbying invariably calls for bargaining at some point, 'It is essential to be prepared for any opportunity to trade that might present itself. The jargon of the bargaining process ... speaks of "trade-offs", "fall-back positions" and "sticking points"'. Moreover many of the details that bodies might wish to alter are the subject of secondary or subordinate legislation. This is yet another reason to build up a consultative relationship with the Government Department concerned as extensive consultation takes place over these sorts of changes.

Holbeche of the NFU argues later in his chapter,

> I think although it is nice to have this reputation of being effective if you look at the evidence we lose far more cases than we win. I would like to suggest that this also applies to any other pressure group. What I think is a reasonable aim is to get some of what we want most of the time ... one of the techniques involved is to get the best deal going and then to explain to the farmers that this is the best deal in the present circumstances.... Some lobbies seem to have difficulty in judging well the art of the possible – to see what is on and what is not – and they tend to be very plaintive about a compromise solution that may have been worked out that does not meet all their requirements.

Judith Hampson of the RSPCA has been quoted (Faulder, p.185) along similar lines, 'A firm proponent of co-operation not confrontation ... So the charges of "collaboration" which she inevitably attracts she accepts with equanimity, meanwhile beavering away on committees, producing reports for the Home Office, etc. ...'

These are British covers of an American song. Phil Cates (1988, p.240-243) advises, 'Those who do not accept political realities do not have a chance to be even mediocre lobbyists.' He quoted a description by a senior Vice President corporate of their lobbying activities, 'They lay out options and deal in the art of the possible. It's rare that we obtain what seems the ideal solution to us.' Jeffrey Berry has a section headed 'SUCCESS = COMPROMISE' in which he makes the same point that no interest group gets all that it wants, and so the difference between success and failure is achieving an acceptable compromise.

6. Trust

Holbeche also expresses the importance of maintaining the continuity of good professional relationships; that persistence and a sense of proportion over any one particular issue is needed. He says that they want to look good with the membership, '... but not at the expense of damaging relationships with Government and politicians. Tomorrow is another day and another issue.' Berry in his American account again offers similar advice, 'Never Burn Your Bridges'. He did note that some public interest groups would publicly identify a 'villain' in the administration. This was partly because the moral indignation that was associated with the public interest field made pragmatism difficult, but also Berry saw the portrayal of issues in terms of good versus evil as a means to put opponents on the defensive. Berry referred to this as a high risk strategy and one of no credibility for corporations and trade associations. Also from a US perspective, Cates (1988, p.250) quotes a lobbyist:

> One cannot expect every legislator to agree on all bills, amendments and procedures. For in the future there will be other issues, bills and causes, and lobbyists will then need all the friends they can get. Those who burn their bridges behind them will soon lose their effectiveness.

As noted above, Miller's book lays emphasis on working with Whitehall. He claims that there are few civil servants at Principal grade or above who do not spend some time of every day giving advice to, engaging in commercial negotiations with, or simply meeting with representatives of their sponsoring area of responsibility. He notes that officials need information and that they cannot be confident about their policy or its efficient administration without knowing who will benefit or be affected. He also stresses the need for good relations with officials and argues for the relationship of trust. Miller says that officials must satisfy themselves of the bona fides of those who deal with them and that the outsiders have to behave in such a way as to maintain their access. He argues the need for total honesty – not however simply from an ethical position but also from the needs of long term effectiveness. He says that the cost of deliberate misinformation is the denial of further credibility. Smith too warns that it can be damaging to longer term interests if politicians have cause to feel that they have been misled.

The American advice is again similar, 'A good lobbyist is an honest and accurate broker of needed information.' (quoted in Cates, 1988, p.246). Cates says:

The credibility of a lobbyist can be tried and found lacking by an elected official only once. A lobbyist can lie or mislead an elected official only one time. A lobbyist's personal credibility must be consistently maintained to have legislative clout.' (1988, p.247)

Berry's American propositions are again similar. He suggests as themes – 'Credibility Comes First' and 'Only the Facts Count'. He tells moral tales of the type familiar in Britain, 'Mislead a member of Congress and, "you can expect a member never to listen to you seriously, ...".'...For the lobbyist, then, honesty is not so much a matter of virtue as it is of necessity. Lobbyists simply cannot do the job if there are any doubts about their credibility.' Writing in 1969 Dexter similarly argued, 'And, above everything else, a competent Washington representative does not exaggerate his case much.' (1969, p.7). The lobbyist who is 'found out' to be over-egging his case will lose future respect. The goal of the lobbying firm is to have such a reputation that the civil servants will trust them to have winnowed out the weak and nonsensical.

7. Professionalise the issue

One technique of the lobbyist might be to underline the electoral and political costs of a particular policy – for example tobacco companies are keen to remind Ministers of the number of jobs involved in cutting back tobacco production. In fact a more common feature of the lobbying trade is to attempt to make the issue under discussion as apolitical as possible. When a policy is 'de politicised' it can be resolved in industry/departmental negotiations more easily than when it is treated as a matter of political principle.

In his first chapter in this collection Charles Miller made the point that the greatest part of the time spent by organisations in dealing with Government is devoted to informing the system about their activities *without necessarily seeking to influence policy or legislation.*

In that chapter Charles Miller also discussed the demise of the 'Establishment' type policy resolution. Post and Kelley (1988) claim that in the US:

> The 'old boy, cigar chomping network' in which favors were traded has given way to an era of professionals who have more substantive experience in business and government and who are increasingly able to make a real career out of public affairs. Thus, trade-offs, negotiations, and compromises are easier to develop.

The Public Affairs Manager at IBM United Kingdom Ltd. Gerry Wade, told a Royal Institute of Public Administration conference in 1988 that, 'There is a remarkable similarity between the work of my team and that of senior civil servants.' A lobbyist in the public campaign business is resorting to his last card.

But at the same time sometimes the public channel is the effective one. Professor Philip Norton told the Select Committee on Members' Interests that the large Conservative vote (72) against the *Shops Bill* was influenced by the fact that both sides hired consultants – but the Sunday Shopping coalition also adopted the technique of telling supporters in the country to write to their own Member or to talk with their own Member. The Home Office received 50,000 letters against and 20,000 for, (HC 518 iii). But the first tactic must be 'professionalise'; to 'politicise' is to admit that success is unlikely.

8. Create a Dependency

The extension of this line of thought is expressed by Berry when he describes how the optimal role for a lobbyist is that of trusted source of information upon whom policy makers come to rely. He quoted one public interest representative as saying, 'Churn out a lot of material at their request. Create a dependency.' (1984, p.122).

Although in general Government is 'big', it is surprising how few civil servants may deal with a specific policy area: the civil service team is then grateful to the lobbyist or interest group who can simplify their job by providing data or picking flaws in early drafts.

9. Find friends

It is useful for any single interest to find partners in lobbying: this can transform what is seen as 'special pleading' into something more politically useful – 'public opinion'. Holbeche gives an example of the NFU aligning itself with the Department of Transport over the Okehampton by-pass – against the environmental protests which wanted 'lines' which made more demands on agricultural land. The trade unions and those in favour of Sunday observance made equally unlikely partners opposing Sunday trading.

As at December 1988 the 'Keep Sunday Special' campaign had as associate members 19 bodies, from the Association of Independent Retailers, to the British Council of Churches, the National Federation of Sub-Postmasters and the Union of Shop, Distributive and Allied Workers. It also had the support of the Baptist Union, the Mothers Union and 9 other 'moral' bodies. It hired Extel as its consultants (with a fee of £40,000 for 4 months work). The opposing group the DIY Federation reported to the Select Committee that it spent £410,000 in a four year campaign – mainly aimed at Parliament. They reported having hired GJW as their consultants. (HC 44-iii).

This 'find friends' has as its reverse face 'do not invent opponents'. Cates has noted, 'The truth is that oil and gas company lobbyists sometimes seem to dislike one another more even than they dislike their enemies outside the industry.' The point here is both obvious and relevant to the UK – that causes can be weakened by unnecessary schisms.

The consultancy can often 'run' a one off alliance by industrial opponents against a common foe. Thus Westminster Strategy administered the Home Taping Rights Campaign which opposed the introduction of a levy on blank audio tapes – against commercial performing rights. (Although HTRC was superficially a consumer based organisation, it was at least in part financed by Japanese audio firms.) Evidence to the Select Committee in 1989 from

Michael Burrell of Westminster Strategy (HC 44-iv) gave the example of the *Copyright Bill* when,

> ... we put them (a number of manufacturers) in touch with other interests – consumer interests and other special-interest groups who had an interest in the subject. We then helped that alliance, as it were, of manufacturers and other groups to put their case ...

10. Institutionalise Access – e.g. The All Party Committee

According to Evie Soames of Charles Barker (quoted in Carolyn Faulder's article in *Good HouseKeeping*) a useful tactic is to set up and run an all party group representing a particular commercial interest which will then be funded by the client industry or cause. She says, 'It's an arrangement that suits everybody. MPs get more information and they are getting much closer to the big companies; equally the companies are getting to know the MPs.' For example, at the request of the General Council of the Bar, Political Relations provides secretariat services for the All Party Barristers Group in Parliament.

In the first investigation of the Select Committee on Members' Interests the chairman Sir Geoffrey Johnson Smith argued, 'Some people think that All Party groups would not exist if it were not for the fact that they are really an extension of lobbying and that they only exist because their salaried work is financed and that they are only alive by the fact that visits to various countries are financed basically by outside groups.' Another member noted that the secretarial services of some groups was given as from a commercial address.

In its conclusions the 1984/5 Committee noted the increase in the number of the 'registered groups'. It noted that they had evidence from Age Concern who seconded one of their staff to be unpaid secretary to the chairman of the relevant All Party group. This gave him access to Parliament and its services even although he did not perform any of the duties normally expected of a Member's secretary. In view of suspicions of this practice, the Committee suggested that the Commons officers of All Party and Registered Groups be required to register the name and the role of the lobbying firm. By 1988 there were 172 Registered Party Groups. The 'gate keeper' lobbyist is criticised by other lobbying organisations who also see a danger that their clients will not be given adequate access when their views counter those of the clients of organising lobby firms. In evidence to the Select Committee in 1988 it was again suggested that when All Party groups allow the provision of administrative services and sponsorship by lobbyists (on behalf of clients), there was a *potential* that the secretariats would act as a barrier hindering access to groups by the public or by other lobbyists. It was argued by Charles Miller:

> We also feel it to be unjust that the membership lists of some All Party Groups are not freely available or that such lists are occasionally in the control of outside organisations who carefully restrict access ...

Similar concern was expressed by Jenny Jeger of GJW Ltd.

Though it is sometimes casually asserted that British lobbyists lack the opportunities to influence legislators that are available to their American counterparts, the All Party Committee access is one largely unheralded opening. Perhaps of growing importance are the equally low profile *party backbench* committees. One source describes them operating as follows: 'The members invite organisations to meetings, and in turn, receive frequent requests for consultations. In this way, the interested MPs are kept informed of developments.' (Mackintosh, 1978, p.67). In April 1989 there was concern by some MPs reported in *The Observer* that Ian Greer was attending a meeting of the Conservative Industry Committee and taking notes. His attendance – to support one of his clients Sir John Clark, the Chairman of Plessey, was described as 'a disturbing commercial intrusion'.

The All Party Committee is an example of a general tactic; that the lobbyist should attempt to create a situation in which access is so taken for granted that it is not recognised as being an issue. Another example might be the participation on departmental committees or a place on the consultation list of the Department. The new Departmental Select Committees are another channel for the group. Again the relationship is reciprocal; the committees are as in need of the information as the groups are in need of the access.

Obviously the policy consultant will attempt to 'sell' his client's case wherever he gets access – with civil servants, Ministers, press articles, back bench party committees, in the Lords or whatever. It may be a minor point but Greer talks in several places of meetings with members of the relevant Standing Committee to discuss the Bill in question. This opens up the prospect of the informal development of legislative hearings.

The party conferences are another opportunity for interest groups to display their wares. In spite of the advice (above) that interests cannot eat their way out of trouble, it is true that the conference hospitality is a means to ensure later access – if not influence – with MPs.

Was this a Thatcher phenomenon?

While it is true that the scale of lobbying has increased since 1979 it is unclear as to whether this linked with the fact that there is a Conservative Government or not. It is true that a disproportionate number of lobbyists appear to have close links with the Conservative party, but this could be explained by the fact that they are the party of Government. The attraction of the Conservatives as targets is also perhaps explained by the fact that most of the lobbying is mobilised for pro-business purposes. This makes them more sympathetic recipients of the lobbying.

Within the industry it is not thought that a Labour Government would view 'Tory Lobbyists' with suspicion. It is argued that the good lobbyists already argue in terms of facts and figures. These realities will be as compelling for Labour Ministers.

While the in-phrase may be 'parliamentary lobbyist' Miller (1987) seems most convincing when he concludes, 'Think Government, not Parliament ...'. But this conclusion should really be sustained by more detailed examples of the *impact* of these increasingly expensive activities – as should our views on the importance of the phenomenon. After all if there are lobbyists active on both sides of a question there are bound to be plenty of cases where the lobbyists can claim to have been effective ... Whether the client wins because of the impact of the lobbying or whether the lobbying was merely incidental is something that requires detailed investigation. Such an assessment however requires more detailed case study evidence than is yet available. The power of lobbyists is not measured by the assertions of the consultancies in their marketing campaigns.

NOTE: This chapter is an expanded version of a review article first published in *Political Studies*, Volume XXXVII, No 1, 1989. The editor is thanked for permission.

Bibliography

Gordon Adams	(1981) *The Iron Triangle* (New York: Council on Economic Priorities)
Paul Addison	(1987) 'The Road from 1945', in P. Hennessy and A. Seldon (eds) *Ruling Performance* (Oxford: Basil Blackwell)
Geoffrey Alderman	(1984) *Pressure Groups and Government in Great Britain* (London: Longman)
Stephen Aris	(1986) 'The Political Fixers', *In The City*, November/December, 1986
Kate Ascher	(1987) *The Politics of Privatisation* (Basingstoke: Macmillan)
Richard Baker	(1988) 'The Politics of Energy: the Layfield Report on Sizewell B', *Political Quarterly*, Vol. 59
Joel Barnett	(1982) *Inside the Treasury* (London: Deutsch)
Raymond Bauer, I de Sola Pool L.A. Dexter	(1968) *American Business and Public Policy* (New York: Atherton)
Jeffrey Berry	(1984) *The Interest Group Society* (Boston: Little, Brown)
J.H. Birnbaum and M.S. Murray	(1988) *Showdown at Gucci Gulch* (New york: Vintage Books)
Jock Bruce-Gardyne	(1986) *Ministers and Mandarins*(London: Sidgwick and Jackson)
Jock Bruce-Gardyne and Nigel Lawson	(1976) *The Power Game* (London: Macmillan)
James Bryce	(1888) *The American Commonwealth* (London: Macmillan)
B. Cain, J. Ferejohn and M. Fiorina	(1987) *The Personal Vote* (Harvard: Harvard University Press)
G. Cannon	(1987) *The Politics of Food*(Century)
H.D. Clarke *et al* (eds)	(1980) *Parliament, Policy and Representation* (Toronto: Methuen)
Phil Cates	(1988) 'Realities of Lobbying and Governmental Affairs', in R.L. Heath (ed)

	Strategic Issues Management(San Francisco; Jossey-Bass)
Cyril Coffin	(1987) *Working with Whitehall* (London: CBI)
M. Colquhoun	(1980) *A Woman in the House* (Scan Books)
A. Courtney	(1968) *Sailor in a Russian Frame* (Johnson)
R. Cowles	(1988) 'Whitehall and the Commercial World', *RIPA Report*, 9,1
R.H.S. Crossman	(1975, 1976, 1977) *The Diaries of a Cabinet Minister* (London: Hamish Hamilton/Jonathan Cape)
Malcolm Davies	(1985) *Politics of Pressure* (London: BBC)
Helen J. Dawson	(1967) 'Relations Between Farm Organizations and the Civil Service in Canada and Great Britain' *Canadian Public Administration* 4, 450-471, 454
Lewis Dexter	(1969) *How Organizations are Represented in Washington* (Indianapolis and New York: Bobbs)
Alan Doig	(1984) *Corruption and Misconduct in Contemporary British Politics* (Penguin Books)
Alan Doig	(1986) 'Access to Parliament and the Rise of Professional Lobbying', *Public Money*, Vol 5
Elizabeth Drew	(1983) 'Charlie, Portrait of a Lobbyist', in Alan J. Cigler and Burdett Loomis, *Interest Group Politics* (Washington: C.Q. Press)
G. Drewry, (ed)	(1985) *The New Select Committees* (Oxford: Oxford University Press)
D. Englefield	(1984) *Select Committees: Catalysts for Change?* (London: Longman)
S. Finer	(1958) *Anonymous Empire* (London: Pall Mall)
C.E.S. Franks	(1987) *The Parliament of Canada* (Toronto: UTP)
Joseph Goulden	(1973) *The Super Lawyers* (New York: Dell)
J.L. Granatstein	(1982) *The Ottawa Men: The Civil Service Mandarins, 1935 – 1957* (Toronto: Oxford University Press)

Wyn Grant	(1981) 'The Development of the Government Relations Function in UK Firms, a Pilot Study of UK Based Companies', Berlin, International Institute of Management Labour Market Policy Discussion paper 81/20
Wyn Grant with Jane Sargent	(1987) *Business and Politics in Britain* (London: Macmillan)
C. Grantham and C. Moore Hodgson	(1985) 'The House of Lords: Structural Changes', in P. Norton (ed) *Parliament in the 1980s* (Oxford: Basil Blackwell)
C. Grantham and C. Seymour-Ure	(1989) 'Parliament and Political Consultants', in M. Rush (ed) *Parliament and Pressure Politics* (Oxford: O.U.P.)
C.S. Greenwald	(1977) *Group Power* (New York: Praegar)
Ian Greer	(1985) *Right to be Heard* (London: Ian Greer Associates)
Mick Hamer	(1987) *Wheels Within Wheels* (Routledge and Kegan Paul)
E. Pendleton Herring	(1929) *Group Representation Before Congress* (Baltimore: John Hopkins U.P.)
Peter Hennessy	(1987) 'The Attlee Government' in P. Hennessy and A. Seldon, *Ruling Performance* (Oxford: Basil Blackwell)
J. Hogrefe	(1986) *Wholly Unacceptable* (London: Harrop)
Grant Jordan	(1985) 'Parliament Under Pressure', *Political Quarterly*, Vol. 56, 2
Grant Jordan and Jeremy Richardson	(1982) 'The British Policy Style or the Logic of Negotiation', in J.J. Richardson (ed), *Policy Style in Western Europe* (London: Allen and Union)
Grant Jordan and Jeremy Richardson	(1979) 'Pantouflage: a Civil Service Perk', *New Society*
Grant Jordan and Jeremy Richardson	(1987) *Government and Pressure Groups in Britain* (Oxford: Clarendon)
N. Kochan and H. Pym	(1987) *The Guinness Affair* (Bromley, Helm)
Robert Lewis	(1977) 'The Hidden Persuaders: Guns Don't Make Laws, but Gun Lobbies Damn Well Do', *MacLeans*

Magnus Linklater & David Leigh	(1986) *Not with Honour* (London: Sphere Books)
L. Lynn and T.J. McKean	(1988) *Trade Associations in America and Japan* (Washington: AEI)
P.S. McGrath	(1979) *Redefining Corporate-Federal Relations* (New York: the Conference Board)
R.T. McKenzie	(1958) 'Parties Pressure Groups and the British Political Process', *Political Quarterly*, 29, 1
J.P. Mackintosh	(1978) *People and Parliament* (Farnborough: Saxon House)
Paul Malvern	(1985) *Persuaders: Lobbying, Influence Peddling and Political Corruption in Canada* (Toronto: Methuen)
Lester Milbrath	(1963) *The Washington Lobbyists* (Chigago: Rand McNally)
Charles Miller and Roger Hayes	(1984) 'Lobbyists – Public Service or Expensive Sham', Bow Group Publications
Charles Miller	(1987) *Lobbying Government* (Oxford: Basil Blackwell)
A. Mueller	(1985) 'A Civil Servant's View', in D. Englefield (ed) *Today's Civil Service* (Harlow: Longman)
E.A. Murray Jnr.	(1982) 'The Public Affairs Function', in L.E. Preston (ed) *Research in Corporate Social Performance and Policy : A Research Annual*, Volume 4 (Greenwich, Conn.: Jai), 129-55
P. Noel-Baker	(1961) 'The Grey Zone: The Problems of Business Affiliations of Members of Parliament', *Parliamentary Affairs*, Vol. 15
E. Nordlinger	(1981) *On the Autonomy of the Democratic State* (Cambridge (Mass): Harvard U.P.)
P. Norton	(1978) *Conservative Dissidents* (London: Temple Smith)
P. Norton	(1980) *Dissension in the House of Commons 1974-79* (Oxford: Oxford U.P.)
P. Norton	(1984) 'Parliament and Policy in Britain: The House of Commons as a Policy Influencer', in *Teaching Politics*, 13 (2)

P. Norton	(1987) *Parliament in Perspective* (Hull: Hull University Press)
M. Olson	(1982) *The Rise and Decline of Nations* (Cambridge: Mass: Harvard U.P.)
E. & A. Porritt	(1903) *The Unreformed House of Commons* (Oxford: OUP)
J. Post and P. Kelly	(1988) 'Lessons from the Learning Curve', in R. Heath (ed) *Strategic Issues Management* (San Francisco: Jossey Bass)
R. Presthus	(1974) 'Interests Groups and Lobbying: Canada and the United States', *Annals of the American Academy of Political & Social Science*, 413
A. Paul Pross	(1975) *Pressure Group Behaviour in Canadian Politics* (Toronto: McGraw-Hill)
A. Paul Pross	(1986) *Group Politics and Public Policy* (Oxford: O.U.P.)
Public Policy Consultants	(1987) *The Government Report*, published by authors
Henry Rhodes	(1949) *The Lynskey Tribunal* (Leigh on Sea: Thames Bank Publishing)
J.J. Richardson and G. Jordan	(1979) *Governing Under Pressure* (Oxford: Martin Robertson)
K.G. Robertson	(1982) *Public Secrets* (London: Macmillan)
Richard Rose	(1984) *Do Parties Make a Difference* (Basingstoke: Macmillan) Second Edition
Andrew Roth	(1981) 'Quagmire at the Interface' in *The Business Background of MPs*, Parliamentary Profile
M. Rush, P. Norton, C. Seymour-Ure and M. Shaw	(1988) Memorandum of Evidence, *Select Committee on Members' Interests*, HC 518-iii (London: HMSO)
Anthony Sampson	(1971) *The New Anatomy of Britain*(London: Hodder and Stoughton)
James Saunders	(1990) *Nightmare* (London: Arrow Books)
John Sawatsky	(1987) *The Insiders: Government, Business and the Lobbyists* (Toronto: McClelland and Stewart)

K. Schlozman and J.T. Tierney	(1986) *Organized Interests and American Democracy* (New York: Harper Row)
Peter Self and H. Storing	(1971 ed) *The State and the Farmer* (London: Allen and Unwin)
D. Shackleton	(1977) *Power Town: Democracy Discarded* (Toronto: Methuen)
Theda Skocpol	(1985) *Bringing the State Back In* (Cambridge: Cambridge U.P.)
Hedrick Smith	(1988) *The Power Game* (New York: Random House)
Martin Smith	(1986) 'The Lobbyist's Business', *Government and Industry* (Harlow: Longman)
Norman Tebbit	(1985) 'Lobbying – Influencing the Parliamentary Process', *The House Magazine*, 29th November
David Truman	(1971 ed) *The Governmental Process* (New York: Alfred Knopf)
J. Turner and G. Pearson	(1966) *The Persuasion Industry* (Eyre and Spottiswoode)
Michael Useem	(1984) *The Inner Circle: large corporations and the rise of business political activity in the US and UK* (New York, O.U.P)
David Vogel	(1978) 'Why Businessmen Distrust Their State', *British Journal of Political Science*, 8, Part 1
David Vogel	(1983) 'The Power of Business in America: A Reappraisal', *British Journal of Political Science*, Vol 13, Part 1
S. Walkland and M. Ryle (eds)	(1977) *The Legislative Process in Great Britain* (London: Fontana)
Sir Douglas Wass	(1984) *Government and the Governed* (London: Routledge and Kegan Paul)
D. Willis and W. Grant	(1987) 'The United Kingdom: Still a Company State?' in MPC Van Schendelen & R Jackson (eds) *The Politicisation of Business in Western Europe* (Croom Helm)
Graham Wilson	(1981) *Interest Groups in the USA* (Oxford: Clarendon Press)

Graham Wilson   (1985) *Business and Politics* (London:
                       Macmillan)

Graham Wilson   (1987) 'The Political Behaviour of Large
                       Corporations', paper presented to the annual
                       meeting of the American Political Science
                       Association, Chicago

H.H. Wilson   (1961) *Pressure Group* (London: Secker and
                       Warburg)

A. Wise   (1989) *Punishment, Prisons & the Private Sector*,
                       undergraduate dissertation, Newcastle
                       Polytechnic

D.B. Yoffie and   (1985) 'Creating Political Advantage: the
S. Bergenstein   Rise of the Corporate Political Entrepreneur',
                       California Management Review, 28, 124-39